D1245893

Southern Country

270 Home Plans

Historic Colonials • Southern Farmhouses
Georgian Classics • Greek Revivals • Coastal Cottages
Plantation Homes • Floridian Designs • And More!

Athens Regional Library
2025 Baxter Street
Athens, GA 30606

Published by Hanley Wood
One Thomas Circle, NW, Suite 600
Washington, DC 20005

DISTRIBUTION CENTER
PBD
Hanley Wood Consumer Group
3280 Summit Ridge Parkway
Duluth, Georgia 30096

GROUP PUBLISHER Andrew Schultz
ASSOCIATE PUBLISHER, EDITORIAL DEVELOPMENT, Jennifer Pearce
MANAGING EDITOR Hannah McCann
EDITOR Simon Hyoun
ASSISTANT EDITOR Kimberly Johnson
PUBLICATIONS MANAGER Brian Haefs
PRODUCTION MANAGER Melissa Curry
DIRECTOR, PLANS MARKETING Mark Wilkin
SENIOR PLAN MERCHANDISER Nicole Phipps
PLAN MERCHANDISER Hillary Huff
GRAPHIC ARTIST Joong Min
PLAN DATA TEAM LEADER Susan Jasmin
SENIOR MARKETING MANAGER Holly Miller
MARKETING MANAGER Bridgit Kearns

NATIONAL SALES MANAGER Bruce Holmes

Most Hanley Wood titles are available at quantity discounts with bulk
purchases for educational, business, or sales promotional use. For information, please contact Bruce Holmes at bholmes@hanleywood.com.

BIG DESIGNS, INC.
PRESIDENT, CREATIVE DIRECTOR Anthony D'Elia
VICE PRESIDENT, BUSINESS MANAGER Megan D'Elia
VICE PRESIDENT, DESIGN DIRECTOR Chris Bonavita
EDITORIAL DIRECTOR John Roach
ASSISTANT EDITOR Carrie Atkinson
SENIOR ART DIRECTOR Stephen Reinfurt
PRODUCTION DIRECTOR David Barbella
PRODUCTION MANAGER Rich Fuentes
PHOTO EDITOR Christine DiVuolo
ART DIRECTOR Frank Augugliaro
GRAPHIC DESIGNER Billy Doremus
GRAPHIC DESIGNER Jacque Young

PHOTO CREDITS

Front Cover: Photo courtesy of William E. Poole Designs, Inc. and the
Islands of Beaufort, SC. For details, see page 129.
Back Cover, Top and Left Inset: Photo courtesy of William E. Poole
Designs, Inc. For details, see page 75.
Back Cover, Middle Inset: Photo by Peter Montanti, courtesy of William E.
Poole Designs, Inc. and General Shale Brick. For details, see page 132.

10 9 8 7 6 5 4 3 2 1

All floor plans and elevations copyright by the individual designers and may not be
reproduced by any means without permission. All text, designs, and illustrative material copyright ©2006 by Home Planners, LLC, wholly owned by Hanley-Wood, LLC. All
rights reserved. No part of this publication may be reproduced in any form or by any
means — electronic, mechanical, photomechanical, recorded, or otherwise — without
the prior written permission of the publisher.

Printed in the United States of America

Library of Congress Control Number: 2005938831

ISBN-13: 978-1-931131-56-8
ISBN-10: 1-931131-56-2

Southern Country

6 Historic Colonials
Bring a piece of history to your neighborhood
with one of these Colonial treasures

70 Charleston-Style Homes
These elegant homes recall grand
southern plantations and estates

126 Creole Influences
Discover bright and airy designs made
for the warmest of southern climates

186 Southern Farmhouses
This classic American style suits any landscape

220 Small-Town Cottages
Stylish, practical designs that are big
on charm and comfort

278 Floridian Designs
Enjoy relaxing on the lanai of your own
Mediterranean-style villa

310 How to Order Blueprints

AT HOME IN THE SOUTH

There's something about the South that recalls visions of grand plantation homes and romantic balconies, of Scarlett O'Hara capering down the curved staircase to stand on the columned terrace of Tara. The South is rich with such imagery, and its influence abounds in the architecture of countryside, and even urban, southern homes. In *The American Collection: Southern Country*, we explore the styles and designs from across the southern landscape, and illustrate the details that make them such memorable, sought-after homes.

The Historic Colonials section, beginning on page 6, shows early American styles from Georgian to Federal to Classical Revival. These traditionally red-brick homes date back to the days of Thomas Jefferson's Monticello and his University of Virginia Rotunda. Likewise, Charleston-Style Homes (page 70) derive much of their influence from the Colonial period but incorporate the aspects into a form all their own. The tell-tale signs of a Charleston home are a narrow, front-gable facade for the "single" house, a more square shape for the "double" houses, and, of course, the signature full-length first- and second-floor porches. Adorned with columns and pediments, these stately manors and plantation beauties provide modern neighborhoods with a nod to the past.

The Gulf city of New Orleans has always been a gathering place of eclectic music, style, and culture, so it's logical that the architecture of the city and its surrounding areas should reflect that individuality. A confluence of architectural styles from France, the Caribbean, and Africa brought home the "Creole" look (page 126) of wide porches, hipped roofs, and French doors—features to accommodate the sweltering Louisiana sun and humidity. Many homes were influenced by French Colonial designs, but others, with pier foundations and above-ground living spaces, are obvious coastal homes appropriate alongside any ocean.

Southern Farmhouses, beginning on page 186, highlight a design form that has become a staple in the American landscape. Characterized by asymmetrical facades, wrapping porches, and Victorian turrets, these homes can be found along the east coast as well as the more central states. The Small-Town Cottages, on page 220, replicate the modest and efficient homes built by hardworking families from the Civil War to World War II. The modified Tudor, Victorian, and Italian designs made popular during that time were first homes to new Americans immigrating from all over the world.

With acknowledgements to Georgia, South Carolina, Louisiana, and other members of the Deep South, how could we forget everyone's favorite vacation state? Floridian designs borrow largely from Mediterranean and Spanish architecture, although coastal and tidewater styles are not uncommon. Colorful stucco and red clay tiles are must-haves, and the rear lanais are the perfect spots for poolside naps and sunbathing. This section begins on page 278.

There are so many inspirational styles offered from the famed and historic South; we hope you will find the perfect home plan to help you bring a touch of southern charm to your neighborhood—whatever the climate.

Full-height windows and a two-tiered porch are features in this Early Classical Revival design. See more on page 12.

plan# **HPK2000004**

First Floor: 3,439 sq. ft.
Second Floor: 803 sq. ft.
Total: 4,242 sq. ft.
Bedrooms: 4
Bathrooms: 4½ + 3 Half Baths
Width: 95' - 0"
Depth: 90' - 0"
Foundation: Slab, Unfinished
Basement, Crawlspace

ORDER ONLINE @ EPLANS.COM

Living History

In the 17th and 18th Centuries, America was still a new idea, trying to develop its identity but still borrowing many influences from London, which in turn derived many of its architectural styles from Ancient Greece. These styles, known today simply as Colonial, include Georgian, Federal (or Adam), Greek Revival, and Neoclassical. Characterized by red brick, white columns, window and entryway pediments, and a symmetrical facade and chimneys, they were the homes of the wealthy "leisure" class popularized by such founding fathers as George Washington and Thomas Jefferson. They can range from stately plantation homes and manors to narrow urban townhomes, but all carry with them the spirit of a young nation.

This home possesses every aspect a Colonial home should: four chimneys placed symmetrically throughout the home; wings and windows placed symmetrically along the brick facade; the broad, two-story-tall, Greek-inspired columns; and a grand pediment crowning it all. While the exterior of this classic estate is pure Colonial, the floor plan successfully integrates every modern convenience. The grand foyer with double staircase opens up to the sunken two-story living room, detailed with columns, a fireplace, and access to the rear property. To the left, a sunny bayed eating area joins a unique kitchen (with a butler's pantry) and the formal dining room for casual or formal meals. The veranda includes an outdoor grill and bar, perfect for dining alfresco. The right wing is devoted to relaxing spaces, such as a guest room, study, and master suite. Enter the master bedroom through a private sitting room with a two-sided fireplace. The sunken sleeping area flows into a bath with dual vanity sinks, separate tub and shower, and a generous walk-in closet. Upstairs, two generous bedrooms each have a private bath and study area, and the balcony's built-ins can accommodate a library of books.

Tricornered hats and Betsy-Ross bonnets may help bring the past alive, but they're hardly necessary. A Colonial-style home, however, does bring a reminder of how our country began to today's neighborhoods—a little piece of history right on your street.

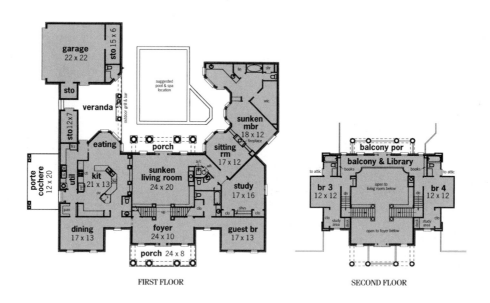

FIRST FLOOR   SECOND FLOOR

This home's facade revels in the look of historic Colonial design.

THIS HOME, AS SHOWN IN THE PHOTOGRAPH, MAY DIFFER FROM THE ACTUAL BLUEPRINTS. FOR MORE DETAILED INFORMATION, PLEASE CHECK THE FLOOR PLANS CAREFULLY.

The double wings, twin chimneys, and center portico of this home work in concert to create a classic architectural statement. The two-story foyer is flanked by the spacious dining room and formal living room, each containing their own fireplaces. A large family room with a full wall of glass opens conveniently to the kitchen and breakfast room. The master suite features a tray ceiling and French doors that open to a covered porch. A grand master bath completes the master suite. Two family bedrooms share a bath, and another has a private bath. Bedroom 4 features a nook for sitting or reading.

plan# HPK2000006

First Floor: 1,455 sq. ft.
Second Floor: 1,649 sq. ft.
Total: 3,104 sq. ft.
Bedrooms: 4
Bathrooms: 3½
Width: 54' - 4"
Depth: 46' - 0"
Foundation: Finished Walkout Basement

ORDER ONLINE @ EPLANS.COM

FIRST FLOOR

SECOND FLOOR

PHOTOGRAPHY COURTESY OF STEPHEN FULLER, INC. THIS HOME, AS SHOWN IN THE PHOTOGRAPH, MAY DIFFER FROM THE ACTUAL BLUEPRINTS. FOR MORE DETAILED INFORMATION, PLEASE CHECK THE FLOOR PLANS CAREFULLY.

plan# HPK2000007

First Floor: 1,981 sq. ft.
Second Floor: 1,935 sq. ft.
Total: 3,916 sq. ft.
Bedrooms: 5
Bathrooms: 4
Width: 65' - 0"
Depth: 64' - 10"
Foundation: Unfinished Walkout Basement

ORDER ONLINE @ EPLANS.COM

Take one look at this Early American Colonial home and you'll fall in love with its beauty, functionality and luxuries. From the covered front porch, continue to the great room, where a fireplace and a bay window with wonderful rear property views await. The kitchen will delight, with a wraparound counter that provides plenty of workspace for easy meal preparation. Up the grand staircase, the master suite revels in a private deck and pampering spa bath. Three additional bedrooms complete this level. Don't miss the first-floor guest room with an adjacent full bath.

SECOND FLOOR

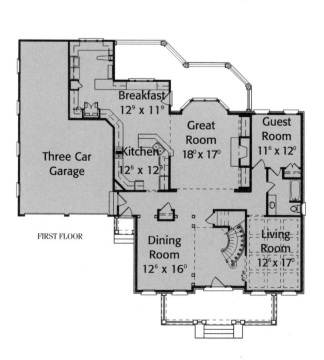

FIRST FLOOR

THIS HOME, AS SHOWN IN THE PHOTOGRAPH, MAY DIFFER FROM THE ACTUAL BLUEPRINTS. FOR MORE DETAILED INFORMATION, PLEASE CHECK THE FLOOR PLANS CAREFULLY.

plan# HPK2000008

First Floor: 2,270 sq. ft.
Second Floor: 685 sq. ft.
Total: 2,955 sq. ft.
Bonus Space: 563 sq. ft.
Bedrooms: 3
Bathrooms: 2½
Width: 75' - 1"
Depth: 53' - 6"

ORDER ONLINE @ EPLANS.COM

Hipped rooflines, sunburst windows, and French-style shutters are the defining elements of this home's exterior. Inside, the foyer is flanked by the dining room and the study. Further on, the lavish great room can be entered through two stately columns and is complete with a fireplace, built-in shelves, a vaulted ceiling, and views to the rear patio. The island kitchen easily accesses a pantry and a desk and flows into the bayed breakfast area. The first-floor master bedroom enjoys a fireplace, two walk-in closets, and an amenity-filled private bath. Two additional bedrooms reside upstairs, along with a sizable bonus room.

REAR EXTERIOR

FIRST FLOOR

SECOND FLOOR

© 2000 DONALD A. GARDNER, INC., PHOTOGRAPHY COURTESY OF DONALD A. GARDNER ARCHITECTS, INC. THIS HOME AS SHOWN IN THE PHOTOGRAPH MAY DIFFER FROM THE ACTUAL BLUEPRINTS.

plan# HPK2000009

First Floor: 2,183 sq. ft.
Second Floor: 993 sq. ft.
Total: 3,176 sq. ft.
Bedrooms: 4
Bathrooms: 3½
Width: 66' - 0"
Depth: 84' - 0"
Foundation: Slab

ORDER ONLINE @ EPLANS.COM

This home combines French styling with Colonial influences to produce a magnificent picture of elegance. A grand two-story foyer introduces the living room to the left and the dining room to the right. The family room reveals a fireplace flanked by two sets of French doors leading to the rear porch. The island kitchen provides plenty of workspace and functions well with a breakfast room, a convenient utility room, and a powder room. The first-floor master suite is a secluded place to relax. Upstairs, three family bedrooms—all with walk-in closets—and two full baths complete the sleeping quarters. An unfinished bonus room above the two-car garage is great for future space.

FIRST FLOOR

SECOND FLOOR

THIS HOME, AS SHOWN IN THE PHOTOGRAPH, MAY DIFFER FROM THE ACTUAL BLUEPRINTS. FOR MORE DETAILED INFORMATION, PLEASE CHECK THE FLOOR PLANS CAREFULLY.

plan# HPK2000283

First Floor: 3,129 sq. ft.
Second Floor: 1,058 sq. ft.
Total: 4,187 sq. ft.
Bonus Space: 551 sq. ft.
Bedrooms: 4
Bathrooms: 4½
Width: 68' - 0"
Depth: 117' - 10"
Foundation: Slab

ORDER ONLINE @ EPLANS.COM

Once inside the welcoming facade, an open floor plan between the foyer, the dining room, and the family room leads directly out to the screened porch and patio in the rear of the house. The L-shaped kitchen includes an island and a walk-in pantry, and nearby breakfast nook. A secondary bedroom, with its own private bath, and a utility room leads to the three-car garage. The luxurious master suite includes two walk-in closets, a fireplace, and access to the back porch. The second floor boasts two bedrooms and baths and a media room.

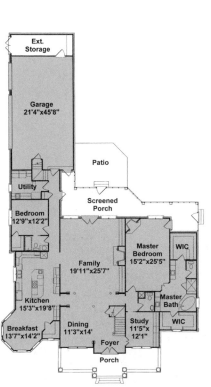

FIRST FLOOR

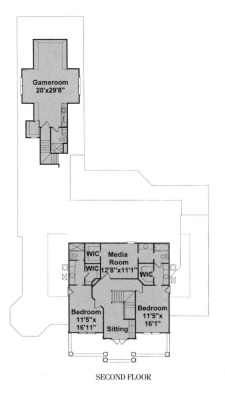

SECOND FLOOR

PHOTOGRAPHY BY STEVE GORUM/"STUDIO G," MOBILE, ALABAMA
THIS HOME, AS SHOWN IN THE PHOTOGRAPH, MAY DIFFER FROM THE ACTUAL BLUEPRINTS.

plan# HPK2000284

First Floor: 3,129 sq. ft.
Second Floor: 1,812 sq. ft.
Total: 4,941 sq. ft.
Bedrooms: 4
Bathrooms: 4½
Width: 85' - 0"
Depth: 61' - 6"
Foundation: Crawlspace

ORDER ONLINE @ EPLANS.COM

This classic entry announces an open interior decked with both comfort and style. The foyer leads to a gallery hall that opens to the grand room through decorative columns. This flexible space offers a warming fireplace and French doors to the rear terrace. Sunlight opens the breakfast bay for a sense of the outdoors and brightens the kitchen, which has a walk-in pantry. The right wing of the plan is dedicated to a deluxe master suite with a spacious bath that features a dressing area, two walk-in closets, and a garden tub.

FOR MORE DETAILED INFORMATION, PLEASE CHECK THE FLOOR PLANS CAREFULLY.

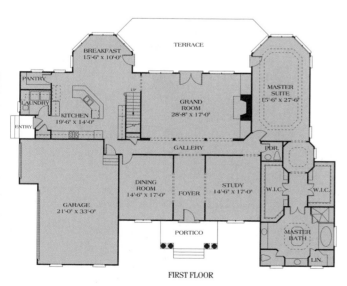

FIRST FLOOR

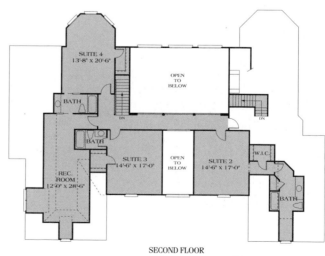

SECOND FLOOR

PHOTO BY ANDREW LAUTMAN, LAUTMAN PHOTOGRAPHY

plan# HPK2000010

First Floor: 1,559 sq. ft.
Second Floor: 1,404 sq. ft.
Total: 2,963 sq. ft.
Bedrooms: 4
Bathrooms: 2½ + ½
Width: 66' - 10"
Depth: 44' - 10"
Foundation: Unfinished Basement

ORDER ONLINE @ EPLANS.COM

Reminiscent of the stately character of Federal architecture during an earlier period in our history, this two-story home is replete with exquisite detailing. The cornice work, pediment gable, dentils, brick corner quoins, beautifully proportioned columns, front-door detailing, window treatment, and massive twin chimneys are among the features that make this design so unique and appealing. Livability is great as well. Notice the quiet study, the beamed-ceiling family room, and the large formal living room. The four bedrooms are located upstairs.

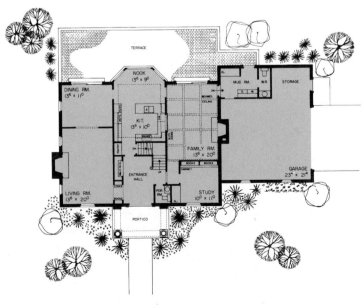

FIRST FLOOR

SECOND FLOOR

plan# HPK2000011

First Floor: 1,930 sq. ft.
Second Floor: 1,807 sq. ft.
Total: 3,737 sq. ft.
Bonus Space: 372 sq. ft.
Bedrooms: 4
Bathrooms: 4
Width: 55' - 2"
Depth: 60' - 2"
Foundation: Crawlspace

ORDER ONLINE @ EPLANS.COM

Classic Georgian stylings create a stately feel on this brick two-story home. A portico entry leads to a gracious foyer and formal rooms on either side. Ahead, a guest suite/home office has a semi-private bath. The kitchen aims to please with a large serving bar island and plenty of counter space. A casual breakfast nook and hearth-warmed gathering room with deck access complete this level. Upstairs, two bedrooms share a Jack-and-Jill bath, and the bonus room contains an additional full bath. The master suite is a remarkable getaway, with a tray ceiling, His and Hers walk-in closets, and an opulent bath with an elegant ceiling treatment. A laundry room nearby is the ultimate convenience.

THIS HOME, AS SHOWN IN THE PHOTOGRAPH, MAY DIFFER FROM THE ACTUAL BLUEPRINTS. FOR MORE DETAILED INFORMATION, PLEASE CHECK THE FLOOR PLANS CAREFULLY.

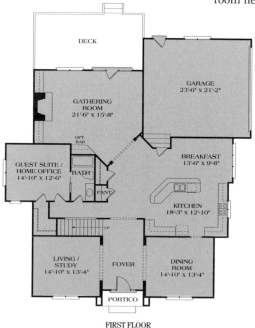

FIRST FLOOR

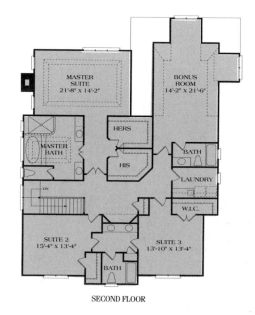

SECOND FLOOR

plan⊞ **HPK2000012**

First Floor: 2,081 sq. ft.
Second Floor: 940 sq. ft.
Total: 3,021 sq. ft.
Bedrooms: 4
Bathrooms: 3½
Width: 69' - 9"
Depth: 65' - 0"
Foundation: Finished Walkout Basement

ORDER ONLINE @ EPLANS.COM

This Georgian country-style home displays an impressive appearance. The front porch and columns frame the elegant elliptical entrance. Georgian symmetry balances the living room and dining room off the foyer. The first floor continues into the two-story great room, which offers built-in cabinetry, a fireplace, and a large bay window that overlooks the rear deck. A dramatic tray ceiling, a wall of glass, and access to the rear deck complete the master bedroom. To the left of the great room, a large kitchen opens to a breakfast area with walls of windows. Upstairs, each of three family bedrooms features ample closet space as well as direct access to a bathroom.

FIRST FLOOR

SECOND FLOOR

PHOTO COURTESY OF STEPHEN FULLER, INC.
THIS HOME AS SHOWN IN THE PHOTOGRAPH, MAY DIFFER FROM THE ACTUAL BLUEPRINTS.

plan# HPK2000285

First Floor: 1,992 sq. ft.
Second Floor: 1,458 sq. ft.
Total: 3,450 sq. ft.
Bonus Space: 380 sq. ft.
Bedrooms: 5
Bathrooms: 3½
Width: 108' - 0"
Depth: 64' - 0"
Foundation: Unfinished Basement

ORDER ONLINE @ EPLANS.COM

The origin of this house dates back to 1787 and George Washington's stately Mount Vernon. The unusual design features curved galleries leading to matching wings. In the main house, the living and dining rooms provide a large open area, with access to the rear porch for additional entertaining possibilities. A keeping room features a pass-through to the kitchen and a fireplace with a built-in wood box. Four bedrooms, including a master suite with a fireplace, are found upstairs. One wing contains separate guest quarters with a full bath, a lounge area, and an upstairs studio, which features a spiral staircase and a loft area. On the other side of the house, the second floor over the garage can be used for storage or as a hobby room.

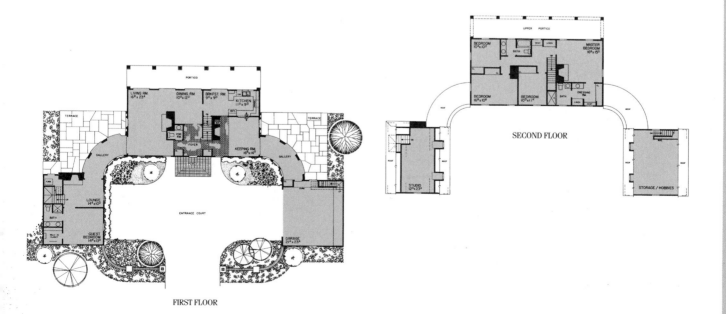

FIRST FLOOR

SECOND FLOOR

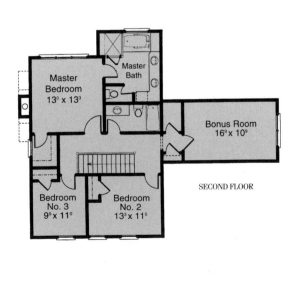

plan# HPK2000286

First Floor: 900 sq. ft.
Second Floor: 870 sq. ft.
Total: 1,770 sq. ft.
Bonus Space: 198 sq. ft.
Bedrooms: 3
Bathrooms: 2½
Width: 45' - 0"
Depth: 36' - 11"
Foundation: Unfinished Basement

ORDER ONLINE @ EPLANS.COM

A pediment gable, echoed over the entry and the garage, and pilastered corners reveal the Georgian heritage of this design. Inside, columned arches mark the boundaries of the massive great room, where a triple window over-looks the rear deck and the kitchen and breakfast rooms. The second floor offers three bedrooms, including a master suite with a deluxe bath. Two family bedrooms share a full bath and adjoin a spacious bonus room.

© William E. Poole Designs, Inc.

plan# HPK2000013

First Floor: 1,876 sq. ft.
Second Floor: 1,396 sq. ft.
Total: 3,272 sq. ft.
Bonus Space: 405 sq. ft.
Bedrooms: 4
Bathrooms: 3½
Width: 63' - 4"
Depth: 51' - 0"
Foundation: Crawlspace,
Unfinished Basement

ORDER ONLINE @ EPLANS.COM

Come home to this classical yet casual Colonial. A center-gabled porch echoes the main roofline and softens the formal symmetry of the facade. Inside, a traditional floor plan presents the living and dining rooms on either side of the foyer. Continue through to the gallery, however, and you'll find all the modern conveniences of a comfortable home. The cathedral-ceilinged great room, anchored by a fireplace and lit by a rose window, is connected to the breakfast nook by a pair of decorative columns. The kitchen offers plenty of counter and cabinet space, plus a walk-in pantry and built-in planning desk. A first-floor bedroom would make a cozy guest suite or study. Upstairs, two additional bedrooms share a hall bath, where a separate area housing dual sinks will help alleviate the morning rush. The master suite is a true retreat, with a corner fireplace and plush bath.

FIRST FLOOR

SECOND FLOOR

© William E. Poole Designs, Inc.

plan# HPK2000014

First Floor: 2,603 sq. ft.
Second Floor: 1,660 sq. ft.
Total: 4,263 sq. ft.
Bonus Space: 669 sq. ft.
Bedrooms: 4
Bathrooms: 4½ + ½
Width: 98' - 0"
Depth: 56' - 8"
Foundation: Unfinished Basement

ORDER ONLINE @ EPLANS.COM

This fine example of the Georgian style of architecture offers a wonderful facade with Southern charm. The foyer is flanked by the formal dining room and the living room. The efficient kitchen is situated between the sunny breakfast nook and the dining room. The family room opens to the backyard. The master suite enjoys an opulent bath and large walk-in closet. The second floor presents three bedrooms and two baths.

FIRST FLOOR

SECOND FLOOR

© William E. Poole Designs, Inc.

plan# HPK2000015

First Floor: 2,359 sq. ft.
Second Floor: 1,112 sq. ft.
Total: 3,471 sq. ft.
Bonus Space: 559 sq. ft.
Bedrooms: 4
Bathrooms: 3½
Width: 81' - 8"
Depth: 77' - 8"
Foundation: Crawlspace

ORDER ONLINE @ EPLANS.COM

Three dormers and a classic front porch define the style of this Southern beauty. The family room is centrally located with a fireplace on the left wall and a built-in entertainment system. The open kitchen features an island snack bar, built-in desk, a bayed breakfast nook, and a walk-in pantry. The mudroom offers a space to doff coats and soiled shoes. Access to a powder room is an added convenience. A separate utility room houses the washer/dryer. Upstairs houses two bedrooms with a Jack-and-Jill bath and a third bedroom with a full bath. The master suite, nestled in the far left corner of the first floor, is a quiet retreat for the homeowners.

FIRST FLOOR

SECOND FLOOR

© William E. Poole Designs, Inc.

Designed for old-fashioned comfort, this two-story home has plenty of modern amenities. The front covered porch and rear deck extend the living space outward, creating a sense of roominess. The family room, furnished with a fireplace, flows smoothly into the breakfast bay and kitchen. A front living room and formal dining area offer convenient space for entertaining. The resplendent master suite comes with a walk-in closet, dual-sink vanity, and separate tub and shower. Two bedrooms on the second floor share a bath and loft. Extra space can be developed into a recreation room. Access to the two-car garage is through the laundry.

plan# HPK2000016

First Floor: 1,714 sq. ft.
Second Floor: 683 sq. ft.
Total: 2,397 sq. ft.
Bonus Space: 287 sq. ft.
Bedrooms: 3
Bathrooms: 2½
Width: 53' - 8"
Depth: 56' - 8"
Foundation: Crawlspace

ORDER ONLINE @ EPLANS.COM

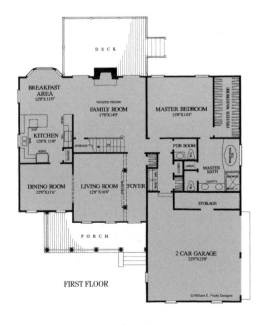

FIRST FLOOR

SECOND FLOOR

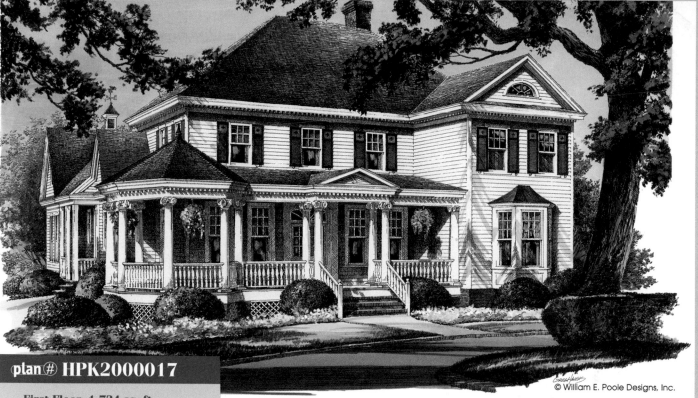

© William E. Poole Designs, Inc.

plan# HPK2000017

First Floor: 1,734 sq. ft.
Second Floor: 1,091 sq. ft.
Total: 2,825 sq. ft.
Bonus Space: 488 sq. ft.
Bedrooms: 4
Bathrooms: 3½
Width: 57' - 6"
Depth: 80' - 11"
Foundation: Crawlspace,
Unfinished Basement

ORDER ONLINE @ EPLANS.COM

Wonderful Victorian charm combines with the flavor of country in this delightful two-story home. A wraparound porch with a gazebo corner welcomes you into the foyer, where the formal dining room waits to the left and a spacious, two-story great room is just ahead. Here, a fireplace, built-ins, and backyard access add to the charm. The L-shaped kitchen features a work-top island, a walk-in pantry, and a breakfast area. Located on the first floor for privacy, the master suite offers a large walk-in closet and a pampering bath. Upstairs, three bedrooms—one with a private bath—share access to a study loft.

FIRST FLOOR

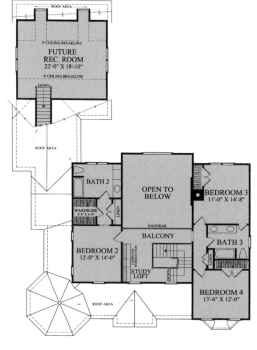

SECOND FLOOR

© William E. Poole Designs, Inc.

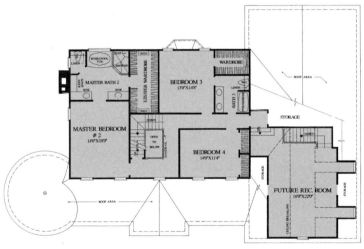

SECOND FLOOR

FIRST FLOOR

© William E. Poole Designs

plan # HPK2000018

First Floor: 2,099 sq. ft.
Second Floor: 1,260 sq. ft.
Total: 3,359 sq. ft.
Bonus Space: 494 sq. ft.
Bedrooms: 4
Bathrooms: 3½
Width: 68' - 4"
Depth: 54' - 0"
Foundation: Crawlspace

ORDER ONLINE @ EPLANS.COM

This Colonial home gets a Victorian treatment with an expansive covered porch complete with a gazebo-like terminus. Inside, the impressive foyer is flanked by the living room and the formal dining room. The spacious island kitchen is ideally situated between the dining room and the sunny breakfast area. Completing the living area, the family room enjoys a fireplace, built-ins, and a generous view. The lavish master suite resides on the far right with a private bath and a huge walk-in closet. A second master suite is found on the upper level, along with two additional bedrooms that share a full bath.

© William E. Poole Designs, Inc.

plan# HPK2000019

First Floor: 2,442 sq. ft.
Second Floor: 1,286 sq. ft.
Total: 3,728 sq. ft.
Bonus Space: 681 sq. ft.
Bedrooms: 4
Bathrooms: 3½ + ½
Width: 84' - 8"
Depth: 60' - 0"
Foundation: Crawlspace

ORDER ONLINE @ EPLANS.COM

With a gazebo-style covered porch and careful exterior details, you can't help but imagine tea parties, porch swings, and lazy summer evenings. Inside, a living room/library will comfort with its fireplace and built-ins. The family room is graced with a fireplace and a curved, two-story ceiling with an overlook above. The master bedroom is a private retreat with a lovely bath, twin walk-in closets, and rear-porch access. Upstairs, three bedrooms with sizable closets—one bedroom would make an excellent guest suite or alternate master suite—share access to expandable space.

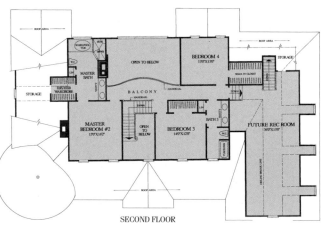

SECOND FLOOR

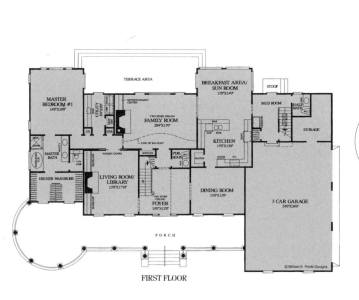

FIRST FLOOR

© William E. Poole Designs, Inc.

plan# HPK2000020

First Floor: 1,291 sq. ft.
Second Floor: 1,087 sq. ft.
Total: 2,378 sq. ft.
Bonus Space: 366 sq. ft.
Bedrooms: 3
Bathrooms: 2½
Width: 65' - 4"
Depth: 40' - 0"
Foundation: Crawlspace

ORDER ONLINE @ EPLANS.COM

This home exudes Early American elegance. Inside, a central fireplace in the family room conveniently warms the adjacent island kitchen and cathedral-ceilinged breakfast area. A built-in entertainment center is an added bonus to this area. Upstairs, the master suite features a sitting area, a dual-sink vanity, a private toilet, whirlpool tub, separate shower, and His and Hers walk-in closets. Two additional family bedrooms share a full hall bath.

SECOND FLOOR

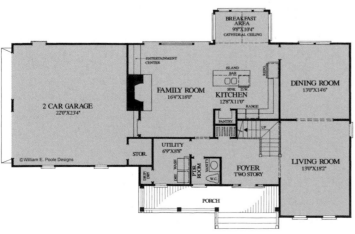

FIRST FLOOR

© William E. Poole Designs, Inc.

plan# HPK2000021

First Floor: 1,028 sq. ft.
Second Floor: 843 sq. ft.
Total: 1,871 sq. ft.
Bonus Space: 304 sq. ft.
Bedrooms: 3
Bathrooms: 2½
Width: 40' - 0"
Depth: 61' - 0"
Foundation: Crawlspace,
Unfinished Basement

ORDER ONLINE @ EPLANS.COM

A pedimented entry and fanlights above the door and in the dormers bring a Federal-style formality to this family home. A partially open stairway creates a soft divide between the dining room and the spacious great room, which features a central fireplace and a wall of windows punctuated by a pair of french doors leading to the back yard. An island kitchen extends into a breakfast nook and planning area. Conveniences are tucked between here and the garage. The second floor is efficiently designed to include two bedrooms and a hall bath as well as a master suite with a private spa and a huge walk-in closet.

FIRST FLOOR

SECOND FLOOR

© William E. Poole Designs, Inc.

plan# **HPK2000022**

First Floor: 2,168 sq. ft.
Second Floor: 1,203 sq. ft.
Total: 3,371 sq. ft.
Bonus Space: 452 sq. ft.
Bedrooms: 4
Bathrooms: 4½
Width: 71' - 2"
Depth: 63' - 4"
Foundation: Crawlspace,
Unfinished Basement

ORDER ONLINE @ EPLANS.COM

This stately two-story beauty offers the utmost in style and livability. The grand columned entryway is topped by a railed roof, making it the centerpiece of the facade. Formal space resides at the front of the plan, with a living room and dining room flanking the foyer. Secluded behind the staircase is the elegant master suite, with a huge walk-in closet and swank private bath. The hearth-warmed family room flows into the island kitchen and breakfast nook, making this space the comfortable hub of home life. A laundry room and half-bath are convenient to this area. Upstairs, three bedrooms all have access to separate baths and share space with a future recreation room.

FIRST FLOOR

SECOND FLOOR

© William E. Poole Designs, Inc.

plan# HPK2000023

First Floor: 2,209 sq. ft.
Second Floor: 1,136 sq. ft.
Total: 3,345 sq. ft.
Bonus Space: 462 sq. ft.
Bedrooms: 5
Bathrooms: 3½
Width: 60' - 2"
Depth: 78' - 2"
Foundation: Crawlspace,
Unfinished Basement

ORDER ONLINE @ EPLANS.COM

This handsome brick Colonial would be majestic in any neighborhood—today as well as yesterday and tomorrow. The pedimented entry leads to an open foyer flanked by rooms for formal entertaining. But guests and family members alike may tend to gravitate towards the family room, drawn by the fireplace and its surrounding entertainment center, or by the views provided through the massive Palladian window topped with a spectacular fanlight. This room shares its assets with the open island kitchen and adjoining breakfast bay. The master suite is secluded in a corner of the first floor. The second level provides three family bedrooms and two full baths, with an optional fifth bedroom and rec room, which is reached by a separate stair near the garage.

FIRST FLOOR

SECOND FLOOR

© William E. Poole Designs, Inc.

plan # HPK2000024

First Floor: 2,416 sq. ft.
Second Floor: 1,535 sq. ft.
Total: 3,951 sq. ft.
Bonus Space: 552 sq. ft.
Bedrooms: 5
Bathrooms: 3½
Width: 79' - 2"
Depth: 63' - 6"
Foundation: Crawlspace,
Unfinished Basement

ORDER ONLINE @ EPLANS.COM

A curved front porch, graceful symmetry in the details, and the sturdiness of brick all combine to enhance this beautiful two-story home. Inside, the two-story foyer introduces the formal rooms—the living room to the right and the dining room to the left—and presents the elegant stairwell. The L-shaped kitchen provides a walk-in pantry, an island with a sink, a butler's pantry, and an adjacent breakfast area. Perfect for casual gatherings, the family room features a fireplace and backyard access. Located on the first floor for privacy, the master suite offers a large walk-in closet and a lavish bath. Upstairs, four bedrooms—each with a walk-in closet—share two full baths and access to the future recreation room over the garage.

FIRST FLOOR

SECOND FLOOR

© William E. Poole Designs, Inc.

plan # HPK2000025

First Floor: 2,327 sq. ft.
Second Floor: 1,431 sq. ft.
Total: 3,758 sq. ft.
Bonus Space: 473 sq. ft.
Bedrooms: 5
Bathrooms: 3½
Width: 78' - 10"
Depth: 58' - 2"
Foundation: Crawlspace,
Unfinished Basement

ORDER ONLINE @ EPLANS.COM

This Early American classic was built with attention to the needs of an active family. The formal entrance allows guests to come and go in splendor, and family members can kick off their shoes in the mudroom. The step-saving kitchen is accented by an island for dinner preparations or school projects, and a pantry with tons of space. In the master suite, homeowners can relax in the whirlpool tub and revel in the ample walk-in closet. Second-floor family bedrooms provide privacy, walk-in closets, and two shared baths, both with dual vanities.

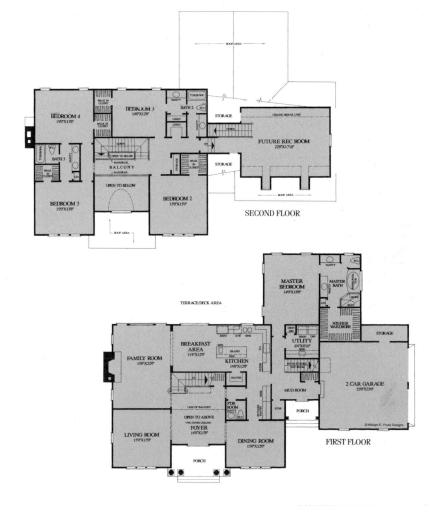

SECOND FLOOR

FIRST FLOOR

© William E. Poole Designs

© 2003 Donald A. Gardner, Inc.

Wrapping traditional brick with two country porches creates a modern exterior that's big on southern charm. Bold columns and a metal roof welcome guests inside to an equally impressive interior. Both the foyer and family room have two-story ceilings. The family room includes such amenities as a fireplace, built-in shelves, and access to the rear porch. A bay window expands the breakfast nook, located adjacent to the U-shaped kitchen. The living room/study and bonus room add flexibility for changing needs. The master suite, conveniently located on the first level, is complete with linen shelves, two walk-in closets, and a master bath featuring a double vanity, garden tub, separate shower, and private privy. The second level holds three more bedrooms, two bathrooms, bonus space, and an overlook to the family room.

plan# HPK2000026

First Floor: 1,809 sq. ft.
Second Floor: 777 sq. ft.
Total: 2,586 sq. ft.
Bonus Space: 264 sq. ft.
Bedrooms: 4
Bathrooms: 3½
Width: 70' - 7"
Depth: 48' - 4"

ORDER ONLINE @ EPLANS.COM

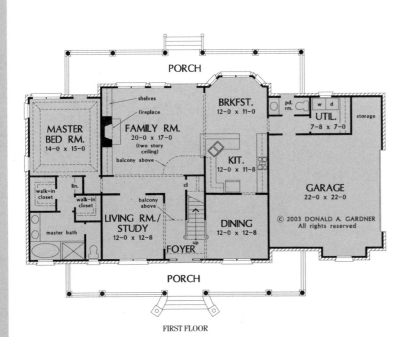

FIRST FLOOR

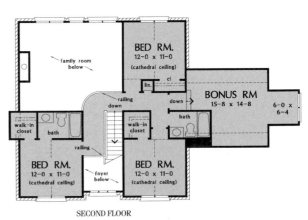

SECOND FLOOR

© 2002 Donald A. Gardner, Inc.

plan# HPK2000027

First Floor: 2,062 sq. ft.
Second Floor: 1,279 sq. ft.
Total: 3,341 sq. ft.
Bonus Space: 386 sq. ft.
Bedrooms: 5
Bathrooms: 4½
Width: 73' - 8"
Depth: 50' - 0"

ORDER ONLINE @ EPLANS.COM

A two-story Colonial Revival home may be exactly what you are looking for to entertain guests in grand style and accommodate a growing family. When visitors pass through the elegant columns on the front porch into the foyer with its spiral staircase and art niche, they know this is a special place. To the left is the formal dining room, and straight ahead is the spacious, two-story-high great room with a centered fireplace flanked by built-in shelves. The huge kitchen with an island counter and handy pantry easily serves the dining room and the sunlit breakfast nook. The absolutely magnificent master suite assumes the entire right wing of the plan. Upstairs, four bedrooms (or make one a study) and three baths offer plenty of comfort. A balcony overlooks the great room.

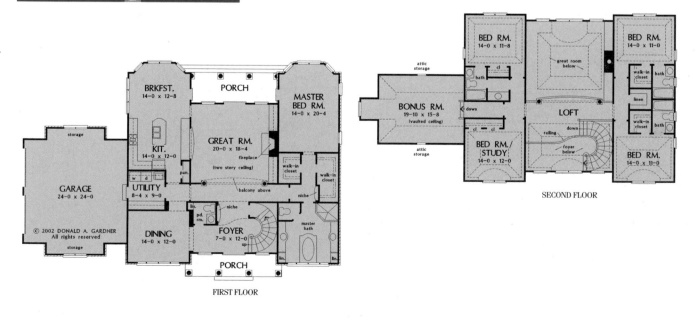

FIRST FLOOR

SECOND FLOOR

© 2003 Donald A. Gardner, Inc.

plan # HPK2000028

First Floor: 2,215 sq. ft.
Second Floor: 981 sq. ft.
Total: 3,196 sq. ft.
Bonus Space: 402 sq. ft.
Bedrooms: 5
Bathrooms: 4
Width: 71' - 11"
Depth: 55' - 10"

ORDER ONLINE @ EPLANS.COM

With a hipped roof, abundant porch space, and custom transoms, this home combines the best of country and traditional styles. The floor plan features well-defined rooms, yet still remains open and family-friendly. Two-story ceilings highlight both the foyer and great room, which are separated by a curved second-floor balcony. Built-in cabinets flank the fireplace, and a counter with a double sink and breakfast bar joins the kitchen to the great room. A butler's pantry connects the kitchen to the dining room, and the mudroom provides access to the bonus room. Special elements include a bay window in the breakfast nook, a shower seat in the master bath, and additional walk-in attic storage upstairs. The study/bedroom allows versatility.

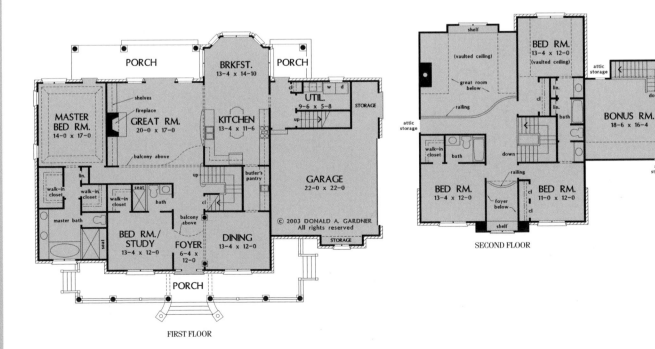

FIRST FLOOR

SECOND FLOOR

© 2001 Donald A. Gardner, Inc.

plan# HPK2000029

First Floor: 1,500 sq. ft.
Second Floor: 1,106 sq. ft.
Total: 2,606 sq. ft.
Bonus Space: 366 sq. ft.
Bedrooms: 4
Bathrooms: 2½
Width: 63' - 3"
Depth: 48' - 1"

ORDER ONLINE @ EPLANS.COM

Elegant and stately, the exterior features a Palladian-style window, which accents the front facade and floods the two-story foyer with light. The floor plan features open spaces with more room definition for those seeking a truly traditional design. Columns separate the formal living and dining rooms, and a bay window extends the breakfast area. French doors access the rear porch as well as connect the family room to the outdoors. Built-ins embrace the fireplace, and an angled counter allows the kitchen to take part in casual entertaining. The master bedroom features a tray ceiling, and additional bedrooms share a full bath with the bonus room. Note the second-floor balcony.

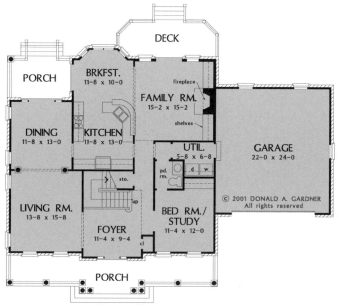

FIRST FLOOR

SECOND FLOOR

© 2001 Donald A. Gardner, Inc.

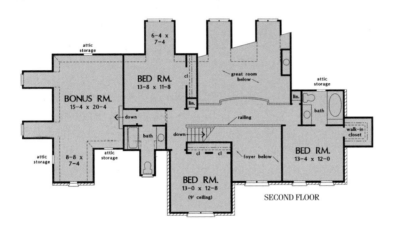

attic storage

BED RM.
13-8 x 11-8

6-4 x 7-4

cl

great room below

attic storage

BONUS RM.
15-4 x 20-4

lin.

bath

down

railing

walk-in closet

attic storage

8-8 x 7-4

attic storage

bath

down

cl   cl

foyer below

BED RM.
13-4 x 12-0

BED RM.
13-0 x 12-8
(9' ceiling)

SECOND FLOOR

© 2001 DONALD A. GARDNER
All rights reserved

plan# HPK2000030

First Floor: 2,511 sq. ft.
Second Floor: 1,062 sq. ft.
Total: 3,573 sq. ft.
Bonus Space: 465 sq. ft.
Bedrooms: 4
Bathrooms: 3½
Width: 84' - 11"
Depth: 55' - 11"

ORDER ONLINE @ EPLANS.COM

An abundance of windows and an attractive brick facade enhance the exterior of this traditional two-story home. Inside, a study and formal dining room flank either side of the two-story foyer. Fireplaces warm both the great room and first-floor master suite. The suite also provides a separate sitting room, two walk-in closets, and a private bath. The island kitchen extends into the breakfast room. The second floor features three additional family bedrooms, two baths, and a bonus room fit for a home office.

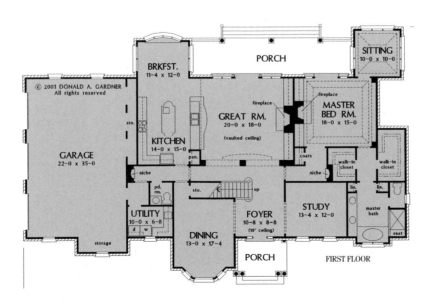

BRKFST.
11-4 x 12-0

PORCH

SITTING
10-0 x 10-0

fireplace

GARAGE
22-0 x 35-0

sto.

KITCHEN
14-0 x 15-0

fireplace

GREAT RM.
20-0 x 18-0
(vaulted ceiling)

MASTER
BED RM.
18-0 x 15-0

pan.

niche

coats

walk-in closet

walk-in closet

pd. rm.

sto.

niche

lin.

lin.

UTILITY
10-0 x 6-8

d   w

up

FOYER
10-8 x 8-8
(18' ceiling)

STUDY
13-4 x 12-0

master bath

storage

DINING
13-0 x 17-4

PORCH

seat

FIRST FLOOR

plan# HPK2000031

First Floor: 1,773 sq. ft.
Second Floor: 1,676 sq. ft.
Total: 3,449 sq. ft.
Bedrooms: 5
Bathrooms: 4
Width: 68' - 7"
Depth: 62' - 8"
Foundation: Crawlspace,
Unfinished Walkout Basement

ORDER ONLINE @ EPLANS.COM

From a Colonial past to a contemporary future, this Southern-style home perfectly combines elements of history and modernity. Brick facing graces the entry, where a double-decker porch invites casual relaxation. A two-story foyer opens on the left to an elegant dining room; a butler's pantry makes entertaining simple. The kitchen is a dream come true for the chef who wants room to move and miles of counter space. Adjacent to the bayed breakfast nook, the vaulted keeping room warms with a cozy hearth. The family room completes the living areas with a fireplace and lots of natural light. Upstairs, the master suite is a romantic getaway with a fireplace, room-sized walk-in closet, and a luxuriant vaulted bath.

© Larry E. Belk Designs

plan# HPK2000287

First Floor: 3,722 sq. ft.
Second Floor: 1,859 sq. ft.
Total: 5,581 sq. ft.
Bedrooms: 5
Bathrooms: 4½
Width: 127' - 10"
Depth: 83' - 9"
Foundation: Slab

ORDER ONLINE @ EPLANS.COM

A richly detailed entrance sets the elegant tone of this luxurious design. Rising gracefully from the two-story foyer, the staircase is a fine prelude to the great room beyond, where a fantastic span of windows on the back wall overlooks the rear grounds. The dining room is located off the entry and has a lovely coffered ceiling. The kitchen, breakfast room, and sunroom are conveniently grouped for casual entertaining. The elaborate master suite enjoys a coffered ceiling, private sitting room, and spa-style bath. The second level consists of four bedrooms with private baths and a large game room featuring a rear stair.

SECOND FLOOR

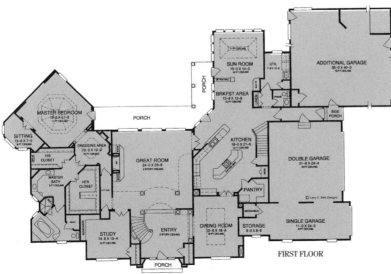

FIRST FLOOR

plan # HPK2000288

First Floor: 2,121 sq. ft.
Second Floor: 920 sq. ft.
Total: 3,041 sq. ft.
Bedrooms: 4
Bathrooms: 3
Width: 63' - 0"
Depth: 63' - 0"
Foundation: Crawlspace, Slab

ORDER ONLINE @ EPLANS.COM

A striking combination of brick and siding complements multi-pane windows and a columned entry to create a fresh face on this classic design. The two-story foyer opens to the formal living and dining rooms, set off by columned archways. Casual living space includes a spacious family area, open to the breakfast room—bright with windows—and the kitchen. The main-level master suite boasts two walk-in closets, an angled whirlpool tub, a separate shower and additional linen storage. A guest suite or family bedroom with a full bath is positioned for privacy on the opposite side of the plan. Each of the two family bedrooms on the upper level boasts a walk-in closet. The bedrooms share a full bath with separate dressing areas and are open to a gallery hall that leads to a sizable game room with attic access.

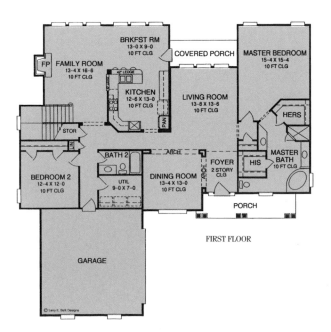

FIRST FLOOR

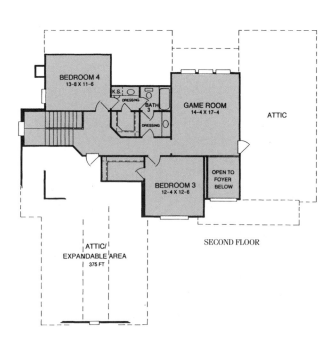

SECOND FLOOR

COPYRIGHT LARRY E. BELK

plan# HPK2000032

First Floor: 3,219 sq. ft.
Second Floor: 1,202 sq. ft.
Total: 4,421 sq. ft.
Bedrooms: 4
Bathrooms: 4½
Width: 86' - 1"
Depth: 76' - 10"
Foundation: Crawlspace

ORDER ONLINE @ EPLANS.COM

Timeless sophistication characterizes this lovely home that's designed for entertaining and family. The columned dining room and the vaulted living room, with a striking two-story window wall, welcome all to this sensational home. The master bedroom is a dream with a cozy sitting room that includes a corner fireplace. A dramatic curved staircase leads upstairs to the secondary sleeping quarters. Here, two bedrooms with private baths, a computer room, and a large game room complete the plan.

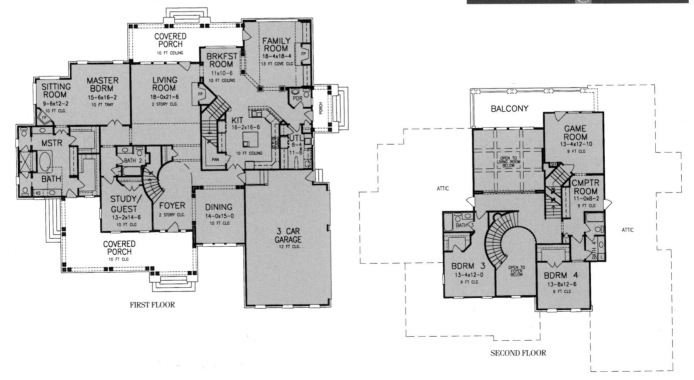

FIRST FLOOR

SECOND FLOOR

plan# HPK2000033

First Floor: 1,205 sq. ft.
Second Floor: 1,160 sq. ft.
Total: 2,365 sq. ft.
Bonus Space: 350 sq. ft.
Bedrooms: 3
Bathrooms: 2½
Width: 52' - 6"
Depth: 43' - 6"
Foundation: Finished
Walkout Basement

ORDER ONLINE @ EPLANS.COM

This charming exterior conceals a perfect family plan. The formal dining and living rooms reside on either side of the foyer. At the rear of the home is a family room with a fireplace and access to a deck and veranda. The modern kitchen features a sunlit breakfast area. The second floor provides four bedrooms, one of which may be finished at a later date and used as a guest suite. Note the extra storage space in the two-car garage.

SECOND FLOOR

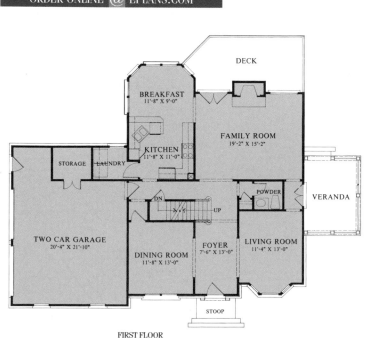

FIRST FLOOR

Gables on the roof really serve as great adornment to the brick facade of this traditional home. Enjoy the dining room fireplace for formal occasions, or retreat to the family room and light that hearth when the family is gathered for a cozy evening together. A walk-in pantry in the counter-filled kitchen is a wonderful touch. Eat casually in the breakfast nook, or bring your coffee to the rear deck. The stairs in the foyer lead to second-floor sleeping areas. Three family bedrooms share a full bath with enough sink and counter space to make everyone happy. The master suite includes a lavish bath and two walk-in closets.

plan# HPK2000289

First Floor: 1,186 sq. ft.
Second Floor: 1,366 sq. ft.
Total: 2,552 sq. ft.
Bedrooms: 4
Bathrooms: 2½
Width: 55' - 0"
Depth: 39' - 0"
Foundation: Unfinished Walkout Basement

ORDER ONLINE @ EPLANS.COM

FIRST FLOOR

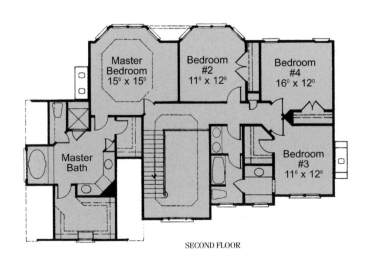

SECOND FLOOR

plan# HPK2000290

First Floor: 2,297 sq. ft.
Second Floor: 1,383 sq. ft.
Total: 3,680 sq. ft.
Bedrooms: 4
Bathrooms: 3½
Width: 65' - 0"
Depth: 55' - 6"
Foundation: Finished Walkout Basement

ORDER ONLINE @ EPLANS.COM

This stately brick home has great curb appeal, from its elegant front entry and multi-pane windows to the private covered porch surprisingly attached to the garage. Inside, the foyer opens to the bayed formal dining room, then leads to the expansive great room with an impressive fireplace and built-ins. A covered back porch is reached from both the great room and the nearby breakfast nook. The informal living area continues with a keeping room and a second fireplace. The efficient island kitchen is just a few steps away from all of these rooms, making entertaining enjoyable for both cook and guests. A sumptuous master suite fills the left side of the plan, while three secondary bedrooms and a library may be found upstairs.

FIRST FLOOR

SECOND FLOOR

plan# HPK2000034

First Floor: 1,465 sq. ft.
Second Floor: 1,332 sq. ft.
Total: 2,797 sq. ft.
Bedrooms: 3
Bathrooms: 2½
Width: 49' - 0"
Depth: 75 - 0"
Foundation: Finished Walkout Basement

ORDER ONLINE @ EPLANS.COM

Brick, horizontal siding, and a columned porch add elements of style to this graceful Georgian design. Formal rooms flank the foyer, which leads to casual living space with a fireplace and French doors to the rear porch. A convenient butler's pantry eases service to the dining room from the well-planned kitchen. Angled counter space allows an overlook to the breakfast room. Upstairs, a rambling master suite has its own hearth and two sets of French doors that lead out to a private porch. The homeowner's bath features a split walk-in closet, an angled shower, a whirlpool tub, and a compartmented bath. Each of two family bedrooms enjoys private access to a shared bath.

Two Car Garage 21³x21³

Storage

Breakfast 11⁶x11⁰

Porch

Porch

Kitchen 13³x12⁶

Family Room 19⁹x14⁹

Dn
Up

Dining Room 12³x15⁰

Foyer

Living Room 12⁰x12⁰

FIRST FLOOR

Porch

Master Bedroom 19⁶x14⁹

Dn

Bedroom No. 2 12³x15⁰

Bedroom No. 3 12⁰x14⁶

SECOND FLOOR

© Stephen Fuller, Inc.

P. Dent

plan# HPK2000035

First Floor: 1,787 sq. ft.
Second Floor: 851 sq. ft.
Total: 2,638 sq. ft.
Bonus Space: 189 sq. ft.
Bedrooms: 3
Bathrooms: 2½
Width: 51' - 3"
Depth: 70' - 6"
Foundation: Finished Walkout
Basement

ORDER ONLINE @ EPLANS.COM

This beautiful brick design displays fine family livability in over 2,600 square feet. The wraparound porch welcomes family and friends to inside living areas. The great room sports an elegant ceiling, a fireplace, and built-ins. The kitchen displays good traffic patterning. An island cooktop will please the house gourmet. The dining room features double doors that open out onto the porch. In the master bedroom, a pampering bath includes a whirlpool tub and separate vanities. A walk-in closet is located at the back of the bath. Two family bedrooms upstairs enjoy peace and quiet and a full hall bath with natural illumination.

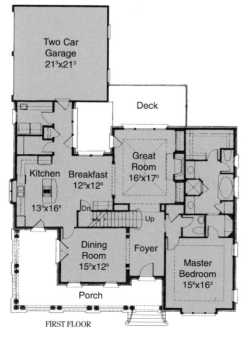

FIRST FLOOR

SECOND FLOOR

plan# **HPK2000036**

First Floor: 1,165 sq. ft.
Second Floor: 1,050 sq. ft.
Total: 2,215 sq. ft.
Bonus Space: 265 sq. ft.
Bedrooms: 3
Bathrooms: 2½
Width: 58' - 0"
Depth: 36' - 0"
Foundation: Finished Walkout Basement

ORDER ONLINE @ EPLANS.COM

No detail is left to chance in this classically designed two-story home. A formal entry opens to the living and dining rooms through graceful arches. For more casual entertaining, the family room provides ample space for large gatherings and features a warming fireplace and access to the rear deck through double doors. The adjacent L-shaped kitchen handles any occasion with ease. Upstairs, the master suite runs the width of the house and includes a generous walk-in closet and a bath with a knee-space vanity, twin lavatories, a garden tub, and a separate shower. A central hall leads to two family bedrooms and a full bath, as well as bonus space, which offers the possibility of a future fourth bedroom and bath.

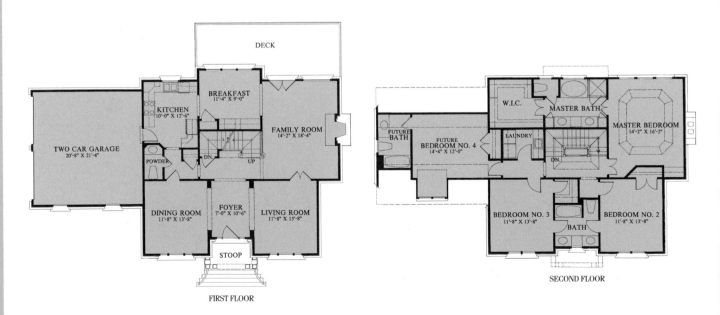

FIRST FLOOR

SECOND FLOOR

plan# HPK2000037

First Floor: 1,270 sq. ft.
Second Floor: 1,070 sq. ft.
Total: 2,340 sq. ft.
Bedrooms: 4
Bathrooms: 3½
Width: 53' - 0"
Depth: 44' - 0"
Foundation: Finished Walkout Basement

ORDER ONLINE @ EPLANS.COM

Grand, welcoming, and cozy—these are the words that describe this two-story brick house. The first floor consists of a family room with an 18-foot ceiling, a dramatic breakfast nook, a deck, and a guest bedroom with a full bath. Family sleeping quarters are located upstairs. Here you'll find a glorious master suite; it includes His and Hers walk-in closets and a bath with a spa tub, shower, and double-bowl vanity. Bedrooms 3 and 4 share a full compartmented bath. The home is completed with a two-car garage.

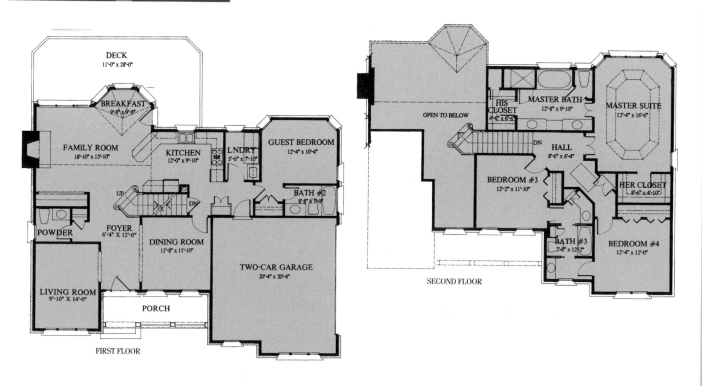

plan# HPK2000291

First Floor: 1,601 sq. ft.
Second Floor: 1,520 sq. ft.
Total: 3,121 sq. ft.
Bedrooms: 4
Bathrooms: 3½
Width: 49' - 3"
Depth: 74' - 3"
Foundation: Finished Walkout
Basement

ORDER ONLINE @ EPLANS.COM

George Washington slept here. Not really, but he may have slept in a home with a Georgian exterior such as this. The amenity-filled interior begins through the columned entry to the formal dining room on the left, and the formal living room on the right. Adjacent to the living room is a more informal family room. An L-shaped kitchen is highlighted by a center cooktop island and access to an office tucked away behind the powder room. The second floor contains three family bedrooms, two full baths and the master suite.

FIRST FLOOR

SECOND FLOOR

plan# HPK2000292

First Floor: 1,355 sq. ft.
Second Floor: 1,442 sq. ft.
Total: 2,797 sq. ft.
Bedrooms: 4
Bathrooms: 3½
Width: 52' - 2"
Depth: 56' - 6"
Foundation: Crawlspace

ORDER ONLINE @ EPLANS.COM

This Southern design begins with a spacious gathering room, complete with an extended-hearth fireplace and lovely French doors. The gathering room opens to a sunny breakfast area, with its own French door to the back terrace and deck. Upstairs, the master suite features a coffered ceiling, two walk-in closets, and a lavish bath with separate vanities. Three family bedrooms, one with a private bath, share a hall that opens to a generous sitting area with space for books and computers

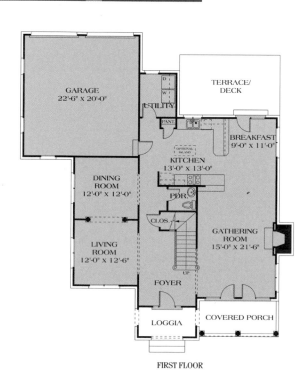

FIRST FLOOR

SECOND FLOOR

plan# HPK2000038

First Floor: 1,611 sq. ft.
Second Floor: 1,687 sq. ft.
Total: 3,298 sq. ft.
Bedrooms: 4
Bathrooms: 3½
Width: 82' - 0"
Depth: 48' - 0"
Foundation: Unfinished Walkout
Basement

ORDER ONLINE @ EPLANS.COM

This home's exterior exudes beauty and sophistication, and those themes are continued inside as well. Up the front steps and past the stately columns, enter the grand foyer. To the left of the foyer sits the parlor, with front-facing windows and access to the welcoming family room—sure to be the heart of this home, with its glowing fireplace. Follow the family room out to the morning room, which connects with the efficient island kitchen—complete with a walk-in pantry. Wrapping up the first floor are a convenient laundry room, powder room, and large, formal dining room. The second level is home to all four bedrooms, three of which have private baths. The spacious master suite includes a pampering master bath—with two sinks on opposite walls, and a separate tub and shower—a massive walk-in closet, and lovely sitting area.

FIRST FLOOR

SECOND FLOOR

plan# HPK2000039

First Floor: 1,332 sq. ft.
Second Floor: 1,331 sq. ft.
Total: 2,663 sq. ft.
Bedrooms: 4
Bathrooms: 3½
Width: 48' - 0"
Depth: 42' - 0"
Foundation: Unfinished Basement

ORDER ONLINE @ EPLANS.COM

Hints of Greek Revivalism blend beautifully with Early American style for a handsome home with world-wide appeal. The entry is gracefully lit by a second-story arched window and leads guests into a bayed living room. The great room is ready to host any occasion, with a corner fireplace and built-in entertainment center. The kitchen has a central island and easily serves the breakfast nook and dining area. Upstairs, three bedrooms line the right side of the plan, and the master suite is on the left. Here, vaulted ceilings and walk-in closets are lovely luxuries, but the real standout is the bath, with a whirlpool tub and a see-through fireplace shared with the bedroom.

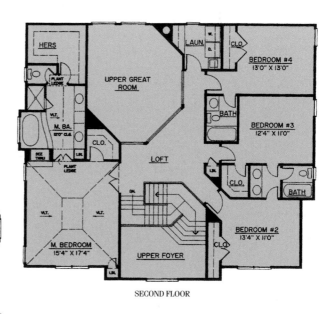

FIRST FLOOR

SECOND FLOOR

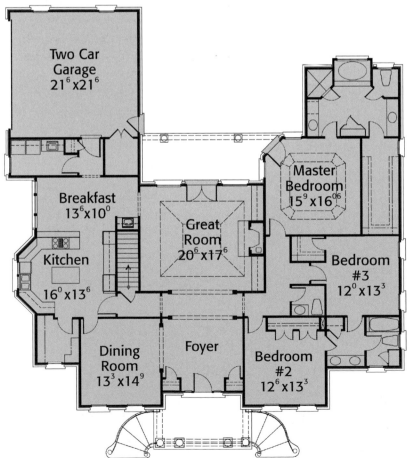

Two Car Garage
21⁶x21⁶

Breakfast
13⁶x10⁰

Kitchen
16⁰x13⁶

Great Room
20⁶x17⁶

Master Bedroom
15⁹x16⁰⁶

Bedroom #3
12⁰x13³

Dining Room
13³x14⁹

Foyer

Bedroom #2
12⁶x13³

plan# HPK2000040

Square Footage: 2,697
Bedrooms: 3
Bathrooms: 2½
Width: 65' - 3"
Depth: 67' - 3"
Foundation: Finished Walkout Basement

ORDER ONLINE @ EPLANS.COM

Dual chimneys (one a false chimney created to enhance the aesthetic effect) and a double stairway to the covered entry of this home create a balanced architectural statement. The sunlit foyer leads straight into the spacious great room, where French doors provide a generous view of the covered veranda in back. The great room features a tray ceiling and a fireplace, bordered by twin bookcases. Another great view is offered from the spacious kitchen with a breakfast bar and a roomy work island. The master suite provides a large, balanced bath and a spacious closet.

plan# HPK2000041

Square Footage: 4,646
Bedrooms: 3
Bathrooms: 2½
Width: 111' - 10"
Depth: 76' - 0"
Foundation: Finished Walkout
Basement

ORDER ONLINE @ EPLANS.COM

Timeless in every detail, this home displays a stately manner through the use of brick, symmetrical design and classic elements. The tremendous foyer offers an ideal location for greeting guests and provides a double entrance to the living room. The kitchen easily serves the formal dining room, the breakfast room and the octagonal den. With a vaulted master bath, access to the study and a private stair to the health spa below, the master suite is complete in every detail. The lower terrace level contains an exercise room with a large bath and a recreation room with a fireplace and wet bar.

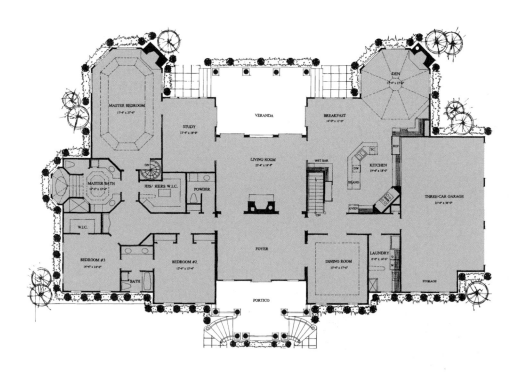

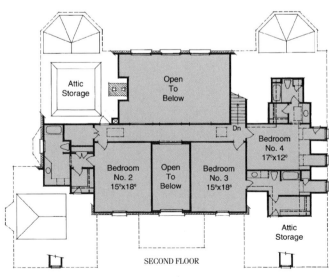

plan # HPK2000042

First Floor: 3,509 sq. ft.
Second Floor: 1,564 sq. ft.
Total: 5,073 sq. ft.
Bedrooms: 4
Bathrooms: 4½ + ½
Width: 86' - 6"
Depth: 67' - 3"
Foundation: Finished Walkout Basement

ORDER ONLINE @ EPLANS.COM

Classic symmetry sets off this graceful exterior, with two sets of double columns framed by tall windows and topped with a detailed pediment. Just off the foyer, the study and dining room present an elegant impression. The gourmet kitchen offers a food-preparation island and a lovely breakfast bay. The central gallery hall connects casual living areas with the master wing. A delightful dressing area with a split vanity and a bay window indulge the lavish master bath. The master bedroom features a bumped-out glass sitting area, a tray ceiling, and a romantic fireplace. Upstairs, three bedroom suites are pampered with private baths.

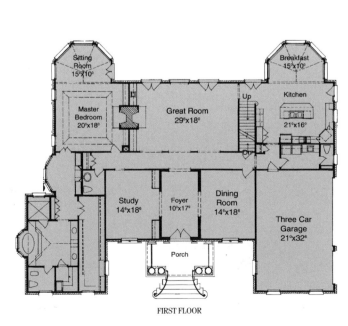

FIRST FLOOR

SECOND FLOOR

plan# HPK2000043

Square Footage: 2,987
Bedrooms: 3
Bathrooms: 2½
Width: 74' - 0"
Depth: 62' - 0"
Foundation: Finished Walkout Basement

ORDER ONLINE @ EPLANS.COM

Reaching back through the centuries for its inspiration, this home reflects the grandeur that was ancient Rome—as it looked to newly independent Americans in the 1700s. The entry portico provides a classic twist: the balustrade that would have marched across the roofline of a typical Revival home trims to form the balcony outside the French doors of the study. Inside, the foyer opens to the study, as well as the formal dining room, then leads to a welcoming great room warmed by a fireplace. The left wing is given over to a private master suite with a bath that offers the ultimate in luxury, including a large walk-in closet. On the right side of the house, two additional bedrooms share a full bath. Separating the sleeping wings is the kitchen, with its nearby keeping/family room.

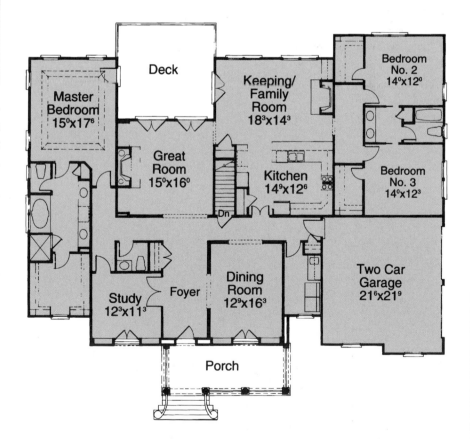

© William E. Poole Designs, Inc

This home takes its cue from the gracious formality indigenous to the typical Mississippi River Delta Planters' Cottage. A noteworthy feature is the rare combination of the Natchez gallery recessed beneath an unbroken slope of gable roof with a triangular pediment. Fanlights span the rear of the home, bringing light to the family room and the first-floor master suite. Future space above the garage allows this plan to be customized or expanded as needed.

plan# **HPK2000044**

First Floor: 2,031 sq. ft.
Second Floor: 1,113 sq. ft.
Total: 3,144 sq. ft.
Bonus Space: 683 sq. ft.
Bedrooms: 4
Bathrooms: 3½
Width: 79' - 10"
Depth: 52' - 4"
Foundation: Crawlspace

ORDER ONLINE @ EPLANS.COM

© William E. Poole Designs

SECOND FLOOR

© William E. Poole Designs, Inc.

plan# HPK2000045

First Floor: 2,337 sq. ft.
Second Floor: 1,016 sq. ft.
Total: 3,353 sq. ft.
Bonus Space: 394 sq. ft.
Bedrooms: 4
Bathrooms: 3½
Width: 66' - 2"
Depth: 71' - 2"
Foundation: Crawlspace

ORDER ONLINE @ EPLANS.COM

With an abundance of natural light and amenities, this home is sure to please. The sunporch doubles as a delightful area to enjoy meals with a view. A mudroom off the utility room accesses a side porch and serves as a place to hang coats or shed dirty shoes before entering the kitchen or family room. The master bedroom, family room, and living room/library each boast a private fireplace. Upstairs houses three additional bedrooms, two sharing a full bath and one with an attached full bath. Future expansion space completes the second floor. Extra storage space in the garage is an added convenience.

FIRST FLOOR

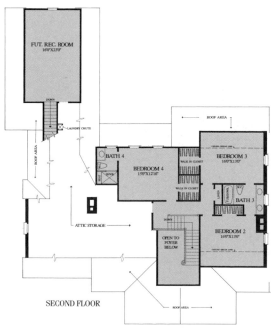

SECOND FLOOR

© William E. Poole Designs, Inc.

plan # HPK2000046

Square Footage: 2,869
Bonus Space: 311 sq. ft.
Bedrooms: 3
Bathrooms: 3½
Width: 68' - 6"
Depth: 79' - 8"
Foundation: Crawlspace

ORDER ONLINE @ EPLANS.COM

Here is a beautiful example of Classical Revival architecture complete with shuttered, jack-arch windows and a column-supported pediment over the entry. Inside, the foyer opens to the living room and leads to the family room at the rear. Here, a panoramic view is complemented by an impressive fireplace framed by built-ins. To the left, the efficient island kitchen is situated between the sunny breakfast nook and the formal dining room. The right side of the plan holds two bedrooms and the lavish master suite.

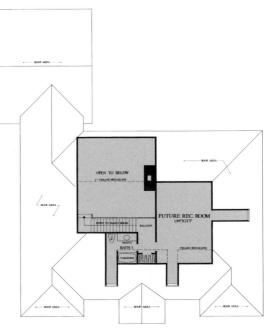

© William E. Poole Designs, Inc

plan# HPK2000047

Square Footage: 2,639
Bonus Space: 396 sq. ft.
Bedrooms: 3
Bathrooms: 2½
Width: 73' - 8"
Depth: 58' - 6"
Foundation: Crawlspace

ORDER ONLINE @ EPLANS.COM

Colonial architecture, like this elegant home, lends a classic air to any neighborhood. The interior offers a completely modern arrangement with the dramatic foyer opening to the spectacular living room with its window wall, cathedral ceiling, and stunning fireplace. To the left, the kitchen is central to the more intimate family/sunroom and breakfast area. The formal dining room, to the left of the foyer, completes the living area. The sleeping quarters on the right include two bedrooms and a romantic master suite with a plush private bath.

© William E. Poole Designs

© William E. Poole Designs, Inc.

plan# HPK2000048

First Floor: 2,320 sq. ft.
Second Floor: 1,009 sq. ft.
Total: 3,329 sq. ft.
Bonus Space: 521 sq. ft.
Bedrooms: 4
Bathrooms: 3½
Width: 80' - 4"
Depth: 58' - 0"
Foundation: Crawlspace

ORDER ONLINE @ EPLANS.COM

Sturdy columns on a spacious, welcoming front porch lend a Greek Revival feel to this design, and three dormer windows provide a relaxed country look. The living and dining rooms, each with a fireplace, flank the two-story foyer; the family room also includes a fireplace, as well as built-in shelves and a wall of windows. The L-shaped kitchen, conveniently near the breakfast area, features a work island and a large pantry. Two walk-in closets highlight the lavish master suite, which offers a private bath with a soothing whirlpool tub. Three family bedrooms—all with dormer alcoves and two with walk-in closets—sit upstairs, along with a future recreation room.

FIRST FLOOR

FIRST FLOOR

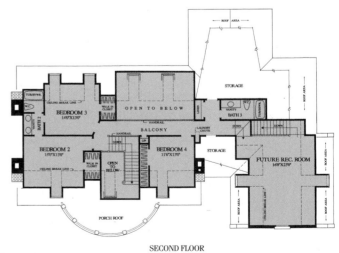

SECOND FLOOR

© William E. Poole Designs, Inc.

plan# HPK2000049

Square Footage: 3,600
Bedrooms: 4
Bathrooms: 3½
Width: 76' - 2"
Depth: 100' - 10"
Foundation: Crawlspace,
Unfinished Basement

ORDER ONLINE @ EPLANS.COM

Graceful columns combine with stunning symmetry on this fine four-bedroom home. Inside, the foyer opens to the formal living room on the left and then leads back to the spacious family room. Here, a fireplace waits to warm cool fall evenings, and built-ins accommodate your book collection. The efficient island kitchen offers plenty of counter and cabinet space, easily serving both the formal dining room and the sunny breakfast area. A separate bedroom resides back by the garage and features a walk-in closet. Two more family bedrooms are at the front right side of the home and share a full bath. The lavish master suite is complete with a huge walk-in closet, a bayed sitting area, and a sumptuous bath.

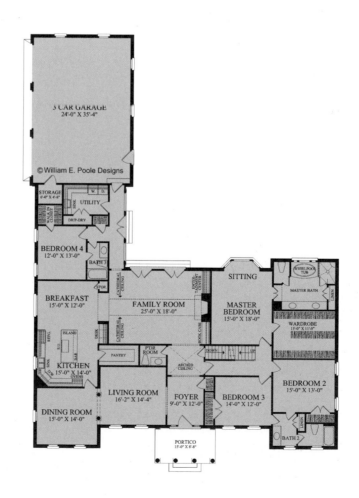

© William E. Poole Designs

plan# HPK2000050

Square Footage: 1,800
Bedrooms: 3
Bathrooms: 2
Width: 65' - 0"
Depth: 66' - 0"
Foundation: Unfinished Basement, Crawlspace, Slab

ORDER ONLINE @ EPLANS.COM

Neoclassic style emerges with columns and a pediment at the porch of this lovely one-story home. An arched transom over the front door lights the foyer—perfect for family photos displayed along the hall. To the right is a cozy living room with a large picture window and fireplace. A bay window gives a backyard view to the dining room. The L-shaped island kitchen adjoins the light-filled dining area. This split-bedroom floor plan includes two family bedrooms sharing a bath. The master suite provides a walk-in closet and two-vanity bath.

Storage 19-6x8-6

Laundry 9-8x5-10

Basement Stair Location
OPTIONAL LAYOUT

Carport 21-10x21-2

Patio 23-9x21-0

Kitchen 11-0x16-0

Dining 12-9x16-0

Master Bedroom 17-6x13-6

Bath

Laundry 9-8x9-3

M.Bath 11-8x11-7

Bedroom 13-8x11-7

Bedroom 12-9x11-3

Foyer

Living Room 15-1x13-6

Planter Box

Stoop

Planter Box

plan# HPK2000051

Square Footage: 1,955
Bedrooms: 3
Bathrooms: 2½
Width: 56' - 4"
Depth: 67' - 4"
Foundation: Crawlspace, Slab,
Unfinished Basement

ORDER ONLINE @ EPLANS.COM

Double pillars, beautiful transoms, and sidelights set off the entry door and draw attention to this comfortable home. The foyer leads to a formal dining room and a great room with two pairs of French doors framing a warming fireplace. The kitchen enjoys a large island/snack bar and a walk-in pantry. Privacy is assured in the master suite—a large walk-in closet and full bath with a separate shower and large tub add to the pleasure of this wing. Two family bedrooms share a full bath at the front of the design.

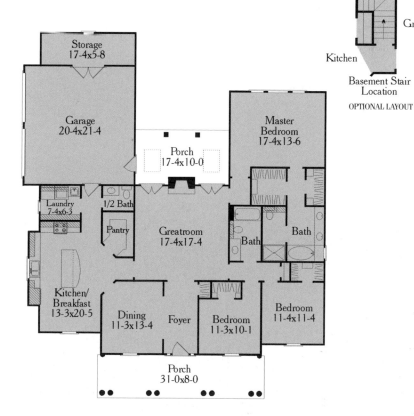

plan⊕ HPK2000293

First Floor: 2,293 sq. ft.
Second Floor: 949 sq. ft.
Total: 3,242 sq. ft.
Bonus Space: 373 sq. ft.
Bedrooms: 3
Bathrooms: 3½
Width: 82' - 6"
Depth: 67' - 2"
Foundation: Finished Walkout Basement

ORDER ONLINE @ EPLANS.COM

From its dramatic front entry to its rear twin-bay turret, this design is as traditional as it is historic. A two-story foyer opens through a gallery to an expansive gathering room, which shares its natural light with a bumped-out morning nook. A formal living room or study offers a coffered ceiling and a private door to the gallery hall that leads to the master suite. The dining room opens to more casual living space, including the kitchen with its angled island counter. Bonus space may be developed later.

REAR EXTERIOR

SECOND FLOOR

FIRST FLOOR

BASEMENT

© The Sater Design Collection, Inc.

plan# HPK2000294

Square Footage: 3,764
Bedrooms: 4
Bathrooms: 3½
Width: 80' - 6"
Depth: 111' - 0"
Foundation: Slab

ORDER ONLINE @ EPLANS.COM

This exquisite Colonial manor will be the showpiece of any neighborhood. Classic brick and stately columns add grandeur to the facade; personal touches and exciting features make the interior a design to call home. The study and dining room border the foyer. Ahead, the living room welcomes guests with a fireplace, rear veranda access, and a coffered ceiling. The step-saving kitchen provides room for more than one chef, and easily serves the dining room and sunny breakfast nook. An entertainment center separates the leisure room from the game room—or make it a bedroom—with extra storage space. The guest suite includes a private bath. Down the gallery (with a window seat) two bedrooms share a full bath. The master suite is resplendent with a defined sitting area, massive walk-in closets, and a soothing spa bath with a whirlpool tub and walk-in shower.

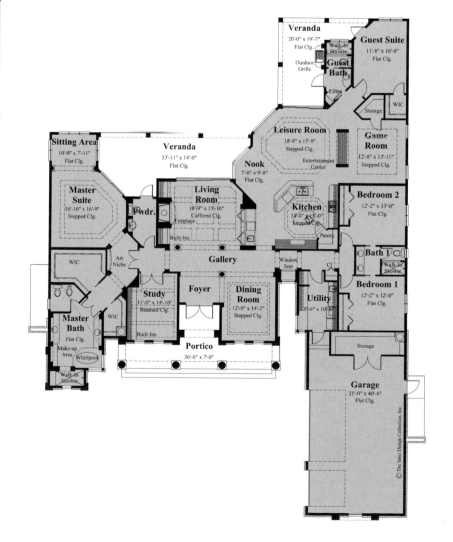

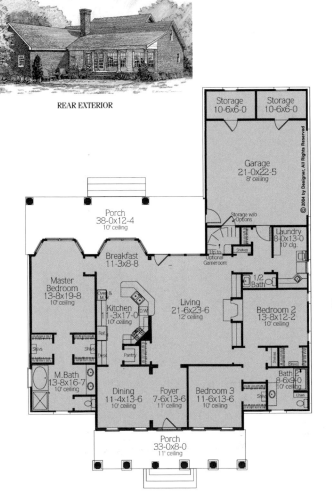

REAR EXTERIOR

Storage
10-6x6-0

Storage
10-6x6-0

Garage
21-0x22-5
8' ceiling

Storage w/o
Options

Porch
38-0x12-4
10' ceiling

Breakfast
11-3x8-8

Master
Bedroom
13-8x19-8
10' ceiling

Kitchen
11-3x17-0
10' ceiling

Living
21-6x23-6
12' ceiling

Laundry
8-0x13-0
10' clg.

1/2
Bath

Bedroom 2
13-8x12-2
10' ceiling

M. Bath
13-8x16-7
10' ceiling

Dining
11-4x13-6
10' ceiling

Foyer
7-6x13-6
11' ceiling

Bedroom 3
11-6x13-6
10' ceiling

Bath
8-6x9-0
10' ceiling

Porch
33-0x8-0
11' ceiling

© 2004 by Designer, All Rights Reserved

Optional
Future
Gameroom
11-11x28-8

OPTIONAL LAYOUT

Garage

Porch

Living

Basement
Stair
Option

OPTIONAL LAYOUT

plan# HPK2000052

Square Footage: 2,379
Bonus Space: 367 sq. ft.
Bedrooms: 3
Bathrooms: 2½
Width: 61' - 0"
Depth: 81' - 9"
Foundation: Crawlspace, Slab,
Unfinished Basement

ORDER ONLINE @ EPLANS.COM

If you are looking for a home that grows with your family, this is it! Six rounded columns grace the front porch and lend a Colonial feel to this great home plan. Inside, the foyer opens to the formal dining space, which is only a few steps to the kitchen. A walk-in pantry, spacious counters and cabinets, snack bar, adjoining breakfast area, and planning desk make this kitchen efficient and gourmet. A private master suite features a sitting bay, twin walk-in closets, and an amenity-filled bath. Two oversized secondary bedrooms enjoy walk-in closets and share a corner bath. The entire second level is future space that will become exactly what you need. Plenty of storage can be found in the garage.

plan# HPK2000295

Square Footage: 1,550
Bedrooms: 3
Bathrooms: 2
Width: 62' - 8"
Depth: 36' - 0"
Foundation: Unfinished Basement

ORDER ONLINE @ EPLANS.COM

A handsome porch dressed up with Greek Revival details greets visitors warmly in this Early American home. The foyer opens to the airy and spacious living room and dining room with vaulted ceilings. The secluded master bedroom also sports a vaulted ceiling and is graced with a dressing area, private bath, and walk-in closet. Two decks located at the rear of the plan are accessed via the master bedroom, kitchen, and living room. A full bath serves the two family bedrooms.

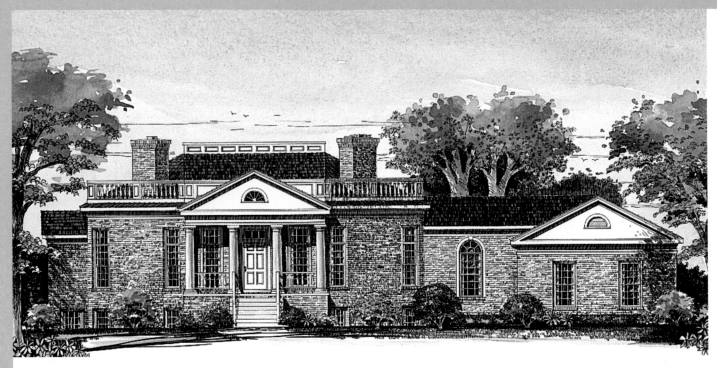

If you're looking to do something a little different for your home-building experience, this adaptation of Jefferson's "Poplar Forest" home may be just the ticket. Originally built in the hills around Lynchburg, Virginia, Poplar Forest served Jefferson as a retreat from the hustle and bustle of a new country. Now, equipped with modern amenities, this home will be your perfect retreat. The entry gives way to a lounge or receiving area on the left and a library on the right. Fireplaces adorn all of the major living areas upstairs-the dining room, the keeping room, the living room the music room and the library. Downstairs bedrooms include a master suite with a fireplace, a private study and a luxurious bath.

plan# HPK2000296

Main Level: 2,434 sq. ft.
Lower Level: 2,434 sq. ft.
Total: 4,868 sq. ft.
Bedrooms: 4
Bathrooms: 2½ + ½
Width: 94' - 8"
Depth: 73' - 2"
Foundation: Slab

ORDER ONLINE @ EPLANS.COM

REAR EXTERIOR

SECOND FLOOR

FIRST FLOOR

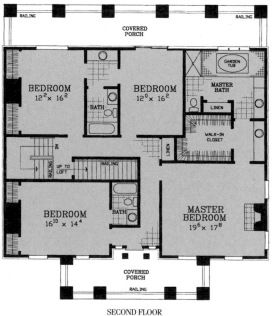

plan# HPK2000053

First Floor: 2,000 sq. ft.
Second Floor: 2,000 sq. ft.
Total: 4,000 sq. ft.
Bonus Space: 264 sq. ft.
Bedrooms: 4
Bathrooms: 3½
Width: 50' - 8"
Depth: 56' - 8"
Foundation: Unfinished Basement

ORDER ONLINE @ EPLANS.COM

From the temple-style front to the angled balustrade on the roof, this home is a standout in any neighborhood. Tall columns support porches on two levels on the front and back of the house. A tiled foyer leads back to the family area, which includes a U-shaped kitchen with a snack bar, a fireplace flanked by window seats, and three sets of sliding glass doors to the rear porch. Fireplaces in the formal living and dining rooms add their welcoming glow for guests, and the master-bedroom fireplace warms the homeowner's quiet time.

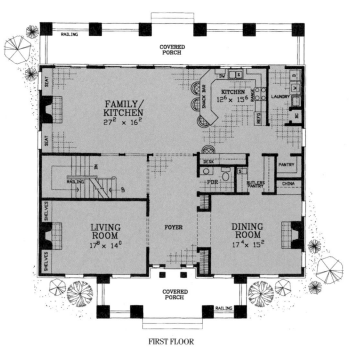

FIRST FLOOR

SECOND FLOOR

plan# **HPK2000001**

First Floor: 2,988 sq. ft.
Second Floor: 1,216 sq. ft.
Total: 4,204 sq. ft.
Bonus Space: 485 sq. ft.
Bedrooms: 4
Bathrooms: 4½ + ½
Width: 83' - 0"
Depth: 70' - 4"
Foundation: Crawlspace,
Unfinished Basement

ORDER ONLINE @ EPLANS.COM

Local Flavor

Once the wealthiest and largest city south of Philadelphia, Charleston bears a footnote in the history of American residential architecture for its highly recognized variation of the Colonial-style home. The example featured here is considered a Double House, so called for its wider floor plan comprising a square center and wings. The Georgian exterior and hipped roof is a typical variation of the Charleston, while the side-loading garage at the rear of the plan is a welcome modification. Note also the significant utility area, which also serves the side entryway as a mud room.

In contrast to the Double House, the more distinctive Single House still thrives as a popular choice in urban and other narrow-lot neighborhoods. The two-tiered porch that runs the length of the home, such as Design HPK200070 on page 88, is the style's signature feature and is meant to overlook a courtyard. Other designs collected here include shorter, wrapping porches that will allow more flexibility on site. In either case, enjoyment of the outdoors is a key component of the Charleston home.

If you're considering a home for an already purchased lot, take note that many of our plans are also available in mirror-reverse packages. Correct orientation of the plan on a lot will ensure the most flattering curbside appearance and ease of use for your new home. In addition, taking into account how sunlight enters the home at different times of the day can have a measurable effect on your heating and cooling needs. Beyond simply mirror-reversing a plan, modifying a design—to add, enlarge, or remove rooms—may also be an option. To find out more about mirror-reverse sets and design customization, turn to page 312 or contact us by phone.

FIRST FLOOR   SECOND FLOOR

A fine Georgian exterior complements the home's historically informed interior.

PHOTO BY: MAURA MCEVOY, COURTESY OF WILLIAM E. POOLE DESIGNS, INC. THIS HOME, AS SHOWN IN THE PHOTOGRAPH, MAY DIFFER FROM THE ACTUAL BLUEPRINTS. FOR MORE DETAILED INFORMATION, PLEASE CHECK THE FLOOR PLANS CAREFULLY.

plan# HPK2000054

First Floor: 2,968 sq. ft.
Second Floor: 1,521 sq. ft.
Total: 4,489 sq. ft.
Bonus Space: 522 sq. ft.
Bedrooms: 4
Bathrooms: 4½ + ½
Width: 82' - 6"
Depth: 81' - 8"
Foundation: Crawlspace

ORDER ONLINE @ EPLANS.COM

This home—showcasing elegant Georgian architecture—is reminiscent of the grand homes in the battery section of Charleston, South Carolina. The entry opens to the foyer with its grand staircase. To the right is the hearth-warmed library and to the left, the formal dining room. The foyer leads to the family room where a window wall looks out to the covered porch. A central hall passes the study and proceeds to the luxurious master suite, featuring a windowed tub and a huge walk-in closet. The left wing holds the sunny breakfast area, island kitchen, spacious mudroom, and garage. Upstairs, three bedrooms enjoy private baths and ample closet space.

FIRST FLOOR

SECOND FLOOR

PHOTO COURTESY OF: WILLIAM E. POOLE DESIGNS, INC. PHOTO BY: JERRY ATNIP.
THIS HOME, AS SHOWN IN THE PHOTOGRAPH, MAY DIFFER FROM THE ACTUAL BLUEPRINTS.

plan# HPK2000055

First Floor: 2,348 sq. ft.
Second Floor: 1,872 sq. ft.
Total: 4,220 sq. ft.
Bedrooms: 4
Bathrooms: 3½ + ½
Width: 90' - 4"
Depth: 44' - 8"
Foundation: Unfinished Basement

ORDER ONLINE @ EPLANS.COM

THIS HOME, AS SHOWN IN THE PHOTOGRAPH, MAY DIFFER FROM THE ACTUAL BLUEPRINTS. FOR MORE DETAILED INFORMATION, PLEASE CHECK THE FLOOR PLANS CAREFULLY.

This classic Georgian design contains a variety of features that make it outstanding: a pediment gable with cornice work and dentils, beautifully proportioned columns, and a distinct window treatment. Inside the foyer, a stunning curved staircase introduces you to this Southern-style home. The first floor contains some special appointments: a fireplace in the living room and another fireplace and a wet bar in the gathering room. A study is offered towards the rear of the plan for convenient home office use. A gourmet island kitchen is open to a breakfast room with a pantry. Upstairs, an extension over the garage allows for a huge walk-in closet in the master suite and a full bath in one of the family bedrooms.

REAR EXTERIOR

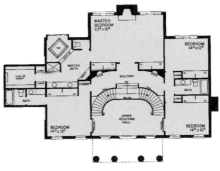

SECOND FLOOR

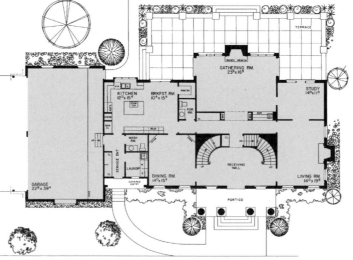

FIRST FLOOR

This magnificent home offers four bedrooms, five baths, one half-bath, and curb appeal to beat the band. The elegant foyer opens to the library, the formal dining room, and the breathtaking living room. To the right, find the kitchen, breakfast nook, and the cozy keeping room. The master suite finds privacy on the far left. The second floor holds three additional bedrooms, four full baths and a rec room.

plan# HPK2000056

First Floor: 3,463 sq. ft.
Second Floor: 1,924 sq. ft.
Total: 5,387 sq. ft.
Bedrooms: 4
Bathrooms: 5½
Width: 88' - 6"
Depth: 98' - 0"
Foundation: Crawlspace, Finished Basement, Unfinished Basement

ORDER ONLINE @ EPLANS.COM

FIRST FLOOR

SECOND FLOOR

PHOTO BY: JEFFREY S. OTTO
THIS HOME, AS SHOWN IN THE PHOTOGRAPH, MAY DIFFER FROM THE ACTUAL BLUEPRINTS.

plan # HPK2000057

First Floor: 3,749 sq. ft.
Second Floor: 1,631 sq. ft.
Total: 5,380 sq. ft.
Bonus Space: 1,171 sq. ft.
Bedrooms: 4
Bathrooms: 4½ + ½
Width: 92' - 4"
Depth: 112' - 0"
Foundation: Crawlspace, Unfinished Basement

ORDER ONLINE @ EPLANS.COM

This stately manor brings to mind the grandeur of a fading age. The pedimented, columned porch commands awe and acts as centerpiece to the perfectly symmetrical facade. Inside, formality reigns at the front of the plan, with an elegant dining room and formal living room flanking the large foyer. Ahead, past the staircase, find the gallery hall, which opens through double columns to the more casual family room. Here, a warming hearth and outdoor access will be enjoyed by family and guests. Another set of double columns on the left introduces the breakfast area and island kitchen. To the rear of these rooms, convenience is provided by a half-bath, mudroom, and utility area. A truly pampering master suite resides on the opposite side of the plan. Upstairs, three bedrooms each have a private bath. An exercise room, and optional rec room and office space complete the second floor.

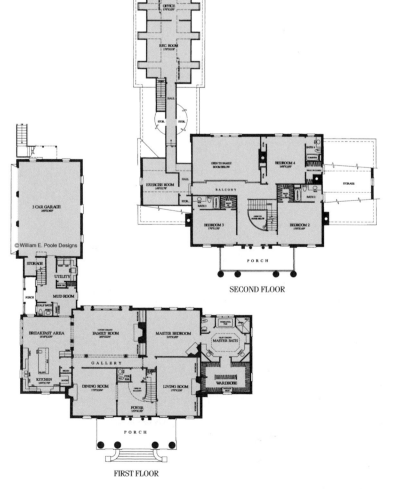

SECOND FLOOR

FIRST FLOOR

© William E. Poole Designs

THIS HOME, AS SHOWN IN THE PHOTOGRAPH, MAY DIFFER FROM THE ACTUAL BLUEPRINTS. FOR MORE DETAILED INFORMATION, PLEASE CHECK THE FLOOR PLANS CAREFULLY.

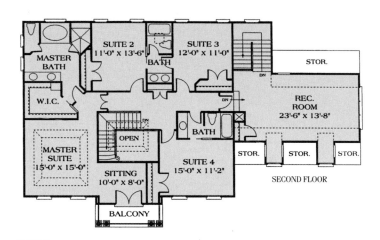

MASTER BATH

SUITE 2
11'-0" x 13'-6"

BATH

SUITE 3
12'-0" x 11'-0"

STOR.

W.I.C.

REC. ROOM
23'-6" x 13'-8"

MASTER SUITE
15'-0" x 15'-0"

OPEN

BATH

SITTING
10'-0" x 8'-0"

SUITE 4
15'-0" x 11'-2"

STOR.   STOR.   STOR.

BALCONY

SECOND FLOOR

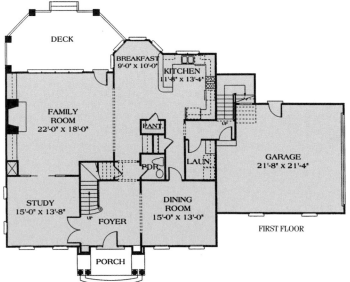

DECK

BREAKFAST
9'-0" x 10'-0"

KITCHEN
11'-8" x 13'-4"

FAMILY ROOM
22'-0" x 18'-0"

PANT.

PDR.

LAUN.

GARAGE
21'-8" x 21'-4"

STUDY
15'-0" x 13'-8"

FOYER

DINING ROOM
15'-0" x 13'-0"

PORCH

FIRST FLOOR

plan# HPK2000058

First Floor: 1,715 sq. ft.
Second Floor: 1,583 sq. ft.
Total: 3,298 sq. ft.
Bonus Space: 410 sq. ft.
Bedrooms: 4
Bathrooms: 3½
Width: 69' - 6"
Depth: 43' - 2"
Foundation: Crawlspace

ORDER ONLINE @ EPLANS.COM

Double columns lend support to a balcony that also creates a sheltering entrance for this stately Colonial home. The interior begins with a formal dining room conveniently located adjacent to the sunny breakfast nook and kitchen, making formal or informal entertaining a breeze. The second floor contains the master suite. Here you can take a relaxing soak in the tub or curl up with a good book in the sitting room while enjoying the sweet scents of nature that waft across the balcony through French doors. Three additional bedrooms, two baths and a bonus recreation room complete this great plan.

PHOTO COURTESY OF LIVING CONCEPTS HOME PLANS
THIS HOME AS SHOWN IN THE PHOTOGRAPH MAY DIFFER FROM THE ACTUAL BLUEPRINTS

plan # HPK2000059

First Floor: 3,487 sq. ft.
Second Floor: 1,945 sq. ft.
Total: 5,432 sq. ft.
Bedrooms: 5
Bathrooms: 5½
Width: 82' - 4"
Depth: 105' - 10"
Foundation: Crawlspace

ORDER ONLINE @ EPLANS.COM

This impressive two-story mansion offers an exquisite floor plan and a traditional Georgian facade. A classic loggia welcomes you inside to a two-story foyer flanked by a formal dining room and a study/guest suite—each warmed by a fireplace. At the rear, the gathering room also provides a fireplace, flanked by built-ins. The island kitchen opens to a breakfast room, which includes a pantry. The bayed den accesses a screened porch that extends to an outdoor deck. The first-floor master suite features a double walk-in closet and a private master bath. A three-car garage and laundry room complete the first floor. The impressive split staircase leads upstairs to a gallery hall overlooking the foyer. Here, three additional family bedrooms each directly access a bath. A few steps up, the bonus room is perfect for a home office or playroom.

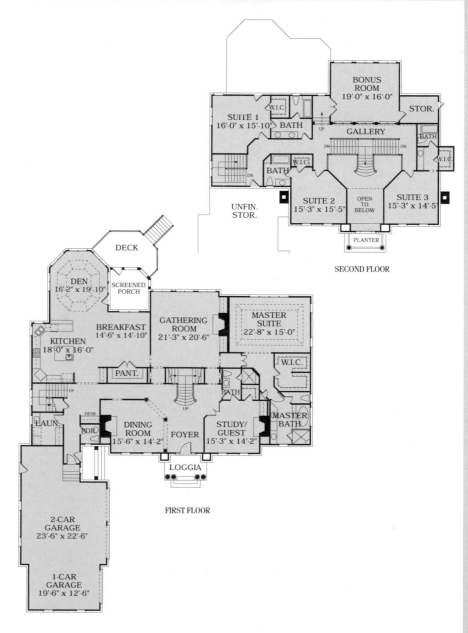

SECOND FLOOR

FIRST FLOOR

plan# HPK2000060

First Floor: 1,670 sq. ft.
Second Floor: 1,741 sq. ft.
Total: 3,411 sq. ft.
Bedrooms: 4
Bathrooms: 3½
Width: 64' - 0"
Depth: 78' - 2"
Foundation: Unfinished Basement

ORDER ONLINE @ EPLANS.COM

Symmetry is everything in the Georgian style, and this home is a classic Georgian in both plan and exterior. The facade as a whole balances a one-story extended porch under a two-story hipped roof box. Inside, a traditional foyer with a central staircase is flanked by the living/dining rooms on one side and the great room on the other. Rear stairs allow private access to a secluded guest suite over the garage.

Guest Bedroom
21³ x 14³

Bedroom #2
14⁶ x 12³

WIC

Master Bathroom

Bedroom #3
12³ x 13⁶

Master Suite
14⁶ x 20⁶

Open to Below

SECOND FLOOR

Two Car Garage
21⁶ x 23⁶

Porte Cochère

Porch

Kitchen
14³ x 14³

Breakfast
12³ x 12³

Dining Room
14⁶ x 11⁶

Living Room
14⁶ x 13⁶

Foyer

Great Room
14⁶ x 20⁹

Porch

FIRST FLOOR

PHOTO COURTESY OF: STEPHEN FULLER, INC.

plan # HPK2000061

First Floor: 1,554 sq. ft.
Second Floor: 1,648 sq. ft.
Total: 3,202 sq. ft.
Bedrooms: 4
Bathrooms: 3½
Width: 60' - 0"
Depth: 43' - 0"
Foundation: Finished Walkout Basement

ORDER ONLINE @ EPLANS.COM

The classic styling of this brick American traditional home will be respected for years to come. The formidable, double-door, transomed entry and a Palladian window reveal the shining foyer within. The spacious dining room and the formal study or living room flank the foyer; a large family room with a full wall of glass conveniently opens to the breakfast room and the kitchen. The master suite features a spacious sitting area with its own fireplace and a tray ceiling. Two additional bedrooms share a bath, and a fourth bedroom has its own private bath.

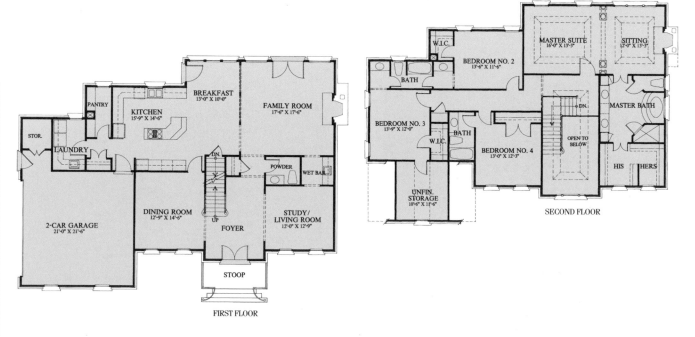

FIRST FLOOR

SECOND FLOOR

THIS HOME, AS SHOWN IN THE PHOTOGRAPH, MAY DIFFER FROM THE ACTUAL BLUEPRINTS. FOR MORE DETAILED INFORMATION, PLEASE CHECK THE FLOOR PLANS CAREFULLY.

plan# HPK2000062

First Floor: 1,576 sq. ft.
Second Floor: 1,334 sq. ft.
Total: 2,910 sq. ft.
Bedrooms: 3
Bathrooms: 2½ + ½
Width: 31' - 8"
Depth: 51' - 7"
Foundation: Crawlspace

ORDER ONLINE @ EPLANS.COM

Perfect for a narrow lot, this distinctive home captures the best of Charlestonian architecture to produce an innovative style with classic good looks. A recessed entry reveals French doors to the bayed sun room, and an open formal dining room. The living room is bathed in natural light for year-round enjoyment. To the rear, the kitchen and family room are defined by an island serving bar. A breakfast nook is a great place to start the day. A central staircase leads to two family bedrooms and an indulgent master suite with a splendid private bath. The master balcony is a wonderful place to relax. The third-floor loft also enjoys a private balcony.

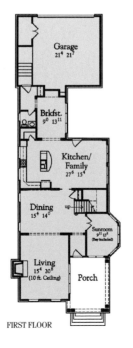

FIRST FLOOR

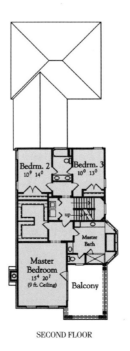

SECOND FLOOR

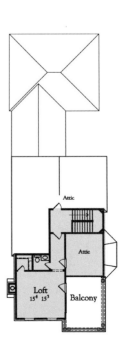

© LOONEY RICKS KISS ARCHITECTS, INC.
THIS HOME AS SHOWN IN THE PHOTOGRAPH MAY DIFFER FROM THE ACTUAL BLUEPRINTS.

plan# HPK2000063

First Floor: 1,108 sq. ft.
Second Floor: 677 sq. ft.
Total: 1,785 sq. ft.
Bedrooms: 3
Bathrooms: 2½
Width: 26' - 1"
Depth: 80' - 2"
Foundation: Slab

ORDER ONLINE @ EPLANS.COM

Like the famous "single houses" of Charleston, this lovely Colonial would be perfect for a narrow lot. The window-lined entry porch opens directly into the living room, where a two-story ceiling enhances the sense of spaciousness. The kitchen and dining area lie beyond the staircase, and the master bedroom occupies the far end of the main floor. Here, a wall of windows provide views to the side porch and garden. On the second floor, two family bedrooms share a compartmented bath. Both open onto a covered balcony that runs the length of the home.

FIRST FLOOR

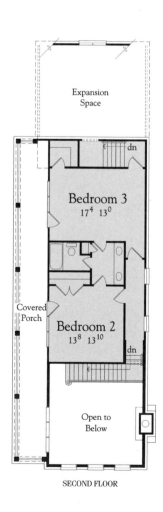

SECOND FLOOR

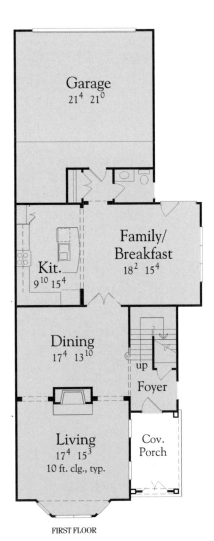

plan# HPK2000064

First Floor: 1,237 sq. ft.
Second Floor: 1,098 sq. ft.
Total: 2,335 sq. ft.
Bedrooms: 3
Bathrooms: 2½
Width: 29' - 4"
Depth: 73' - 0"
Foundation: Slab

ORDER ONLINE @ EPLANS.COM

The curb appeal of this home can be found in the dazzling details: a bay window, twin sconces illuminating a columned porch, a pretty portico, and classic shutters. The foyer opens to the formal living and dining rooms, subtly defined by a central fireplace. The gourmet kitchen overlooks a spacious family/breakfast area, which leads outdoors. The second floor includes a lavish master suite with a spa-style tub and a private covered balcony. The secondary sleeping area is connected by a gallery hall and a stair landing.

Garage
21⁴ 21⁰

Family/ Breakfast
18² 15⁴

Kit.
9¹⁰ 15⁴

Dining
17⁴ 13¹⁰

up

Foyer

Living
17⁴ 15³
10 ft. clg., typ.

Cov. Porch

FIRST FLOOR

Bedroom 2
11⁰ 14⁶

Bedroom 3
11⁰ 13⁰

Master Bedroom
17⁴ 15³
9 ft. clg., typ.

Cov. Bal.

SECOND FLOOR

plan# **HPK2000065**

First Floor: 1,587 sq. ft.
Second Floor: 1,191 sq. ft.
Total: 2,778 sq. ft.
Bedrooms: 3
Bathrooms: 2½
Width: 21' - 8"
Depth: 93' - 8"
Foundation: Slab

ORDER ONLINE @ EPLANS.COM

Box-paneled shutters add a touch
of class to this Town design—a home that
is simply the ultimate in comfort and
style. A winding staircase highlights a
refined foyer that sets the pace for the
entire home. Fireplaces warm the formal
and casual rooms, which can accommodate all occasions. The well-organized
kitchen provides a snack bar for easy
meals and serves the formal dining room
with ease. Upstairs, two secondary bedrooms share a full bath and a study that
could be used as a computer room. The
master suite boasts two walk-in closets,
an indulgent bath and a private porch.

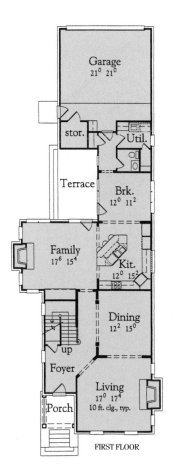

FIRST FLOOR

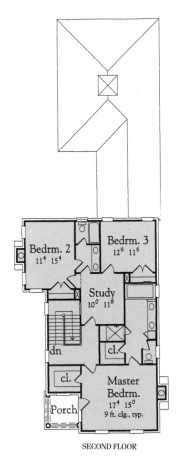

SECOND FLOOR

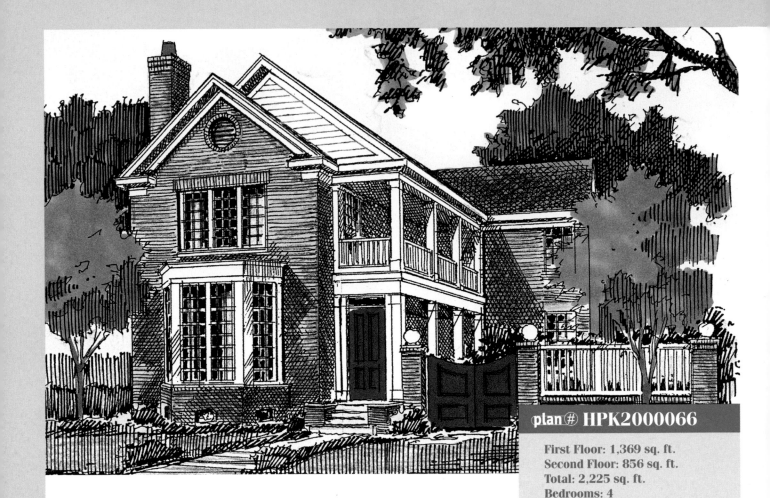

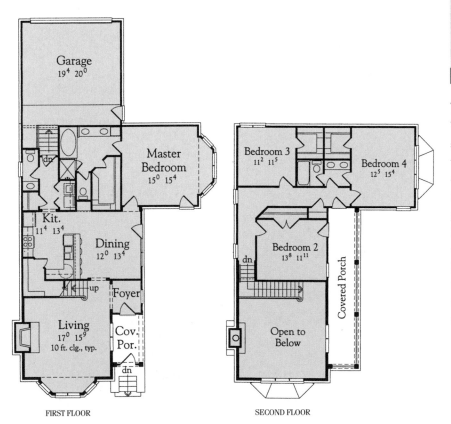

plan# HPK2000066

First Floor: 1,369 sq. ft.
Second Floor: 856 sq. ft.
Total: 2,225 sq. ft.
Bedrooms: 4
Bathrooms: 2½
Width: 36' - 2"
Depth: 71' - 6"
Foundation: Slab

ORDER ONLINE @ EPLANS.COM

The lovely facade of this Town or Village home is beautifully decorated with a double portico. A front bay window provides a stunning accent to the traditional exterior, while allowing natural light within. The formal living room features a fireplace and opens to the dining room, which leads outdoors. The gourmet kitchen has a walk-in pantry. The master suite is a relaxing space that includes a sitting bay, access to the side grounds, walk-in closet and soothing bath. A winding staircase offers an overlook to the living room.

Garage
19⁴ 20⁰

Master Bedroom
15⁰ 15⁴

Kit.
11⁴ 13⁴

Dining
12⁰ 13⁴

Foyer

Living
17⁰ 15⁹
10 ft. clg., typ.

Cov. Por.

FIRST FLOOR

Bedroom 3
11² 11⁵

Bedroom 4
12⁵ 15⁴

Bedroom 2
13⁸ 11¹¹

Open to Below

Covered Porch

SECOND FLOOR

plan# **HPK2000067**

First Floor: 1,792 sq. ft.
Second Floor: 899 sq. ft.
Total: 2,691 sq. ft.
Bedrooms: 4
Bathrooms: 2½
Width: 32' - 9"
Depth: 99' - 5"
Foundation: Slab

ORDER ONLINE @ EPLANS.COM

Tall, elegant windows and a stately chimney deck out the facade of this stunning Town home. The robust mix of Colonial balance and natural symmetry lends an inviting look to the exterior. Inside, a row of columns sets off the dining area, which provides views to the side courtyard. Informal spaces share a door to the side property—a great place to linger or start a walk into town. The secluded master suite provides a dressing area and two walk-in closets. Upstairs, a cluster of secondary bedrooms share a spacious hall bath.

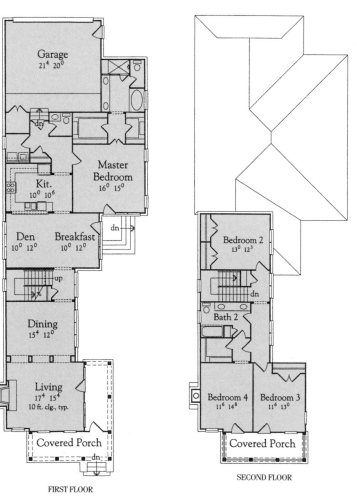

FIRST FLOOR

SECOND FLOOR

plan# HPK2000068

First Floor: 1,660 sq. ft.
Second Floor: 943 sq. ft.
Total: 2,603 sq. ft.
Bedrooms: 3
Bathrooms: 3½
Width: 30' - 10"
Depth: 102' - 10"
Foundation: Slab

ORDER ONLINE @ EPLANS.COM

Grand arch-top windows set off the lovely facade of this gently French design, and promote the presence of natural light within. The open formal rooms blend traditional style with supreme comfort, with a centered fireplace and French doors to the covered porch. A secluded study or secondary bedroom has a splendid bath with a dressing area and a walk-in closet. Upstairs, an additional bedroom has its own door to the covered balcony. The master suite includes two walk-in closets and access to the balcony.

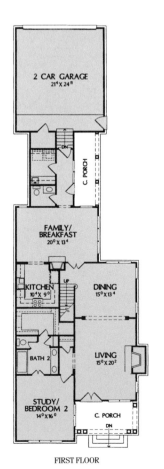

FIRST FLOOR

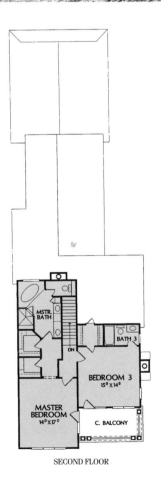

SECOND FLOOR

plan# HPK2000069

First Floor: 1,260 sq. ft.
Second Floor: 1,160 sq. ft.
Total: 2,420 sq. ft.
Bedrooms: 4
Bathrooms: 3
Width: 43' - 5"
Depth: 68' - 3"
Foundation: Crawlspace

ORDER ONLINE @ EPLANS.COM

A wealth of outdoor living space extends the confines of this narrow-lot home, creating a sense of spaciousness. A fireplace in the living room adds ambiance and warmth. A second fireplace in the family room is a nice touch. The U-shaped kitchen is both practical and efficient. A first-floor bedroom, with full bath, can be used as a study or guest suite. On the second floor, the master bedroom shares access to a screened porch with bedroom 4. An additional bedroom and a full bath complete this level.

FIRST FLOOR

SECOND FLOOR

plan# HPK2000070

First Floor: 1,901 sq. ft.
Second Floor: 1,874 sq. ft.
Total: 3,775 sq. ft.
Bedrooms: 4
Bathrooms: 3½
Width: 50' - 0"
Depth: 70' - 0"
Foundation: Pier (same as Piling)

ORDER ONLINE @ EPLANS.COM

This elegant Charleston townhouse is enhanced by Southern grace and three levels of charming livability. Covered porches offer outdoor living space at every level. The first floor offers a living room with fireplace, an island kitchen serving a bayed nook, and a formal dining room. A first-floor guest bedroom is located at the front of the plan, along with a laundry and powder room. The second level offers a sumptuous master suite boasting a private balcony, a master bath, and enormous walk-in closet. Two other bedrooms sharing a Jack-and-Jill bath are also on this level. The basement level includes a three-car garage.

Foyer

GROUND LEVEL

Three-Car Garage
20'x 36'

Porch

Kitchen
14'6"x 18'11"

Breakfast
13'7"x 12'3"

Living Room
19'2"x 21'5"

Dining
16'7"x 13'1"

Porch

Util.

1/2 Ba.

Bath

Bedroom
21'5"x 12'1"

FIRST FLOOR

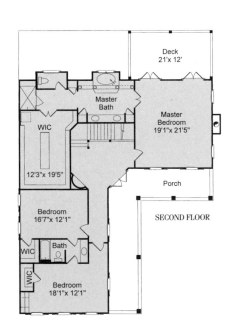

Deck
21'x 12'

Master Bath

WIC
12'3"x 19'5"

Master Bedroom
19'1"x 21'5"

Porch

Bedroom
16'7"x 12'1"

WIC

Bath

WIC

Bedroom
18'1"x 12'1"

SECOND FLOOR

plan# HPK2000071

First Floor: 1,742 sq. ft.
Second Floor: 1,624 sq. ft.
Total: 3,366 sq. ft.
Bedrooms: 4
Bathrooms: 3
Width: 42' - 10"
Depth: 77' - 0"
Foundation: Pier (same as Piling)

ORDER ONLINE @ EPLANS.COM

Elegant Southern living is the theme of this seaside townhouse. The narrow-lot design allows for comfortable urban living. Inside, the living room is warmed by a fireplace, while the island kitchen serves the breakfast room and casual den. A first-floor guest bedroom is located at the front of the design. The dining room is reserved for more formal occasions. Upstairs, the gracious master suite features a private second-floor porch, two walk-in closets, and a private bath. Two additional bedrooms share a hall bath on this floor.

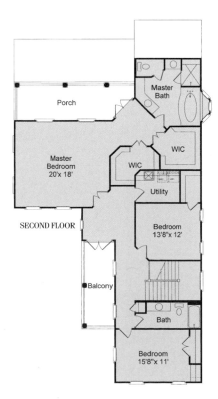

FIRST FLOOR

Deck 25'8"x 9'

Porch 25'8"x 8'

Den 13'8"x 12'9"

Breakfast 16'6"x 10'

Living 25'4"x 18'

Kitchen 13'8"x 15'

Porch

Dining 13'8"x 12'

Bath

Bedroom 15'8"x 11'

SECOND FLOOR

Porch

Master Bath

WIC

Master Bedroom 20'x 18'

WIC

Utility

Porch

Bedroom 13'8"x 12'

Bath

Bedroom 15'8"x 11'

plan# HPK2000072

First Floor: 1,742 sq. ft.
Second Floor: 1,624 sq. ft.
Total: 3,366 sq. ft.
Bedrooms: 4
Bathrooms: 3
Width: 42' - 10"
Depth: 77' - 6"
Foundation: Pier (same as Piling)

ORDER ONLINE @ EPLANS.COM

Porches abound upon this grand, two-story home—perfect for nature enthusiasts. The first floor holds the entertaining spaces with the island kitchen acting as a hub around which all activity revolves. The den, with a cozy corner fireplace, and the breakfast nook are ideal for more intimate situations. On the second floor, the master suite pampers with a luxurious bath and a private porch. Two additional bedrooms share a full bath on this floor; the first-floor bedroom works well as a guest bedroom.

plan# HPK2000073

First Floor: 2,578 sq. ft.
Second Floor: 1,277 sq. ft.
Total: 3,855 sq. ft.
Bonus Space: 347 sq. ft.
Bedrooms: 4
Bathrooms: 3½
Width: 53' - 6"
Depth: 97' - 0"
Foundation: Pier (same as Piling)

ORDER ONLINE @ EPLANS.COM

This charming Charleston design is full of surprises! Perfect for a narrow lot, the raised foundation is ideal for a waterfront location. An entry porch introduces a winding staircase. To the right is a living room/library that functions as a formal entertaining space. A large hearth and two sets of French doors to the covered porch enhance the great room. The master suite is positioned for privacy and includes great amenities that work to relax the homeowners. Upstairs, three family bedrooms, two full baths, an open media room, and a future game room create a fantastic casual family space.

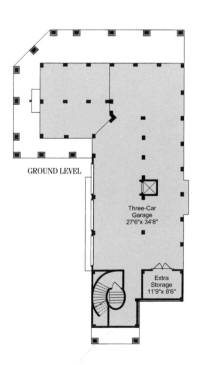

GROUND LEVEL

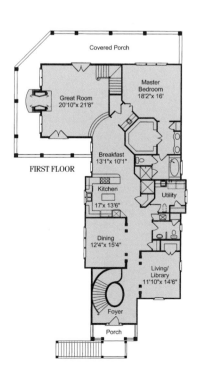

FIRST FLOOR

SECOND FLOOR

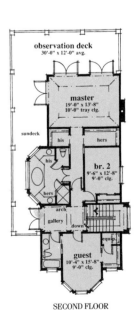

plan# HPK2000074

First Floor: 1,305 sq. ft.
Second Floor: 1,215 sq. ft.
Total: 2,520 sq. ft.
Bonus Space: 935 sq. ft.
Bedrooms: 3
Bathrooms: 2½
Width: 30' - 6"
Depth: 72' - 2"
Foundation: Slab

ORDER ONLINE @ EPLANS.COM

This elegant Old Charleston row design blends high vogue with a restful character that says shoes are optional. A flexible interior enjoys modern space that welcomes sunlight. Wraparound porticos on two levels offer views to the living areas, and a "sit-and-watch-the-stars" observation deck opens from the master suite. Four sets of French doors bring the outside into the great room. The second-floor master suite features a spacious bath and three sets of doors that open to the observation deck. A guest bedroom on this level leads to a gallery hall with its own access to the deck. Bonus space awaits development on the lower level, which—true to its Old Charleston roots—opens gloriously to a garden courtyard.

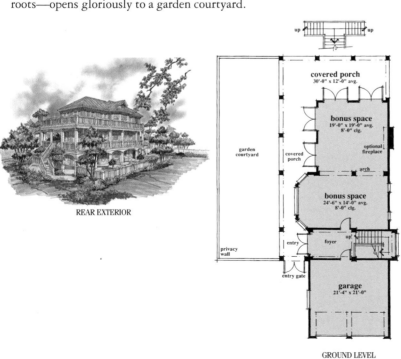

REAR EXTERIOR

GROUND LEVEL

FIRST FLOOR

SECOND FLOOR

plan# HPK2000075

First Floor: 1,266 sq. ft.
Second Floor: 1,324 sq. ft.
Total: 2,590 sq. ft.
Bedrooms: 3
Bathrooms: 2½
Width: 34' - 0"
Depth: 63' - 2"
Foundation: Crawlspace

ORDER ONLINE @ EPLANS.COM

This Charleston-style home boasts an impressive balcony that is sure to catch the eye. A large veranda borders two sides of the home. The entry leads into a long foyer, which runs from the entrance to the rear of the design. The coffered great room enjoys a fireplace, built-in cabinetry, and French doors to the veranda; the dining room also accesses the veranda. The island kitchen leads into a bayed nook, perfect for Sunday morning breakfasting. The second floor is home to two family bedrooms—both with access to the deck—a study, and a luxurious master suite. A vaulted sitting area, full bath, and deck access are just some of the highlights of the master suite.

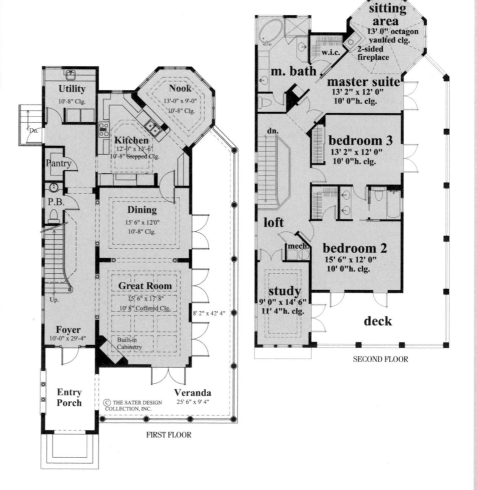

plan# HPK2000076

First Floor: 1,135 sq. ft.
Second Floor: 1,092 sq. ft.
Total: 2,227 sq. ft.
Bedrooms: 3
Bathrooms: 2½
Width: 28' - 8"
Depth: 74' - 2"
Foundation: Crawlspace

ORDER ONLINE @ EPLANS.COM

Stylish square columns line the porch and portico of this townhome, which has received the Builder's Choice National Design and Planning Award and the Award of Merit in Architecture. Inside, an open arrangement of the formal rooms is partially defined by a through-fireplace. Brightened by a triple window, the breakfast nook is an inviting place for family and friends to gather. A single door opens to the outside, where steps lead down to the rear property—a good place to start a walk into town. The kitchen features a food-prep island and a sizable pantry. Upstairs, the master suite offers a fireplace and access to the portico.

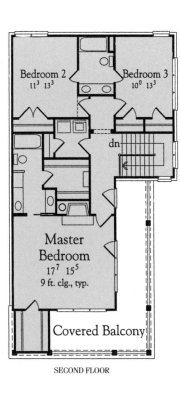

Garage
21⁰ 21⁰

Study / Guest
10⁰ 15⁸

Kit.
12³ 12⁹

dn

Dining
17⁷ 11¹⁰

up

Foyer

Living
17⁷ 15⁵
10 ft. clg., typ.

Porch

dn

FIRST FLOOR

Bedroom 2
11³ 13³

Bedroom 3
10⁰ 13³

dn

Master Bedroom
17⁷ 15⁵
9 ft. clg., typ.

Covered Balcony

SECOND FLOOR

plan# HPK2000077

First Floor: 1,282 sq. ft.
Second Floor: 956 sq. ft.
Total: 2,238 sq. ft.
Bedrooms: 2
Bathrooms: 3
Width: 30' - 2"
Depth: 74' - 2"
Foundation: Crawlspace

ORDER ONLINE @ EPLANS.COM

There won't be any chilly mornings for the homeowner within this lovely townhome. The second-floor master suite boasts a massive hearth, flanked by built-in shelves. French doors open from the bedroom to a private balcony, where gentle breezes may invigorate the senses. A gallery hall leads to a secondary bedroom, which offers its own bath and a walk-in closet. On the first floor, formal rooms share a through-fireplace and offer doors to the veranda and garden court. A secluded study easily converts to a guest suite or home office, and convenient storage space is available in the rear-loading garage.

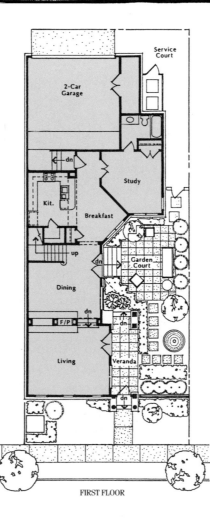

FIRST FLOOR

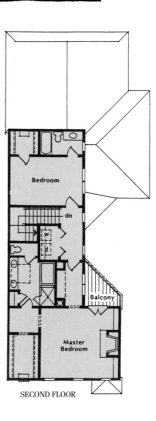

SECOND FLOOR

plan# HPK2000078

First Floor: 2,174 sq. ft.
Second Floor: 1,109 sq. ft.
Total: 3,283 sq. ft.
Bonus Space: 526 sq. ft.
Bedrooms: 5
Bathrooms: 3½
Width: 52' - 0"
Depth: 84' - 0"
Foundation: Slab, Unfinished
Basement

ORDER ONLINE @ EPLANS.COM

This magnificent take on Early American tradition will excite and inspire before you even enter the home. Once inside, a foyer reveals a sophisticated hearth-warmed library on the right, and an elegant dining room on the left. Continue beneath a dramatic spiral staircase to find a grand room with a lovely coffered ceiling and prominent fireplace. The kitchen is designed to accommodate more than one cook and is situated conveniently between the dining room and sunny morning nook. The master suite is accessed on the far right. Here, a romantic two-way fireplace, intricate ceiling treatment, and indulgent bath will pamper any homeowner. The upper level includes four bedrooms and two well-appointed baths. An apartment over the three-car garage is perfect for guests or live-in help, and features a bedroom, separate living area, and full bath.

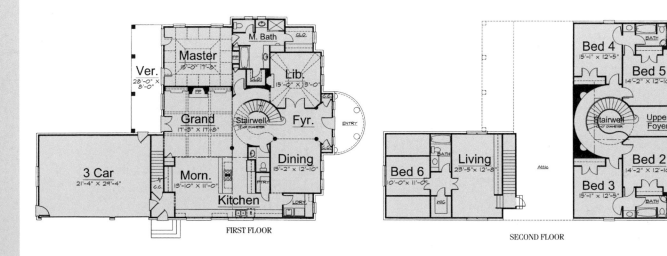

FIRST FLOOR

SECOND FLOOR

ptan# HPK2000079

First Floor: 3,365 sq. ft.
Second Floor: 1,456 sq. ft.
Total: 4,821 sq. ft.
Bonus Space: 341 sq. ft.
Bedrooms: 4
Bathrooms: 3½
Width: 81' - 0"
Depth: 71' - 9"
Foundation: Finished Walkout
Basement

ORDER ONLINE @ EPLANS.COM

The graceful lines of this formal Georgian brick manor are an inviting presence in any neighborhood. An open foyer enjoys views of the back property through the living room, which features a fireplace framed with built-in bookshelves. Dinner guests will want to linger on the rear terrace, which opens through French doors from formal and casual areas. The gourmet kitchen has a cooktop island, a walk-in pantry and a breakfast area that's open to the bright family room. Homeowners will enjoy the master bedroom's private sitting area, which features two skylights, a fireplace, and access to the terrace.

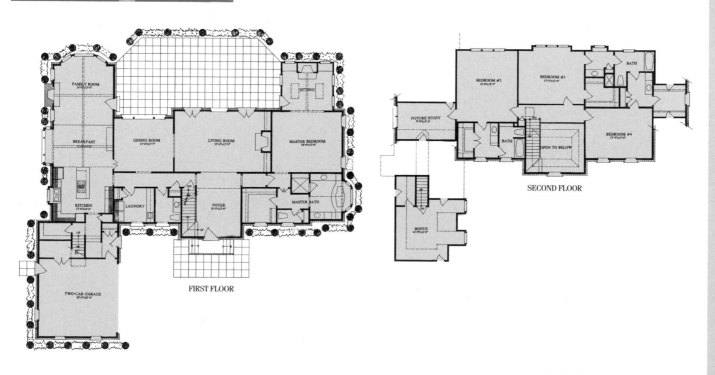

FIRST FLOOR

SECOND FLOOR

plan# HPK2000080

First Floor: 3,902 sq. ft.
Second Floor: 2,159 sq. ft.
Total: 6,061 sq. ft.
Bedrooms: 5
Bathrooms: 3½
Width: 85' - 3"
Depth: 74' - 0"
Foundation: Finished Walkout Basement

ORDER ONLINE @ EPLANS.COM

The entry to this classic home is framed with a sweeping double staircase and four large columns topped with a pediment. The two-story foyer is flanked by spacious living and dining rooms. The two-story family room, which has a central fireplace, opens to the study and a solarium. A spacious U-shaped kitchen features a central island cooktop. An additional staircase off the breakfast room offers convenient access to the second floor. The impressive master suite features backyard access and a bath fit for royalty. Four bedrooms upstairs enjoy large proportions.

FIRST FLOOR

SECOND FLOOR

© William E. Poole Designs, Inc.

plan# HPK2000081

First Floor: 3,064 sq. ft.
Second Floor: 1,726 sq. ft.
Total: 4,790 sq. ft.
Bonus Space: 793 sq. ft.
Bedrooms: 4
Bathrooms: 4½ + ½
Width: 94' - 2"
Depth: 92' - 2"
Foundation: Crawlspace

ORDER ONLINE @ EPLANS.COM

You'll add a bit of stately Southern charm to the neighborhood with this gorgeous plan. Pass through the grand Ionic columns into the charming two-story foyer, with the formal dining room and living room/library on either side. Fireplaces warm up both rooms, as well as the family room and the master suite. Occupying much of the right-hand side of the plan, the master suite accesses the rear covered porch, and includes a spacious bath and enormous closet. Three bedrooms upstairs each have a private bath, and a sitting area overlooking the family room offers a welcome retreat.

FIRST FLOOR

SECOND FLOOR

© William E. Poole Designs, Inc.

plan# **HPK2000082**

First Floor: 2,913 sq. ft.
Second Floor: 1,380 sq. ft.
Total: 4,293 sq. ft.
Bonus Space: 905 sq. ft.
Bedrooms: 4
Bathrooms: 4½
Width: 88' - 4"
Depth: 100' - 8"
Foundation: Crawlspace

ORDER ONLINE @ EPLANS.COM

A classic Southern beauty, grand columns frame the regal entry of this two-story Plantation home. Once inside, the family living spaces are distinguished by decorative interior columns. The L-shaped kitchen easily serves the nearby dining and family rooms. Four fireplaces are peppered throughout the first floor, with one in the master bedroom as a romantic added bonus. Upstairs, three additional family bedrooms each boast a walk-in closet and a full bath. A sewing room and future rec room above the garage complete this plan.

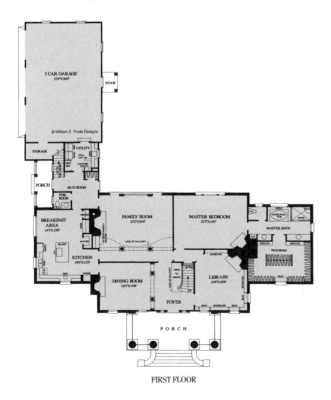

FIRST FLOOR

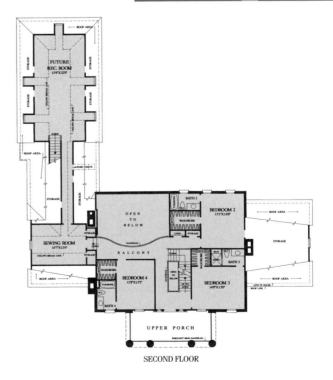

SECOND FLOOR

© William E. Poole Designs, Inc.

plan # HPK2000083

Main Level: 4,556 sq. ft.
Upper Level: 3,261 sq. ft.
Lower Level: 2,918 sq. ft.
Total: 10,735 sq. ft.
Bedrooms: 6
Bathrooms: 7½ + ½
Width: 97' - 2"
Depth: 81' - 2"
Foundation: Finished Walkout Basement

ORDER ONLINE @ EPLANS.COM

Come home to true Southern glamour in this stunning Greek Revival. Imposing columns enclose a double porch, creating a dramatic entrance. The foyer showcases a spiral staircase and opens to a formal dining room on the left and a library on the right—both warmed by fireplaces. The family will love spending quality time in the huge hearth-warmed living room, which opens to a rear triple porch. On the left of the plan, the island kitchen is expanded by a breakfast area and keeping room. Elegance abounds in the right wing, where the master suite takes center stage. The second floor is home to four spacious bedrooms—one with a fireplace—two baths, and a playroom. A balcony that opens to the second-level porch also overlooks the foyer below. The lower level of this home is its own little world, with a pub, rec room, efficiency kitchen, hobby and exercise rooms, and another full bath and bedroom.

LOWER LEVEL

MAIN LEVEL

UPPER LEVEL

© William E. Poole Designs, Inc.

plan# HPK2000084

First Floor: 3,635 sq. ft.
Second Floor: 1,357 sq. ft.
Total: 4,992 sq. ft.
Bonus Space: 759 sq. ft.
Bedrooms: 4
Bathrooms: 4½ + ½
Width: 121' - 6"
Depth: 60' - 4"
Foundation: Unfinished Basement, Crawlspace

ORDER ONLINE @ EPLANS.COM

The grandeur of this Southern estate belies the practical floor plan within. An elegant foyer joins the dining room and oversized living room—both with fireplaces—to welcome guests. The left wing comprises a gourmet kitchen with a walk-in pantry, two powder rooms, and a utility area featuring a mudroom and a separate entrance. The two-story family room, with porch access and a fireplace, is central; the right wing is devoted to a luxurious master suite and a private study, each with a fireplace. An expansive upper level includes three family suites, a balcony overlook, and future space for a fifth bedroom and bath, as well as a game room.

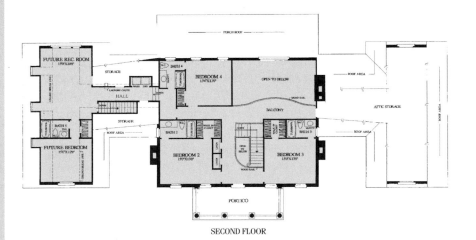

SECOND FLOOR

FIRST FLOOR

© William E. Poole Designs, Inc.

plan # HPK2000085

First Floor: 2,670 sq. ft.
Second Floor: 1,795 sq. ft.
Total: 4,465 sq. ft.
Bonus Space: 744 sq. ft.
Bedrooms: 5
Bathrooms: 4½ + ½
Width: 74' - 8"
Depth: 93' - 10"
Foundation: Crawlspace,
Unfinished Basement

ORDER ONLINE @ EPLANS.COM

A stately brick plantation home, this plan presents all the luxuries that are so desired by today's homeowner. Enter past the columned portico to the formal two-story foyer. To the left is a library with a corner fireplace; to the right, the dining room flows into an enormous kitchen, outfitted with an island serving bar. Exposed wood-beam ceilings in the kitchen, breakfast area, and family room add a vintage element. The master suite is a romantic hideaway, with a corner fireplace, whirlpool tub, and seated shower. Upstairs, four well-appointed bedrooms join a lounge area to finish the plan. Future space above the three-car garage is limited only by your imagination.

FIRST FLOOR

SECOND FLOOR

© William E. Poole Designs, Inc.

plan# HPK2000086

First Floor: 2,696 sq. ft.
Second Floor: 1,518 sq. ft.
Total: 4,214 sq. ft.
Bonus Space: 360 sq. ft.
Bedrooms: 4
Bathrooms: 4½ + ½
Width: 72' - 6"
Depth: 97' - 10"
Foundation: Crawlspace

ORDER ONLINE @ EPLANS.COM

An exquisite exterior is only the beginning for this Southern-style home. The welcoming front porch opens to the family room, complete with a fireplace and French-door access to a rear screen porch. The open kitchen features an island snack bar, built-in desk, a bayed breakfast nook, and a walk-in pantry. The mudroom offers a space to doff coats and soiled shoes. Access to a powder room is an added convenience. A separate utility room houses the washer/dryer, fold-down ironing board, laundry chute, and sink. The lavish master suite, adjacent library/living room, and dining room each boast a private fireplace. Upstairs houses three additional family bedrooms, each with a full bath. A study, storage space, and an area for future expansion can also be found here.

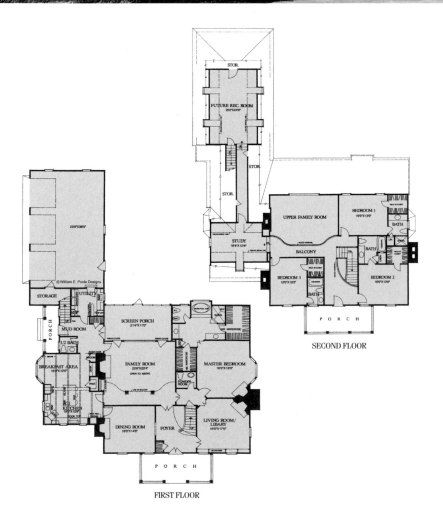

SECOND FLOOR

FIRST FLOOR

© William E. Poole Designs, Inc.

plan# HPK2000087

First Floor: 1,209 sq. ft.
Second Floor: 1,005 sq. ft.
Total: 2,214 sq. ft.
Bonus Space: 366 sq. ft.
Bedrooms: 3
Bathrooms: 2½
Width: 65' - 4"
Depth: 40' - 4"
Foundation: Crawlspace

ORDER ONLINE @ EPLANS.COM

The rebirth of a style—this design salutes the look of Early America. From the porch, step into the two-story foyer, and either venture to the left towards the living room and dining room, or to the right where the family room sits. A central fireplace in the family room warms the island kitchen. The open design allows unrestricted interaction. Upstairs, the master suite boasts a roomy bath with a dual-sink vanity, a whirlpool tub, a private toilet, a separate shower, and His and Hers walk-in closets. Two additional family bedrooms share a full bath. Future expansion space completes this level.

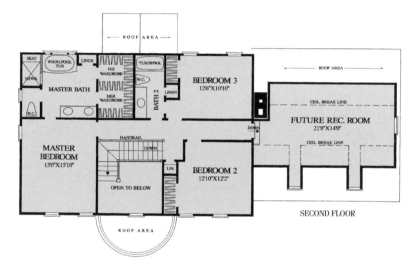

SECOND FLOOR

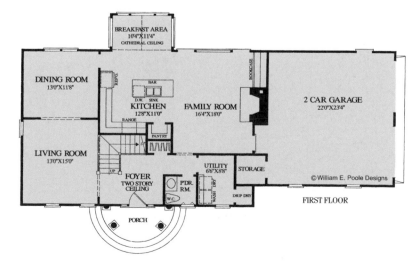

FIRST FLOOR

© William E. Poole Designs, Inc.

plan# HPK2000088

First Floor: 2,064 sq. ft.
Second Floor: 1,521 sq. ft.
Total: 3,585 sq. ft.
Bonus Space: 427 sq. ft.
Bedrooms: 4
Bathrooms: 3
Width: 84' - 8"
Depth: 65' - 0"
Foundation: Crawlspace

ORDER ONLINE @ EPLANS.COM

The best of Southern tradition combines with an easygoing floor plan to make this home a sure neighborhood favorite. The elegant portico at the front is a unique touch. Formal rooms—a library, living room, and dining room—surround the two-story foyer, which leads past the staircase to the hearth-warmed family room. In the very back, the kitchen is amplified by a gorgeous vaulted sunroom featuring two walls of windows to let in light. The second floor is home to a deluxe master suite, as well as two family bedrooms that share a bath. A utility room is conveniently located upstairs as well. Future space is available for expansion over the garage.

FIRST FLOOR

SECOND FLOOR

© William E. Poole Designs, Inc.

plan# HPK2000089

First Floor: 2,767 sq. ft.
Second Floor: 1,179 sq. ft.
Total: 3,946 sq. ft.
Bonus Space: 591 sq. ft.
Bedrooms: 4
Bathrooms: 3½ + ½
Width: 79' - 11"
Depth: 80' - 6"
Foundation: Crawlspace

ORDER ONLINE @ EPLANS.COM

The grandiose entrance is reminiscent of homes from Early America and the exquisite interior does not disappoint. Formal living areas give way to the informal openness of the family room and adjoining breakfast area and island kitchen. Access to the rear terrace from this area makes alfresco meals an option. Upstairs houses three additional family bedrooms—two share a Jack-and-Jill bath—the third boasts a private, full bath. A future rec room completes this level.

FIRST FLOOR

SECOND FLOOR

© William E. Poole Designs, Inc.

plan# HPK2000090

First Floor: 2,492 sq. ft.
Second Floor: 1,313 sq. ft.
Total: 3,805 sq. ft.
Bonus Space: 687 sq. ft.
Bedrooms: 4
Bathrooms: 3½ + ½
Width: 85' - 10"
Depth: 54' - 6"
Foundation: Crawlspace,
Unfinished Basement

ORDER ONLINE @ EPLANS.COM

Although the exterior of this Georgian home is entirely classical, the interior boasts an up-to-date floor plan that's a perfect fit for today's lifestyles. The large central family room, conveniently near the kitchen and breakfast area, includes a fireplace and access to the rear terrace; fireplaces also grace the formal dining room and library. The master suite, also with terrace access, features a spacious walk-in closet and a bath with a whirlpool tub. Upstairs, a second master suite—great for guests—joins two family bedrooms. Nearby, a large open area can serve as a recreation room.

SECOND FLOOR

FIRST FLOOR

© William E. Poole Designs, Inc.

plan# HPK2000091

First Floor: 3,712 sq. ft.
Second Floor: 2,083 sq. ft.
Total: 5,795 sq. ft.
Bonus Space: 409 sq. ft.
Bedrooms: 5
Bathrooms: 5 + 3 Half Baths
Width: 107' - 8"
Depth: 46' - 6"
Foundation: Crawlspace

ORDER ONLINE @ EPLANS.COM

The stately Southerly, a home with presence and impressive refinement, is the type of architecture brought to our shores by the more affluent English people in the later Georgian period. Formality at its best and classic detail that is difficult to surpass, combined with a floor plan which is both gracious and most of all functional—all of these elements merge in the Southerly, an English Georgian home.

SECOND FLOOR

FIRST FLOOR

© William E. Poole Designs, Inc.

The grand appearance of this Greek Revival home is timeless. Inside, the family room is enhanced by a central fireplace, a built-in bookcase, and access to a rear porch. The adjacent master suite boasts His and Hers wardrobes, a whirlpool tub, a dual-sink vanity, and a private toilet and shower. The right side of the first floor features a side porch that leads to the mudroom. The island kitchen will be a family favorite with wrap-around counter space, a built-in desk, a walk-in pantry, and a sunporch that doubles as a breakfast area. The second floor houses a second master suite, or possible guest suite, complete with all of the amenities of the first floor master. Two additional family bedrooms share a full bath. A future rec room above the garage completes this plan.

plan# HPK2000092

First Floor: 2,473 sq. ft.
Second Floor: 1,447 sq. ft.
Total: 3,920 sq. ft.
Bonus Space: 428 sq. ft.
Bedrooms: 4
Bathrooms: 3½
Width: 68' - 8"
Depth: 80' - 0"
Foundation: Crawlspace,
Unfinished Walkout Basement

ORDER ONLINE @ EPLANS.COM

FIRST FLOOR

SECOND FLOOR

© William E. Poole Designs, Inc.

plan# HPK2000093

First Floor: 1,305 sq. ft.
Second Floor: 1,052 sq. ft.
Total: 2,357 sq. ft.
Bonus Space: 430 sq. ft.
Bedrooms: 3
Bathrooms: 2½
Width: 69' - 4"
Depth: 35' - 10"
Foundation: Crawlspace,
Unfinished Basement

ORDER ONLINE @ EPLANS.COM

With a hipped roofline, white-washed brick, and attractive shutters, this fine Colonial will dress up any neighborhood. Inside, the foyer introduces the formal living room to the right, which is separated from the formal dining room by graceful columns—a perfect layout for dinner parties. The spacious family room offers a warming fireplace, built-ins, and backyard access. Designed with an efficient island, the kitchen easily serves the formal dining room as well as the sunny breakfast area. Upstairs, two family bedrooms share a hall bath, and the master suite provides privacy with a lavish bath and His and Hers walk-in closets. Don't miss the future recreation room, perfect as a home office, gym, or playroom.

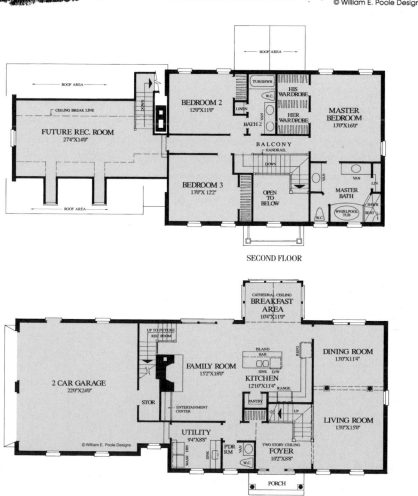

SECOND FLOOR

FIRST FLOOR

© William E. Poole Designs, Inc.

plan# **HPK2000094**

First Floor: 3,027 sq. ft.
Second Floor: 1,509 sq. ft.
Total: 4,536 sq. ft.
Bedrooms: 5
Bathrooms: 4½
Width: 85' - 0"
Depth: 82' - 6"
Foundation: Crawlspace,
Unfinished Basement

ORDER ONLINE @ EPLANS.COM

This home retains an elegant air while presenting a gracious and welcoming facade. Inside find plenty of space for both formal and casual events. A dining room and hearth-warmed living room flank the foyer, and a library is tucked in back to the right. The family room enjoys a fireplace and great views of the outdoors, as well as open flow into the breakfast area and kitchen. A large utility room expands the kitchen's space to the front of the plan. The master suite on the right is made extra-special by its deluxe bath. Plenty of dressing space is surrounded by an enormous double wardrobe, double vanities, a compartmented toilet, and a stunning whirlpool tub set in a curved bay window. Four more bedrooms reside on the second floor, each with its own bath and plenty of closet space. Two handy storage spaces flank the bedrooms, and a wealth of unfinished attic storage awaits above the garage.

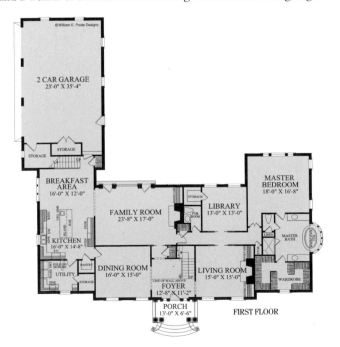

FIRST FLOOR

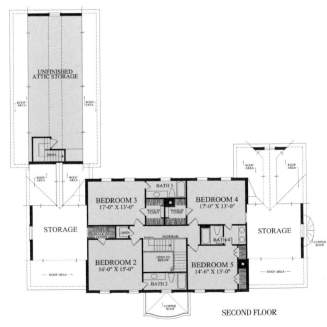

SECOND FLOOR

© 2001 Donald A. Gardner, Inc.

plan # HPK2000095

First Floor: 1,486 sq. ft.
Second Floor: 1,248 sq. ft.
Total: 2,734 sq. ft.
Bonus Space: 455 sq. ft.
Bedrooms: 3
Bathrooms: 2½
Width: 70' - 11"
Depth: 44' - 7"

ORDER ONLINE @ EPLANS.COM

This traditional estate home is accented with heavy crown molding, two sets of dormers, and an exquisite balustrade. Regal columns, sidelights, and a transom frame the entrance, and a beautiful window floods the two-story foyer with light. A striking staircase directs traffic into the varied living areas; the great room with a fireplace, the open dining room down the hall from the bayed breakfast room, and the kitchen, with its versatile island, all flow from this central hub. The powder room is conveniently located to accommodate common rooms. The bonus room can be designated as a home gym or playroom.

SECOND FLOOR

FIRST FLOOR

© 2000 Donald A. Gardner, Inc.

The only thing modest about this home is its square footage. Two gables, a hipped roof and siding combine with an open interior layout to create a design that promotes easy living. Open to the common areas of the house, the dining room is distinguished by a tray ceiling and a single column. A vaulted ceiling starts in the great room and extends into the kitchen and breakfast area. An angled counter separates the kitchen without enclosing space. Highlighting the great room is a fireplace and access to the rear deck through French doors. The washer and dryer have been given their own utility closet, and storage space can be found in the garage.

plan# HPK2000096

First Floor: 985 sq. ft.
Second Floor: 870 sq. ft.
Total: 1,855 sq. ft.
Bonus Space: 331 sq. ft.
Bedrooms: 3
Bathrooms: 2½
Width: 53' - 5"
Depth: 36' - 2"

ORDER ONLINE @ EPLANS.COM

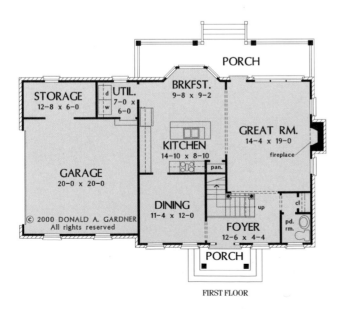

FIRST FLOOR

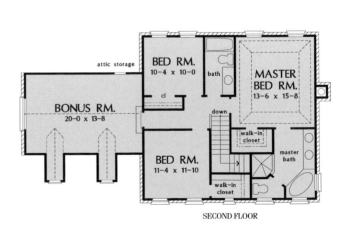

SECOND FLOOR

plan# HPK2000097

First Floor: 2,140 sq. ft.
Second Floor: 1,219 sq. ft.
Total: 3,359 sq. ft.
Bonus Space: 441 sq. ft.
Bedrooms: 4
Bathrooms: 3½
Width: 76' - 0"
Depth: 77' - 9"
Foundation: Finished Walkout Basement

ORDER ONLINE @ EPLANS.COM

With its adjacent two-car garage connected to the main house via a covered walkway and porch, this design would make an excellent home for a corner lot. Inside the main house, the entry leads to a formal living room, a formal dining room, and a massive great room with a fireplace flanked by French doors to the rear porch. The island kitchen includes a large pantry and a breakfast nook with outdoor access. The master bedroom is found on the first floor for privacy and features a luxurious private bath. Three bedrooms, all with large walk-in closets, and two full baths are located upstairs. Additional bonus space is available over the garage for a guest suite or a game room.

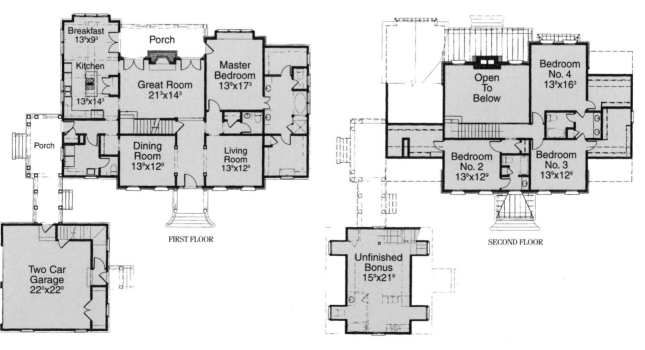

FIRST FLOOR

SECOND FLOOR

The charm of the Old South is designed into this stately Federal manor. A round entry portico leads to the two-story foyer with a circular staircase. The formal living room, dining room, and family room each feature distinctive fireplaces; the latter is also highlighted by a built-in entertainment center, walk-in wet bar, beamed cathedral ceiling, and access to a rear covered patio. Impressive 10-foot ceilings grace the entire first floor. The secluded master bedroom has a vaulted ceiling, three walk-in closets, and porch access. Four additional bedrooms on the second floor share adjoining baths.

plan# HPK2000098

First Floor: 3,294 sq. ft.
Second Floor: 1,300 sq. ft.
Total: 4,594 sq. ft.
Bedrooms: 5
Bathrooms: 3½
Width: 106' - 10"
Depth: 52' - 10"
Foundation: Unfinished Basement

ORDER ONLINE @ EPLANS.COM

plan# HPK2000099

First Floor: 3,116 sq. ft.
Second Floor: 1,997 sq. ft.
Total: 5,113 sq. ft.
Bedrooms: 4
Bathrooms: 4½
Width: 104' - 0"
Depth: 54' - 8"
Foundation: Unfinished Basement

ORDER ONLINE @ EPLANS.COM

An echo of Whitehall, built in 1765 in Anne Arundel County, Maryland, resounds in this home. Its classic symmetry and columned facade herald a grand interior. There's no lack of space whether entertaining formally or just enjoying a family get-together, and all are kept cozy with fireplaces in the gathering room, study and family room. An island kitchen with attached breakfast room handily serves the nearby dining room. Four second-floor bedrooms include a large master suite with another fireplace, a whirlpool tub and His and Hers closets in the bath. Three more full baths are found on this floor.

REAR EXTERIOR

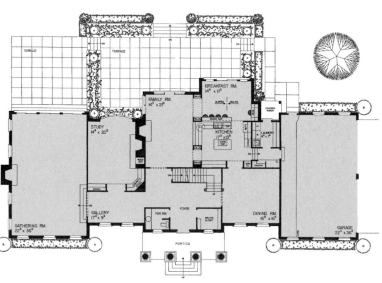

FIRST FLOOR

SECOND FLOOR

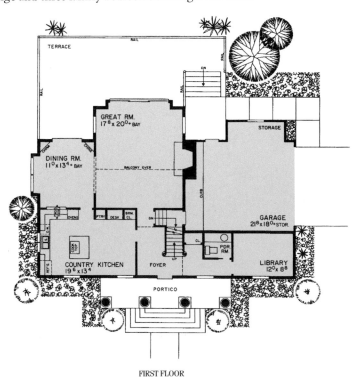

Clapboards, a center entrance, and symmetrically placed shuttered windows give a distinctly Georgian ambiance, until a Greek Revival portico with four soaring columns and a pediment is added. Inside, a library offers a quiet retreat to the right of the foyer. To the left, the country kitchen provides plenty of room for a table, an island cooktop, and a pass-through to the dining room. Between the pantry and the broom closet sits a built-in desk. The great room is outstanding, with a high ceiling, a wall of windows, and a fireplace. Upstairs, the master suite includes a balcony overlooking the foyer and a bath with twin vanities. Laundry facilities are on this floor, as are a lounge and three family bedrooms sharing a full bath.

plan# HPK2000100

First Floor: 1,206 sq. ft.
Second Floor: 1,254 sq. ft.
Total: 2,460 sq. ft.
Bedrooms: 4
Bathrooms: 2½
Width: 52' - 0"
Depth: 42' - 0"
Foundation: Unfinished Basement

ORDER ONLINE @ EPLANS.COM

FIRST FLOOR

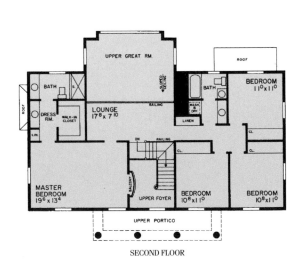

SECOND FLOOR

plan# HPK2000101

First Floor: 3,276 sq. ft.
Second Floor: 1,697 sq. ft.
Total: 4,973 sq. ft.
Bedrooms: 4
Bathrooms: 4½ + ½
Width: 106' - 2"
Depth: 77' - 10"
Foundation: Crawlspace, Slab

ORDER ONLINE @ EPLANS.COM

This antebellum home evokes all the charm and elegance of the enchanting South. The two-story foyer opens to the formal living room and dining room. A nearby study features a spiral staircase to the game room upstairs. The kitchen is enhanced by a cooktop island and a breakfast bar. A double-sided fireplace serves the kitchen, breakfast room, and keeping room. Three family bedrooms—each with a private bath—are located on the second floor.

FIRST FLOOR

SECOND FLOOR

plan# HPK2000102

First Floor: 3,669 sq. ft.
Second Floor: 2,048 sq. ft.
Total: 5,717 sq. ft.
Bonus Space: 375 sq. ft.
Bedrooms: 5
Bathrooms: 4½ + ½
Width: 108' - 10"
Depth: 72' - 0"
Foundation: Crawlspace

ORDER ONLINE @ EPLANS.COM

A massive pillared portico bids entry into this stunning two-story home. While a formal dining room and a quiet study flank the foyer, a dramatic sweeping staircase takes center stage. Beyond it is a columned grand room with a fireplace and access to the rear terrace. A gourmet island kitchen with a large walk-in pantry provides access to the dining room via a butler's pantry or to the breakfast nook and the secluded family room with its central fireplace. The master suite commands the right wing of the home and features terrace access and an opulent master bath with separate walk-in closets and a whirlpool tub. Four family bedrooms and three full baths are available upstairs, as well as bonus space that can be made into a studio or a game room.

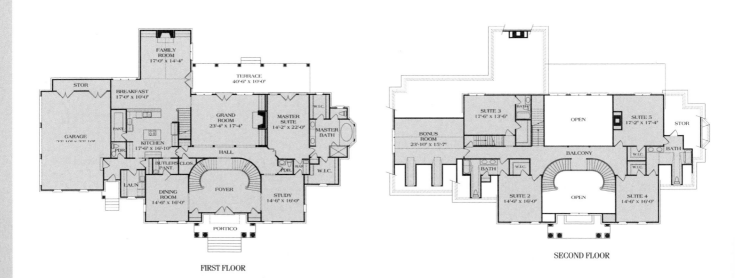

FIRST FLOOR

SECOND FLOOR

plan# HPK2000103

Main Level: 4,528 sq. ft.
Upper Level: 3,590 sq. ft.
Lower Level: 2,992 sq. ft.
Total: 11,110 sq. ft.
Bedrooms: 4
Bathrooms: 5½ + 3 Powder Rooms
Width: 138' - 2"
Depth: 80' - 10"
Foundation: Finished Walkout

ORDER ONLINE @ EPLANS.COM

REAR EXTERIOR

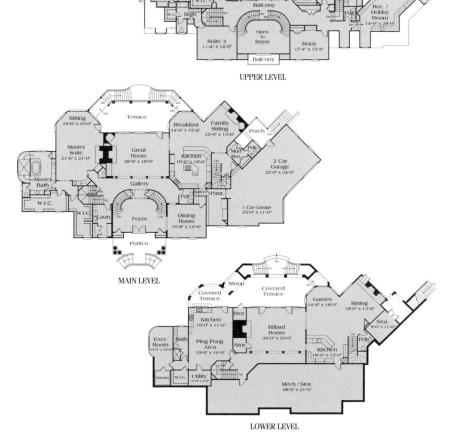

UPPER LEVEL

MAIN LEVEL

LOWER LEVEL

If you're looking for a home that fits a sloping lot, yet retains a strength and character that matches that of our Colonial forefathers, you need look no further. The front elevation reflects a traditional style that incorporates design elements of an earlier period. However, the floor plan and the rear elevation provide a contemporary twist. Beyond the portico, you'll enter a two-story foyer framed by twin curving staircases. Straight ahead, a spacious great room separates the private master suite to the left, and the formal dining room, kitchen, breakfast room and family/sitting room to the right. The second floor contains three suites—two with bay windows—three full baths, one powder room, a study and a recreation room. The basement sports a billiard room, two kitchens, an exercise room, a full bath, a game room and a sitting room.

plan# HPK2000104

First Floor: 1,754 sq. ft.
Second Floor: 1,502 sq. ft.
Total: 3,256 sq. ft.
Bonus Space: 588 sq. ft.
Bedrooms: 4
Bathrooms: 3½
Width: 70' - 4"
Depth: 48' - 0"
Foundation: Crawlspace

ORDER ONLINE @ EPLANS.COM

Behind its elegant Palladian facade, this plan offers a delightful arrangement of rooms for both formal and casual living. In the foyer, look up through the open stairwell to the tray ceiling two stories above. To the right, a formal dining room also boasts a striking ceiling treatment, and to the left, double doors open to a study or parlor. Pocket doors allow this room to be open or closed to the family room, where a fireplace, built-in cabinetry, and a wall of windows create an exciting space for gatherings. The huge kitchen includes an L-shaped island, complete with cooktop and snack counter. Laundry facilities are found in the mudroom-style entry from the three-car garage, along with a back stair to the spacious bonus room. This room's proximity to the fourth suite's bath would allow it to be used as a permanent or occasional bedroom. Two additional bedrooms share a compartmented bath, while the homeowners enjoy the privacy of their luxury suite.

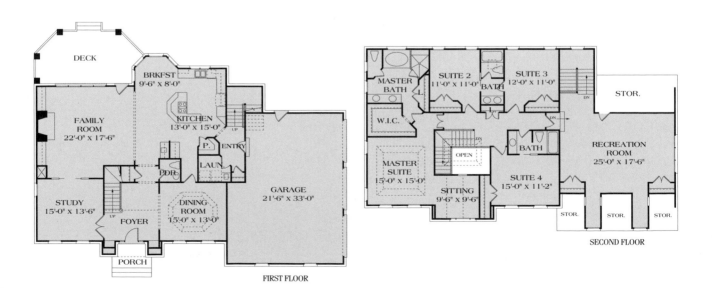

FIRST FLOOR

SECOND FLOOR

© 2004 Donald A. Gardner, Inc.

plan# HPK2000105

First Floor: 2,562 sq. ft.
Second Floor: 805 sq. ft.
Total: 3,367 sq. ft.
Bonus Space: 622 sq. ft.
Bedrooms: 4
Bathrooms: 4
Width: 87' - 7"
Depth: 59' - 6"

ORDER ONLINE @ EPLANS.COM

Evoking stately manors of the past, this traditional plan would be at home in any neighborhood. Inside, the design balances formal and informal spaces. Decorative windows usher in natural light, while columns and built-in cabinetry enhance elegance. A formal dining room and study flank the lofty foyer; beyond, the gallery gives way to a soaring great room. The common spaces offer all the latest amenities to enhance family life, such as a vast island kitchen, walk-in pantry, and a utility/mudroom just inside the garage. A high-ceilinged screened porch will become a favorite place to enjoy the summer breezes. In a quiet corner of the first floor, the master suite offers all the necessary luxuries to help reduce the stress of everyday life. Children or guests will enjoy the privacy of the two upstairs bedrooms and baths, and the generous bonus space is large enough to accommodate several uses.

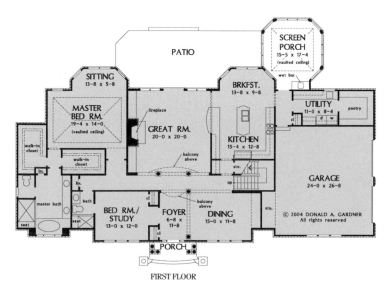

FIRST FLOOR

SECOND FLOOR

plan# HPK2000106

First Floor: 3,599 sq. ft.
Second Floor: 1,621 sq. ft.
Total: 5,220 sq. ft.
Bonus Space: 537 sq. ft.
Bedrooms: 4
Bathrooms: 5½
Width: 108' - 10"
Depth: 53' - 10"
Foundation: Slab, Unfinished
Basement

ORDER ONLINE @ EPLANS.COM

A grand facade detailed with brick corner quoins, stucco flourishes, arched windows, and an elegant entrance presents this home. A spacious foyer is accented by curving stairs and flanked by a formal living room and a formal dining room. For cozy times, a through-fireplace is located between a large family room and a quiet study. The master bedroom is designed to pamper, with two walk-in closets, a two-sided fireplace, a bayed sitting area, and a lavish private bath. Upstairs, three secondary bedrooms each have a private bath and a walk-in closet. Also on this level is a spacious recreation room, perfect for a game room or children's playroom.

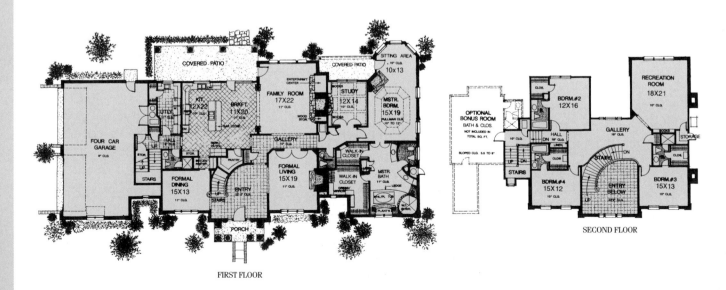

FIRST FLOOR

SECOND FLOOR

plan# HPK2000107

First Floor: 2,814 sq. ft.
Second Floor: 1,231 sq. ft.
Total: 4,045 sq. ft.
Bedrooms: 5
Bathrooms: 3½
Width: 98' - 0"
Depth: 45' - 10"
Foundation: Slab, Unfinished Basement

ORDER ONLINE @ EPLANS.COM

This very formal Georgian home was designed to be admired, but also to be lived in. It features handsome formal areas in a living room and formal dining room, but also an oversized family room with a focal fireplace. The master suite sits on the first floor, as is popluar with most homeowners today. Besides its wealth of amenities, it is located near a cozy study. Don't miss the private patio and sitting area with glass in the master bedroom. Upstairs, there are four family bedrooms with great closet space. A three-car garage contains space for a golf cart and a work bench.

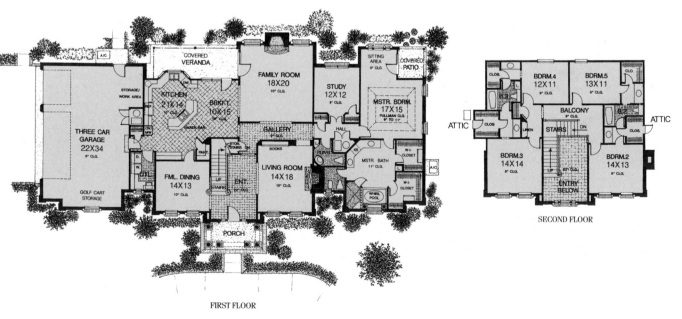

FIRST FLOOR

SECOND FLOOR

plan# **HPK2000002**

First Floor: 2,142 sq. ft.
Second Floor: 960 sq. ft.
Total: 3,102 sq. ft.
Bonus Space: 327 sq. ft.
Bedrooms: 4
Bathrooms: 3½
Width: 75' - 8"
Depth: 53' - 0"
Foundation: Crawlspace

ORDER ONLINE @ EPLANS.COM

PHOTO COURTESY OF: WILLIAM E. POOLE DESIGNS, INC. · ISLANDS OF BEAUFORT, BEAUFORT, SC
THIS HOME, AS SHOWN IN THE PHOTOGRAPH, MAY DIFFER FROM THE ACTUAL BLUEPRINTS.
FOR MORE DETAILED INFORMATION, PLEASE CHECK THE FLOOR PLANS CAREFULLY.

Cajun Flavor

Down in Louisiana where Cajun food is delightfully savored and zydeco music and jazz spill from the balconies of Bourbon Street, the architecture is equally unique and exciting. With a raised foundation, hipped roof, long covered porch, and French-Eclectic details, this cottage is an excellent example of Creole influences and demonstrates how such Cajun touches can be at home anywhere in the country.

Imagine this home among the foliage of a Louisiana bayou, with crickets chirping, music playing, and the spicy aroma of simmering gumbo in the air…. Now imagine this home in your neighborhood, kids riding their bikes along the front sidewalk, friendly neighbors watering their lawns, and you pulling into the driveway after a long day at work. Simple country elements, such as gabled dormers, a decorative porch railing, and muntin windows, are comforting features that are appropriate for any region. The easygoing atmosphere of the South awaits within this design, and so does every desired modern amenity.

Inside, the hearth-warmed family room, beyond the foyer and formal living room, will surely become the hub of the home. The spacious kitchen boasts a worktop island counter, ample pantry space, and a breakfast area. The master suite takes up the entire left wing, with an elegant private bath and a walk-in closet completing the private retreat. There's also room upstairs for family and guests, where three more bedrooms share two full baths, and a future rec room is available for further expansion.

The spirit of New Orleans is alive in the food, music, and architecture of Creole culture. In such an inspired southern design, even among suburban streets or northern pines, you can almost hear the sound of jazz horns playing in the distance.

FIRST FLOOR

SECOND FLOOR

A decorative railing surrounds the porch of this quaint country home derived from Creole-style architecture.

This romantic getaway puts charm into island living. A double-decker terrace and rear porch extend the living space to the outdoors. Views from every room keep the home light and open. The great room sports a fireplace and is within steps of the island kitchen/breakfast room combination. The dining room is to the left of the foyer, which makes entertaining a breeze. Upstairs, two family bedrooms share a compartmented bath with dual vanities. The master suite is indulged with a private bath and a spacious His and Hers walk-in closet.

plan# HPK2000108

First Floor: 1,075 sq. ft.
Second Floor: 994 sq. ft.
Total: 2,069 sq. ft.
Bonus Space: 382 sq. ft.
Bedrooms: 3
Bathrooms: 2½
Width: 56' - 4"
Depth: 35' - 4"
Foundation: Crawlspace,
Unfinished Basement

ORDER ONLINE @ EPLANS.COM

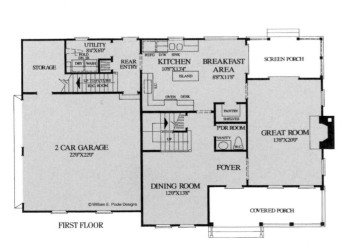

FIRST FLOOR

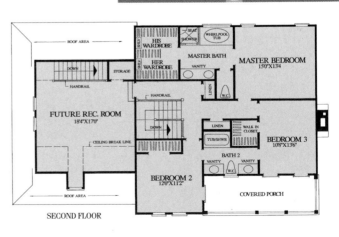

SECOND FLOOR

PHOTO COURTESY OF: WILLIAM E. POOLE DESIGNS, INC. - ISLANDS OF BEAUFORT, BEAUFORT, SC

plan# HPK2000109

First Floor: 1,273 sq. ft.
Second Floor: 1,358 sq. ft.
Total: 2,631 sq. ft.
Bedrooms: 4
Bathrooms: 3½
Width: 54' - 10"
Depth: 48' - 6"
Foundation: Crawlspace

ORDER ONLINE @ EPLANS.COM

This two-story home suits the needs of each household member. Family gatherings won't be crowded in the spacious family room, which is adjacent to the kitchen and the breakfast area. Just beyond the foyer, the dining and living rooms view the front yard. The master suite features its own full bath with dual vanities, a whirlpool tub, and separate shower. Three family bedrooms—one with a walk-in closet—and two full hall baths are available upstairs. Extra storage space is found in the two-car garage.

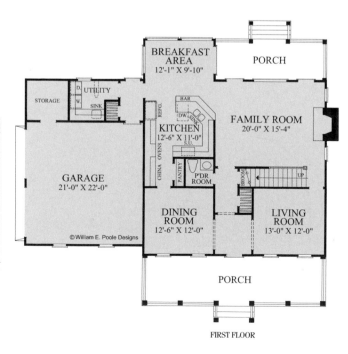

FIRST FLOOR

SECOND FLOOR

THIS HOME, AS SHOWN IN THE PHOTOGRAPH, MAY DIFFER FROM THE ACTUAL BLUEPRINTS. FOR MORE DETAILED INFORMATION, PLEASE CHECK THE FLOOR PLANS CAREFULLY.

plan# **HPK2000110**

First Floor: 2,036 sq. ft.
Second Floor: 1,230 sq. ft.
Total: 3,266 sq. ft.
Bedrooms: 4
Bathrooms: 3½
Width: 57' - 4"
Depth: 59' - 0"
Foundation: Pier (same as Piling)

ORDER ONLINE @ EPLANS.COM

The standing-seam metal roof adds character to this four- (or five-) bedroom home. The covered front porch, screened porch, and rear deck add outdoor living spaces for nature enthusiasts. A flexible room is found to the left of the foyer and the dining room is to the right. The galley kitchen is accessed through an archway with a sunny breakfast nook adjoining at the back. The lavish master suite is on the left with a private bath that includes access to the laundry room. The second floor holds three bedrooms and a multimedia room where the family can spend quality time in a casual atmosphere.

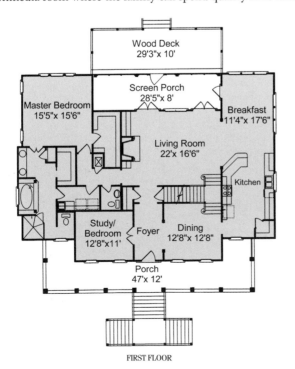

FIRST FLOOR

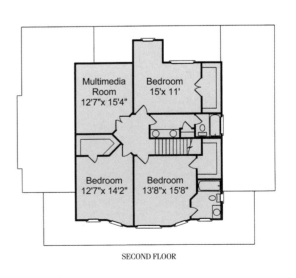

SECOND FLOOR

CHRIS A. LITTLE FROM ATLANTA; COURTESY OF CHATHAM HOME PLANNING, INC.
THIS HOME AS SHOWN IN THE PHOTOGRAPH MAY DIFFER FROM THE ACTUAL BLUEPRINTS.

plan # HPK2000111

First Floor: 2,390 sq. ft.
Second Floor: 1,200 sq. ft.
Total: 3,590 sq. ft.
Bedrooms: 4
Bathrooms: 3
Width: 61' - 0"
Depth: 64' - 4"
Foundation: Pier (same as Piling)

ORDER ONLINE @ EPLANS.COM

REAR EXTERIOR

This luxurious waterfront design sings of southern island influences. A front covered porch opens to a foyer, flanked by a study and dining room. The living room, warmed by a fireplace and safe from off-season ocean breezes, overlooks the rear covered porch. The island kitchen extends into a breakfast room. Beyond the covered porch, the wood deck is also accessed privately from the master suite. This suite includes a private whirlpool bath and huge walk-in closet. A guest suite is located on the first floor, while two additional bedrooms and a multimedia room are located on the second level.

THIS HOME, AS SHOWN IN THE PHOTOGRAPH, MAY DIFFER FROM THE ACTUAL BLUEPRINTS. FOR MORE DETAILED INFORMATION, PLEASE CHECK THE FLOOR PLANS CAREFULLY.

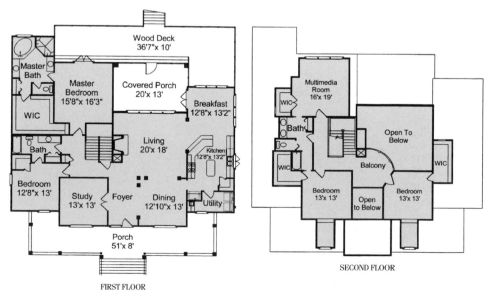

FIRST FLOOR

SECOND FLOOR

PHOTO COURTESY OF: WILLIAM E. POOLE DESIGNS, INC. · GENERAL SHALE BRICK, PHOTO BY: PETER MONTANTI. THIS HOME, AS SHOWN IN THE PHOTOGRAPH, MAY DIFFER FROM THE ACTUAL BLUEPRINTS.

Southern grandeur is evident in this wonderful two-story design with its magnificent second-floor balcony. The formal living spaces—dining room and living room—flank the impressive foyer with its stunning staircase. The family room resides in the rear, opening to the terrace. The sunny breakfast bay adjoins the island kitchen for efficient planning. The right wing holds the two-car garage, utility room, a secondary staircase, and a study that can easily be converted to a guest suite with a private bath. The master suite and Bedrooms 2 and 3 are placed on the second floor.

plan# HPK2000112

First Floor: 2,033 sq. ft.
Second Floor: 1,447 sq. ft.
Total: 3,480 sq. ft.
Bonus Space: 411 sq. ft.
Bedrooms: 3
Bathrooms: 3½
Width: 67' - 10"
Depth: 64' - 4"
Foundation: Crawlspace, Unfinished Basement, Unfinished Walkout Basement

ORDER ONLINE @ EPLANS.COM

FIRST FLOOR

SECOND FLOOR

plan# HPK2000113

First Floor: 2,129 sq. ft.
Second Floor: 1,206 sq. ft.
Total: 3,335 sq. ft.
Bonus Space: 422 sq. ft.
Bedrooms: 4
Bathrooms: 4
Width: 59' - 4"
Depth: 64' - 0"
Foundation: Finished Walkout Basement

ORDER ONLINE @ EPLANS.COM

REAR EXTERIOR

THIS HOME, AS SHOWN IN THE PHOTOGRAPH, MAY DIFFER FROM THE ACTUAL BLUEPRINTS. FOR MORE DETAILED INFORMATION, PLEASE CHECK THE FLOOR PLANS CAREFULLY.

French style embellishes this dormered country home. Stepping through French doors to the foyer, the dining area is immediately to the left. To the right is a set of double doors leading to a study or secondary bedroom. A lavish master bedroom provides privacy and plenty of storage space. The living room sports three doors to the rear porch and a lovely fireplace with built-ins. A secluded breakfast nook adjoins an efficient kitchen. Upstairs, two of the three family bedrooms boast dormer windows. Plans include a basement-level garage that adjoins a game room and two handy storage areas.

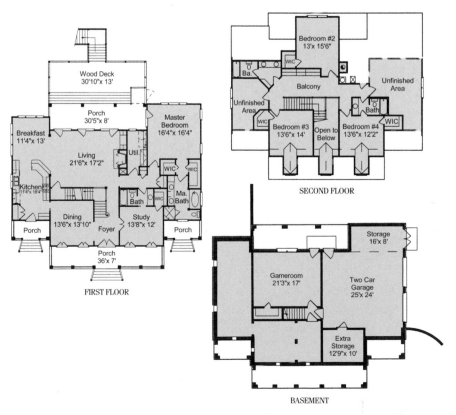

FIRST FLOOR

SECOND FLOOR

BASEMENT

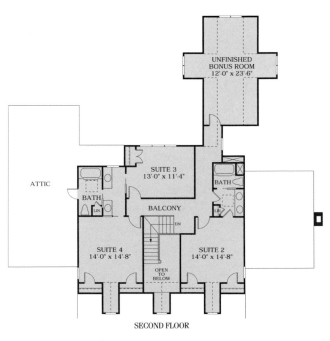

plan# HPK2000114

First Floor: 2,159 sq. ft.
Second Floor: 1,179 sq. ft.
Total: 3,338 sq. ft.
Bonus Space: 360 sq. ft.
Bedrooms: 4
Bathrooms: 3½
Width: 68' - 0"
Depth: 69' - 0"
Foundation: Crawlspace

ORDER ONLINE @ EPLANS.COM

This attractive plantation-style home exhibits a floor plan that is completely up-to-date, beginning with the secluded master suite and its lavish bath. The foyer is flanked by the living room and the dining room and leads ahead to the morning room. The family chef will enjoy the open kitchen and its nearby pantry and wet bar. The family room features a fireplace and built-ins. The second floor contains three bedrooms, two baths, a bonus room, and attic storage.

PHOTO COURTESY OF LIVING CONCEPTS HOME PLANS
THIS HOME AS SHOWN IN THE PHOTOGRAPH MAY DIFFER FROM THE ACTUAL BLUEPRINTS.

plan# HPK2000115

First Floor: 2,092 sq. ft.
Second Floor: 1,027 sq. ft.
Total: 3,119 sq. ft.
Bedrooms: 4
Bathrooms: 3½
Width: 66' - 0"
Depth: 80' - 0"
Foundation: Crawlspace, Slab

ORDER ONLINE @ EPLANS.COM

This Southern plantation home, featuring traditional accents such as front-facing dormers, a covered front porch, and a stucco-and-brick facade, will be the delight of any fine neighborhood. Inside, a study and formal dining room flank the foyer. The family room shares a two-sided fireplace with the refreshing sunroom, which overlooks the rear deck. The kitchen shares space with an eating area overlooking the front yard. The first-floor master suite features a large closet and a private bath. Three additional bedrooms and two baths are located upstairs.

THIS HOME, AS SHOWN IN THE PHOTOGRAPH, MAY DIFFER FROM THE ACTUAL BLUEPRINTS. FOR MORE DETAILED INFORMATION, PLEASE CHECK THE FLOOR PLANS CAREFULLY.

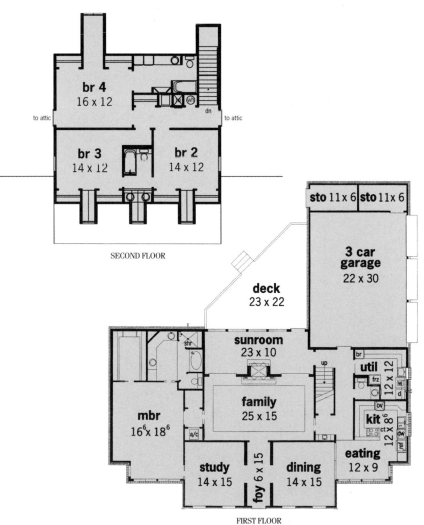

SECOND FLOOR

FIRST FLOOR

plan# HPK2000116

Square Footage: 2,595
Bonus Space: 1,480 sq. ft.
Bedrooms: 4
Bathrooms: 2½
Width: 78' - 8"
Depth: 67' - 0"
Foundation: Unfinished Basement

ORDER ONLINE @ EPLANS.COM

This home has a touch of modernism with all the comforts of country style. The pillared front porch allows for summer evening relaxation. The foyer extends into the bright great room equipped with a fireplace. The large kitchen is stationed between the vaulted dining room and airy breakfast nook. Two walk-in closets, dual vanities, and a spacious bath complement the master suite. Each of the three family bedrooms features closet space. The entire second floor is left for future development, whether it be a guest room, rec room, or study—or all three.

plan# HPK2000117

First Floor: 1,883 sq. ft.
Second Floor: 803 sq. ft.
Total: 2,686 sq. ft.
Bonus Space: 489 sq. ft.
Bedrooms: 3
Bathrooms: 3½
Width: 63' - 0"
Depth: 81' - 10"
Foundation: Crawlspace

ORDER ONLINE @ EPLANS.COM

Where creeks converge and marsh grasses sway in gentle breezes, this is a classical low country home. Steep rooflines, high ceilings, front and back porches, plus long and low windows are typical details of these charming planters' cottages. The foyer is flanked by the formal dining room and the living room, which opens to the family room. Here, several windows look out to the terrace and a fireplace removes the chill on a winter's night. The sunny breakfast room, which adjoins the kitchen, offers a wonderful space for casual dining. Two bedrooms, the lavish master suite, and the two-car garage complete the floor plan.

FIRST FLOOR

SECOND FLOOR

THIS HOME, AS SHOWN IN THE PHOTOGRAPH, MAY DIFFER FROM THE ACTUAL BLUEPRINTS. FOR MORE DETAILED INFORMATION, PLEASE CHECK THE FLOOR PLANS CAREFULLY.

plan# HPK2000118

First Floor: 2,200 sq. ft.
Second Floor: 1,001 sq. ft.
Total: 3,201 sq. ft.
Bonus Space: 674 sq. ft.
Bedrooms: 4
Bathrooms: 3½
Width: 70' - 4"
Depth: 74' - 4"
Foundation: Crawlspace

ORDER ONLINE @ EPLANS.COM

A wide, welcoming front porch and three dormer windows lend Southern flair to this charming farmhouse. Inside, three fireplaces—found in the living, dining, and family rooms—create a cozy atmosphere. The family room opens to the covered rear porch, and the breakfast area opens to a small side porch. Sleeping quarters include a luxurious first-floor master suite—with a private bath and two walk-in closets—as well as three family bedrooms upstairs.

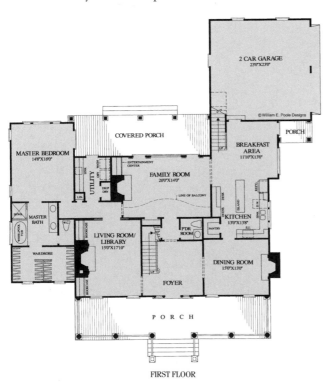

FIRST FLOOR

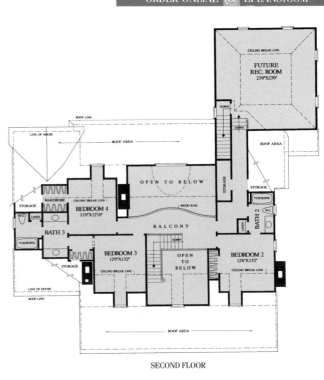

SECOND FLOOR

PHOTO COURTESY OF: WILLIAM E. POOLE DESIGNS, INC. PHOTO BY COLBERT HOWELL
THIS HOME AS SHOWN IN THE PHOTOGRAPH MAY DIFFER FROM THE ACTUAL BLUEPRINTS.

plan# HPK2000119

First Floor: 1,704 sq. ft.
Second Floor: 734 sq. ft.
Total: 2,438 sq. ft.
Bonus Space: 479 sq. ft.
Bedrooms: 3
Bathrooms: 3½
Width: 50' - 0"
Depth: 82' - 6"
Foundation: Crawlspace

ORDER ONLINE @ EPLANS.COM

Elegant country——that's one way to describe this attractive three-bedroom home. Inside, comfort is evidently the theme, with the formal dining room flowing into the U-shaped kitchen and casual dining taking place in the sunny breakfast area. The spacious, vaulted great room offers a fireplace and built-ins. The first-floor master suite is complete with a walk-in closet, a whirlpool tub, and a separate shower. Upstairs, the sleeping quarters include two family bedrooms with private baths and walk-in closets.

THIS HOME, AS SHOWN IN THE PHOTOGRAPH, MAY DIFFER FROM THE ACTUAL BLUEPRINTS. FOR MORE DETAILED INFORMATION, PLEASE CHECK THE FLOOR PLANS CAREFULLY.

FIRST FLOOR

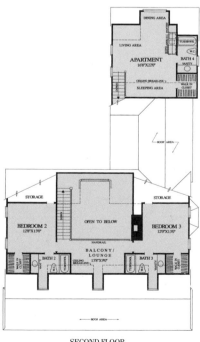

SECOND FLOOR

plan# HPK2000120

First Floor: 1,927 sq. ft.
Second Floor: 879 sq. ft.
Total: 2,806 sq. ft.
Bonus Space: 459 sq. ft.
Bedrooms: 4
Bathrooms: 3½
Width: 71' - 0"
Depth: 53' - 0"
Foundation: Crawlspace

ORDER ONLINE @ EPLANS.COM

This charming Southern plantation home packs quite a punch in 2,800 square feet! The elegant foyer is flanked by the formal dining room and the living room. To the rear, the family room enjoys a fireplace and expansive view of the outdoors. An archway leads to the breakfast area and on to the island kitchen. The luxurious master suite is tucked away for privacy behind the two-car garage. Three additional bedrooms rest on the second floor where they share two full baths. Space above the garage is available for future development.

FIRST FLOOR

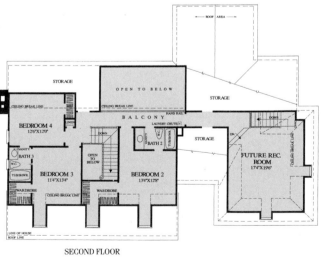

SECOND FLOOR

PHOTO COURTESY OF: WILLIAM E. POOLE DESIGNS, INC. PHOTO BY STEVE DIGGS.
THIS HOME, AS SHOWN IN THE PHOTOGRAPH, MAY DIFFER FROM THE ACTUAL BLUEPRINTS.

plan# HPK2000121

Square Footage: 2,151
Bonus Space: 814 sq. ft.
Bedrooms: 3
Bathrooms: 2
Width: 61' - 0"
Depth: 55' - 8"
Foundation: Crawlspace,
Unfinished Basement

ORDER ONLINE @ EPLANS.COM

Country flavor is well established on this fine three-bedroom home. The covered front porch welcomes friends and family alike to the foyer, where the formal dining room opens to the left. The vaulted ceiling in the great room enhances the warmth of the fireplace and the wall of windows. An efficient kitchen works well with the bayed breakfast area. The secluded master suite offers a walk-in closet and a lavish bath; on the other side of the home, two family bedrooms share a full bath. Upstairs, an optional fourth bedroom is available for guests or in-laws and provides access to a large recreation room.

THIS HOME, AS SHOWN IN THE PHOTOGRAPH, MAY DIFFER FROM THE ACTUAL BLUEPRINTS. FOR MORE DETAILED INFORMATION, PLEASE CHECK THE FLOOR PLANS CAREFULLY.

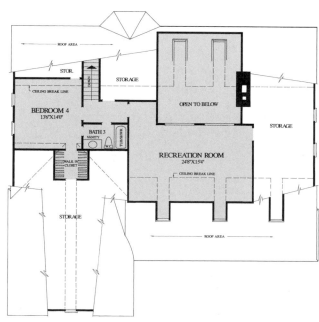

PHOTO COURTESY OF: WILLIAM E. POOLE DESIGNS, INC.; PHOTO BY: TAYLOR LEWIS
THIS HOME AS SHOWN IN THE PHOTOGRAPH, MAY DIFFER FROM THE ACTUAL BLUEPRINTS.

plan# HPK2000122

First Floor: 2,648 sq. ft.
Second Floor: 1,253 sq. ft.
Total: 3,901 sq. ft.
Bonus Space: 540 sq. ft.
Bedrooms: 4
Bathrooms: 3½
Width: 82' - 0"
Depth: 60' - 4"
Foundation: Crawlspace

ORDER ONLINE @ EPLANS.COM

This delightful home packs quite a punch. The grand staircase in the elegant foyer makes a dazzling first impression. To the left is the living room and on the right is the library, which opens to the sunroom overlooking the deck. The angled island kitchen is situated conveniently between the breakfast area and the dining room. The master suite finds privacy on the far right. Here the private bath pampers with spaciousness and twin wardrobes. Three additional bedrooms are found on the second floor, along with two full baths. Future space provides an additional bedroom, bath, and rec room.

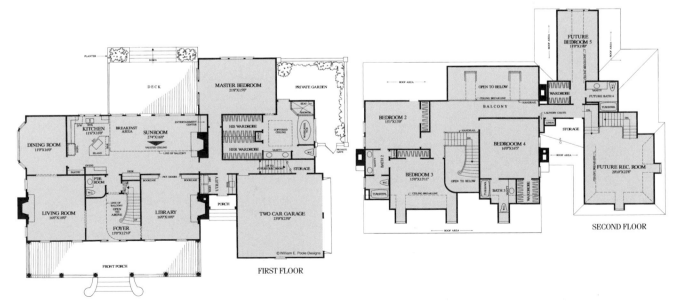

FIRST FLOOR

SECOND FLOOR

© William E. Poole Designs, Inc.

plan# HPK2000123

First Floor: 2,653 sq. ft.
Second Floor: 1,286 sq. ft.
Total: 3,939 sq. ft.
Bonus Space: 583 sq. ft.
Bedrooms: 4
Bathrooms: 3½
Width: 77' - 8"
Depth: 81' - 6"
Foundation: Crawlspace

ORDER ONLINE @ EPLANS.COM

One covered front porch, twin chimneys, and a triplet of dormers add up to create the gorgeous facade of this country cottage. Through the impressive entry and into the foyer, look left to find a convenient powder room, straight ahead to see the friendly family room, and to the right to locate the living room (or library). The kitchen/breakfast area is convenient to the dining room and also provides access to the utility room near a double garage. To the far right of the first level sits the master suite and master bath, complete with a lavish tub and an enormous walk-in closet. The second level includes three bedrooms, two full baths, and a future rec room.

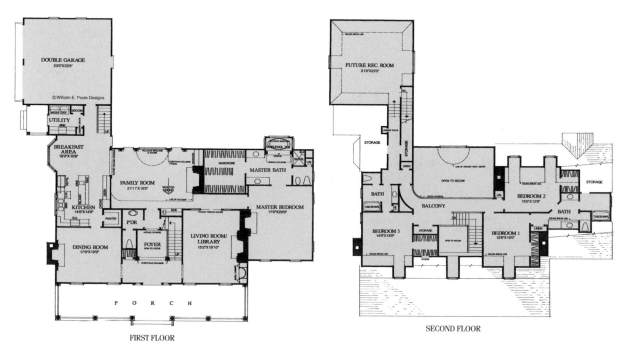

FIRST FLOOR

SECOND FLOOR

© William E. Poole Designs, Inc.

The raised front porch, reached by twin staircases and enhanced by graceful pillars, dominates the exterior of this wonderful Southern Colonial home. A front dining room is perfect for formal dinner parties, and the spacious great room with a fireplace and built-in bookshelves, will host many memorable get-togethers. The kitchen enjoys ample counter space and easily serves the sunlit breakfast alcove. Soothing comfort is guaranteed in the master suite, with a walk-in closet, whirlpool tub, and shower with a seat. Upstairs, two bedrooms share a bath. Space is available for a recreation room, a fourth bedroom, and storage in the basement.

plan# HPK2000124

First Floor: 1,542 sq. ft.
Second Floor: 755 sq. ft.
Total: 2,297 sq. ft.
Bedrooms: 3
Bathrooms: 2½
Width: 48' - 4"
Depth: 39' - 6"
Foundation: Unfinished Walkout Basement

ORDER ONLINE @ EPLANS.COM

GROUND LEVEL

FIRST FLOOR

SECOND FLOOR

© William E. Poole Designs, Inc.

plan# HPK2000125

First Floor: 1,376 sq. ft.
Second Floor: 695 sq. ft.
Total: 2,071 sq. ft.
Bedrooms: 3
Bathrooms: 2½
Width: 47' - 0"
Depth: 49' - 8"
Foundation: Finished Walkout Basement

ORDER ONLINE @ EPLANS.COM

The unique charm of this farmhouse begins with a flight of steps and a welcoming, covered front porch. Just inside, the foyer leads to the formal dining room on the left—with easy access to the kitchen—and straight ahead to the great room. Here, a warming fireplace and built-in entertainment center are balanced by access to the rear screened porch. The first-floor master suite provides plenty of privacy; upstairs, two family bedrooms share a full bath. The lower level offers space for a fourth bedroom, a recreation room, and a garage.

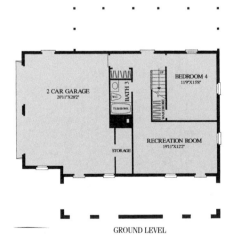

GROUND LEVEL

FIRST FLOOR

SECOND FLOOR

plan# HPK2000126

First Floor: 2,591 sq. ft.
Second Floor: 1,399 sq. ft.
Total: 3,990 sq. ft.
Bedrooms: 4
Bathrooms: 3½
Width: 61' - 4"
Depth: 75' - 0"
Foundation: Slab

ORDER ONLINE @ EPLANS.COM

A dramatic front stairway announces visitors and welcomes all onto a cozy covered porch. The foyer introduces the living room on the right and the dining area on the left. Straight ahead, the family room boasts a fireplace. The kitchen is set between the breakfast room and a petite outdoor porch—perfect for grilling. Secluded on the first floor for privacy, the master suite includes two luxuriously sized walk-in closets, private access to the rear deck, and a master bath with access to another porch out front. Upstairs, dormers enhance sunlight in two family bedrooms that share a full bath between them. A third bedroom uses the hall bath.

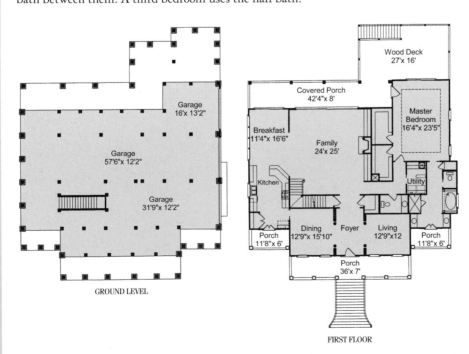

GROUND LEVEL

FIRST FLOOR

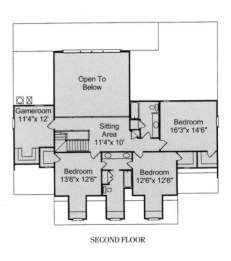

SECOND FLOOR

plan# HPK2000127

First Floor: 3,143 sq. ft.
Second Floor: 901 sq. ft.
Total: 4,044 sq. ft.
Bedrooms: 5
Bathrooms: 4
Width: 80' - 3"
Depth: 66' - 0"
Foundation: Slab

ORDER ONLINE @ EPLANS.COM

This stunning seaside home expresses the regional flavor of the Carolina coast. A wrapping covered front porch welcomes you into the main level. Inside, formal living and dining rooms flank the foyer. A fireplace and built ins arc featured in the family room, which views the rear covered porch. The gourmet island kitchen offers pantry storage and a breakfast nook. The first-floor master bedroom provides a sitting area, private bath, and two walk-in closets. A second bedroom is also located on this level, while three additional bedrooms and attic storage reside upstairs. The basement level provides a spacious garage, second kitchen, game room, guest bedroom, second utility room, and a workshop.

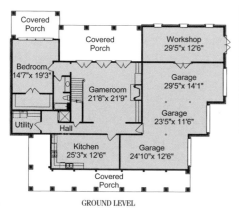

GROUND LEVEL

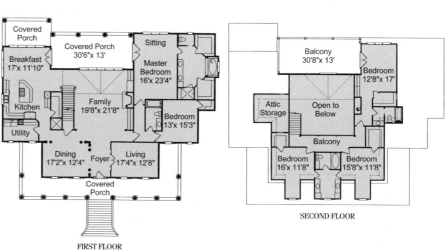

FIRST FLOOR

SECOND FLOOR

plan# **HPK2000128**

First Floor: 1,855 sq. ft.
Second Floor: 901 sq. ft.
Total: 2,756 sq. ft.
Bedrooms: 3
Bathrooms: 3½
Width: 66' - 0"
Depth: 50' - 0"
Foundation: Island Basement

ORDER ONLINE @ EPLANS.COM

This Southern tidewater cottage is the perfect vacation hideaway. An octagonal great room with a multifaceted vaulted ceiling illuminates the interior. The island kitchen is brightened by a bumped-out window and a pass-through to the lanai. Two walk-in closets and a whirlpool bath await to indulge the homeowner in the master suite. A set of double doors opens to the vaulted master lanai for quiet comfort. The U-shaped staircase leads to a loft, which overlooks the great room and the foyer. Two additional family bedrooms offer private baths. A computer center and a morning kitchen complete the upper level.

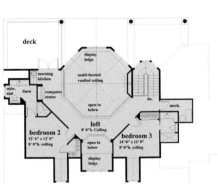

SECOND FLOOR

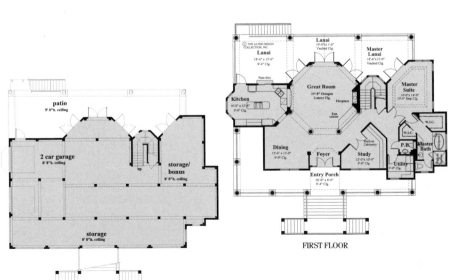

FIRST FLOOR

GROUND LEVEL

plan# HPK2000129

First Floor: 2,146 sq. ft.
Second Floor: 952 sq. ft.
Total: 3,098 sq. ft.
Bedrooms: 3
Bathrooms: 3½
Width: 52' - 0"
Depth: 65' - 4"
Foundation: Island Basement

ORDER ONLINE @ EPLANS.COM

Outdoor spaces, such as the inviting wraparound porch and the rear veranda, are the living areas of this cottage. French doors, a fireplace, and built-in cabinets adorn the great room. A private hall leads to the first-floor master suite. The upper level boasts a catwalk that overlooks the great room and the foyer. A secluded master wing enjoys a bumped-out window, a stunning tray ceiling, and two walk-in closets. The island kitchen conveniently accesses the nook, dining area, and the wet bar.

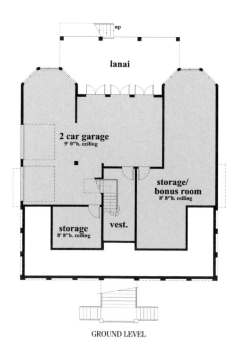

GROUND LEVEL

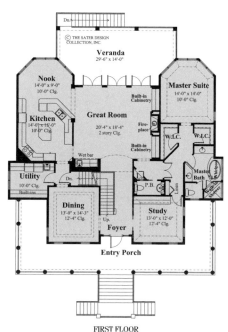

FIRST FLOOR

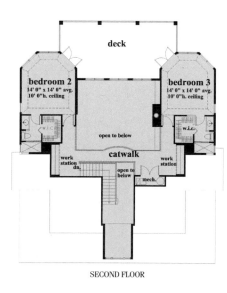

SECOND FLOOR

Hurricane shutters let fresh air in, while five decks make the outside easily accessible. Inside, the open living and dining area is defined by two pairs of French doors that frame a two-story wall of glass, while built-ins flank the living room fireplace. The efficient kitchen features a walk-in pantry, a work island, and a door to the covered porch. Split sleeping quarters offer privacy to the first-floor master suite. Upstairs, a gallery loft leads to a computer area with a built-in desk and a balcony overlook.

plan# HPK2000130

First Floor: 1.642 sq. ft.
Second Floor: 1,165 sq. ft.
Total: 2,807 sq. ft.
Bedrooms: 3
Bathrooms: 3½
Width: 44' - 6"
Depth: 58' - 0"
Foundation: Pier (same as Piling)

ORDER ONLINE @ EPLANS.COM

REAR EXTERIOR

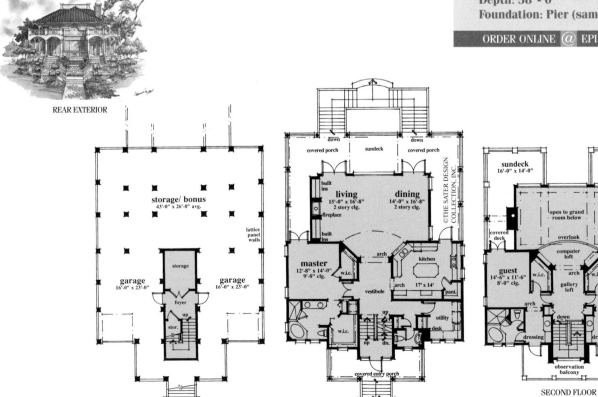

GROUND LEVEL

FIRST FLOOR

SECOND FLOOR

© The Sater Design Collection, Inc.

plan # HPK2000131

First Floor: 2,159 sq. ft.
Second Floor: 1,160 sq. ft.
Total: 3,319 sq. ft.
Bonus Space: 317 sq. ft.
Bedrooms: 5
Bathrooms: 5
Width: 63' - 0"
Depth: 114' - 10"
Foundation: Pier (same as Piling)

ORDER ONLINE @ EPLANS.COM

Triple dormers and a widow's walk set off the standing-seam roof of this New South cottage, inspired by island plantation houses of the early 20th Century. Horizontal siding lends an informal character to the stately facade, which is set off by massive columns and tall shuttered windows. A midlevel landing eases the transition to an L-shaped plan anchored by a forward arrangement of the great room and study. The foyer creates a fluid boundary by connecting the entry veranda with the wrapping rear veranda, pool, and spa. Toward the center of the plan, a winding staircase defines a progresssion from the public realm, which includes a high-tech kitchen and a formal dining room, and the private sleeping quarters. Luxury amenities highlight the master retreat, which offers its own access to the solana and pool.

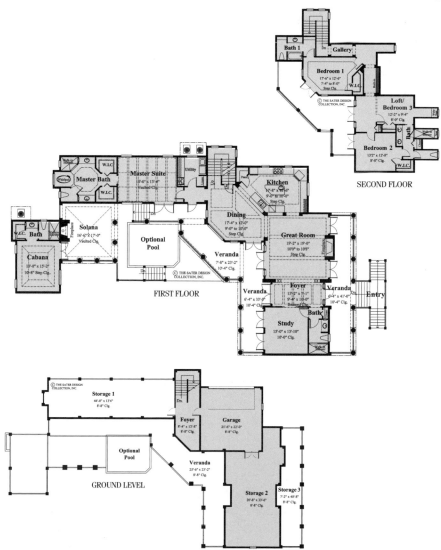

ptan# HPK2000132

First Floor: 2,917 sq. ft.
Second Floor: 1,407 sq. ft.
Total: 4,324 sq. ft.
Bedrooms: 4
Bathrooms: 3½
Width: 59' - 9"
Depth: 79' - 0"
Foundation: Slab

ORDER ONLINE @ EPLANS.COM

This grand Southern home offers an impressive exterior dominated by the colonnaded porch with a full second-floor balcony. The foyer is flanked by the living room, on the right, and the dining room that conveniently adjoins the island kitchen. The breakfast nook opens to the family room that leads out to the rear covered porch. The master suite is found on the right with a lavish bath and large walk-in closet. The second floor holds three family bedrooms, two baths, and a media room. The centered sitting area accesses the front balcony while the media room opens to the balcony on the left.

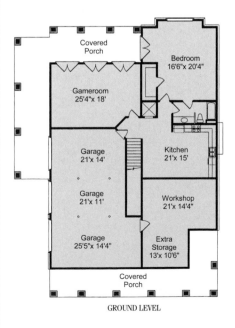

Covered Porch

Gameroom 25'4"x 18'

Bedroom 16'6"x 20'4"

Garage 21'x 14'

Kitchen 21'x 15'

Garage 21'x 11'

Workshop 21'x 14'4"

Garage 25'5"x 14'4"

Extra Storage 13'x 10'6"

Covered Porch

GROUND LEVEL

Covered Porch

Master Bedroom 21'x 16'6"

Family 23'x 18'2"

Hall

Breakfast 16'6"x 11'3"

Utility

Walk-In Closet

Kitchen 16'4"x 15'

Dining 11'8"x 14'6"

Foyer

Living 11'9"x 14'6"

Covered Porch

FIRST FLOOR

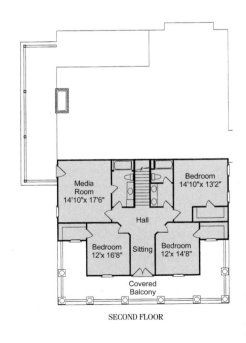

Media Room 14'10"x 17'6"

Bedroom 14'10"x 13'2"

Hall

Bedroom 12'x 16'8"

Sitting

Bedroom 12'x 14'8"

Covered Balcony

SECOND FLOOR

plan# HPK2000133

First Floor: 1,498 sq. ft.
Second Floor: 1,450 sq. ft.
Total: 2,948 sq. ft.
Bonus Space: 423 sq. ft.
Bedrooms: 3
Bathrooms: 2½
Width: 63' - 2"
Depth: 46' - 10"
Foundation: Crawlspace,
Unfinished Basement

ORDER ONLINE @ EPLANS.COM

This stately home achieves grandeur in a modest footprint. The tone is set by a full-facade porches on both levels. Inside, rooms are efficiently arranged around a central stair. The foyer opens to the living room on the right, which leads into a family room designed for cozy gatherings. The flow continues around the back of the house, through the breakfast area and into the island kitchen, ending in the formal dining room to the left of the foyer. Upstairs, an expanded landing with access to the second-level porch serves as a lounge area. There are two family bedrooms with a connecting bath and a master suite with a private bath and dual walk-in closets. The laundry room is also located upstairs for ultimate convenience.

SECOND FLOOR

FIRST FLOOR

© William E. Poole Designs, Inc.

plan# **HPK2000134**

First Floor: 2,945 sq. ft.
Second Floor: 1,353 sq. ft.
Total: 4,298 sq. ft.
Bedrooms: 4
Bathrooms: 4½
Width: 61' - 4"
Depth: 72' - 2"
Foundation: Finished Walkout Basement

ORDER ONLINE @ EPLANS.COM

Nothing is more satisfying and fulfilling than home—and home at the Mount Pleasant is the stuff from which dreams are made. Take advantage of the views from the second-story porch of this grand home. Inside, this home considers everyone's needs with private baths in all the bedrooms. The master bedroom boasts His and Hers closets, a whirlpool tub, separate shower and double sinks. Near the family room (with fireplace), the U-shaped kitchen features a twelve-inch bar top and an island accessing the dining room. Guests have the option of utilizing the stairs or elevator between floors. The basement is designed with a fifth bedroom, recreational, mechanical and storage rooms. A two-car garage protects vehicles from the weather.

GROUND LEVEL

FIRST FLOOR

SECOND FLOOR

© William E. Poole Designs, Inc.

plan# HPK2000135

First Floor: 1,978 sq. ft.
Second Floor: 1,320 sq. ft.
Total: 3,298 sq. ft.
Bonus Space: 352 sq. ft.
Bedrooms: 4
Bathrooms: 3½
Width: 66' - 8"
Depth: 62' - 0"
Foundation: Crawlspace

ORDER ONLINE @ EPLANS.COM

The wide hipped roof of this classic Southern plantation home demonstrates the influence of Creole conventions. Shady porches protect the front rooms from the southern sun and provide pleasant places to sit and enjoy the evening breezes. The traditional center hall plan features formal living and dining rooms flanking the foyer, while the rear of the home is modern as can be, with an open arrangement of family room, breakfast nook, and kitchen. A grand fireplace, built-in cabinetry, and conveniences like a walk-in pantry and planning desk in the kitchen are every homeowner's dream. Upstairs are two spacious bedrooms and a bath, as well as the sumptous master suite.

© William E. Poole Designs, Inc.

plan# **HPK2000136**

First Floor: 1,887 sq. ft.
Second Floor: 1,133 sq. ft.
Total: 3,020 sq. ft.
Bonus Space: 444 sq. ft.
Bedrooms: 4
Bathrooms: 4½
Width: 63' - 4"
Depth: 82' - 2"
Foundation: Crawlspace,
Unfinished Basement

ORDER ONLINE @ EPLANS.COM

This beautiful Southern Colonial home will dazzle with a double-decker porch and generous family space. The family room features built-in bookshelves, a fireplace, and screened-porch access. Separated by pocket doors, the oversized living room makes a great spot to read and relax. The dining room, kitchen, and breakfast nook flow effortlessly; porch access from the breakfast nook invites outdoor dining. In the master bedroom, an elongated walk-in closet and sumptuous bath with a whirlpool tub will soothe and refresh. Three upper-level bedrooms feature private baths and walk-in closets. Don't miss the future space above the garage.

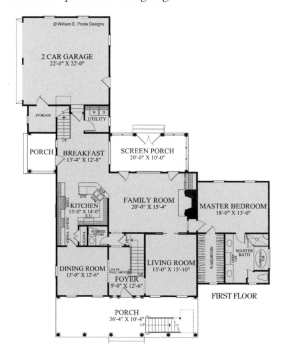

FIRST FLOOR

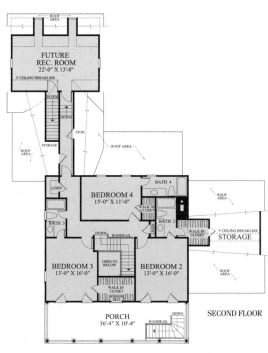

SECOND FLOOR

plan# HPK2000137

First Floor: 1,778 sq. ft.
Second Floor: 1,663 sq. ft.
Total: 3,441 sq. ft.
Bonus Space: 442 sq. ft.
Bedrooms: 4
Bathrooms: 3½
Width: 72' - 0"
Depth: 50' - 0"
Foundation: Unfinished Basement

ORDER ONLINE @ EPLANS.COM

Spring breezes and summer nights will be a joy to take in on the verandas and balcony of this gorgeous Southern Colonial home. Or, if you prefer, sit back and enjoy a good book in the library, or invite a friend over for a chat in the conversation room. The first floor also includes formal dining and living rooms, a service entry with a laundry, and a three-car garage. You'll find a bonus room over the garage; you may decide to turn it into a media room or an exercise room. The master bedroom sports a fireplace, two walk-in closets, a double-bowl vanity, a shower, and a whirlpool tub. Three other bedrooms occupy the second floor—one has its own full bath. Of course, the balcony is just a step away.

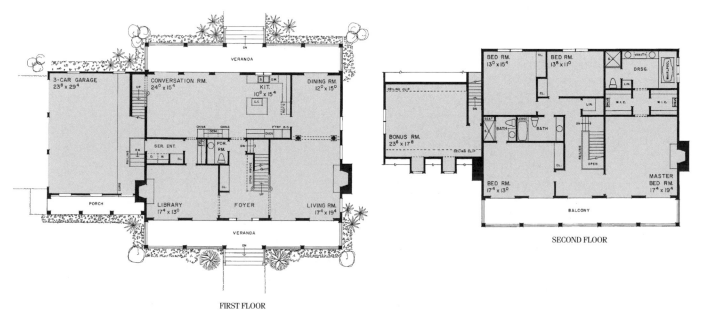

FIRST FLOOR

SECOND FLOOR

© The Sater Design Collection, Inc.

Tall, stately columns wrap around the full front porch on this wonderful Southern Colonial home. The foyer features a gallery colonnade that separates the formal dining space from the great room. A two-sided fireplace is shared between the great room and private library just off the sumptuous master retreat. The gourmet kitchen works in tandem with the breakfast nook and both have excellent views of the amazing rear porch. Upstairs, three generously sized bedrooms—two with access to a private porch—share a study, laundry room, and two bathrooms.

plan# HPK2000138

First Floor: 2,705 sq. ft.
Second Floor: 1,241 sq. ft.
Total: 3,946 sq. ft.
Bedrooms: 4
Bathrooms: 4
Width: 98' - 0"
Depth: 60' - 0"
Foundation: Crawlspace, Slab

ORDER ONLINE @ EPLANS.COM

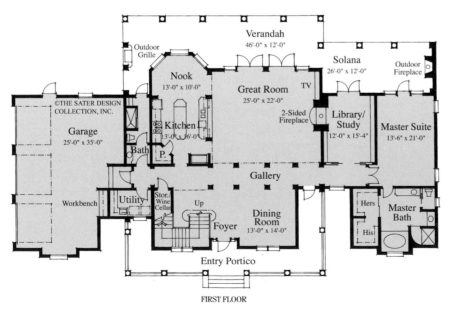

FIRST FLOOR

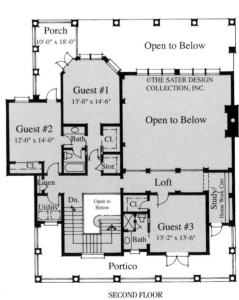

SECOND FLOOR

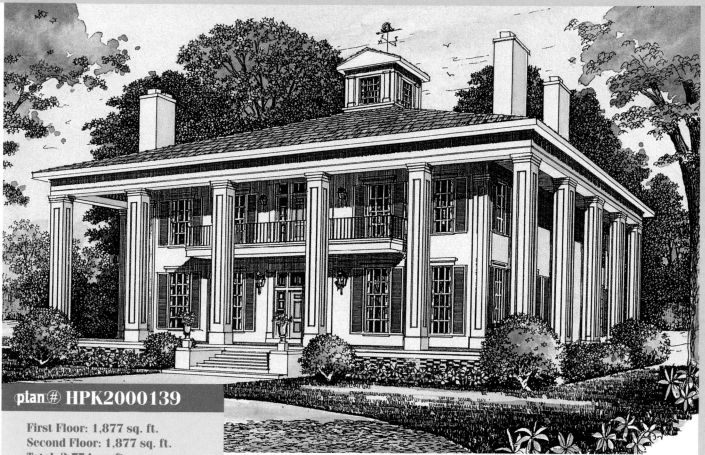

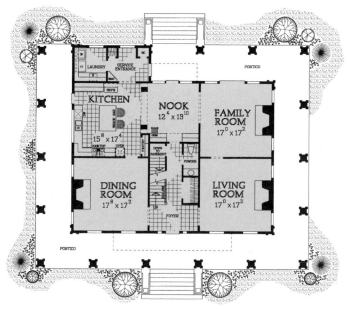

plan# HPK2000139

First Floor: 1,877 sq. ft.
Second Floor: 1,877 sq. ft.
Total: 3,754 sq. ft.
Bedrooms: 4
Bathrooms: 3½
Width: 65' - 0"
Depth: 53' - 0"
Foundation: Unfinished Basement

ORDER ONLINE @ EPLANS.COM

The gracious hospitality and the genteel, easy lifestyle of the South are personified in this elegant Southern Colonial home. Contributing to the exterior's stucco warmth are shutters, a cupola, and square columns surrounding the home. Inside, the warmth continues with six fireplaces throughout the home: in the formal dining room, living room, family room—and on the second floor—in one of the family bedrooms, romantic master bedroom, and master bath. The second floor contains two family bedrooms—each with its own bath—and a lavish master bedroom with a balcony and a pampering bath. A study/bedroom with a balcony completes the upstairs. Plans for a detached garage with an enclosed lap pool are included with the blueprints.

FIRST FLOOR

SECOND FLOOR

HOLZHAUER INC.

A truly grand entry—absolutely stunning on a corner lot—sets the eclectic yet elegant tone of this four-bedroom home. The foyer opens to a dramatic circular stair, then on to the two-story great room that's framed by a second-story balcony. An elegant dining room is set to the side, distinguished by a span of arches. The gourmet kitchen features wrapping counters, a cooktop island, and a breakfast room. A front study and a secondary bedroom are nice accompaniments to the expansive master suite. A through-fireplace, a spa-style bath, and a huge walk-in closet highlight this area. Upstairs, a loft opens to two balconies overlooking the porch and leads to two family bedrooms and a game room.

plan# HPK2000140

First Floor: 2,772 sq. ft.
Second Floor: 933 sq. ft.
Total: 3,705 sq. ft.
Bonus Space: 217 sq. ft.
Bedrooms: 4
Bathrooms: 4½
Width: 74' - 8"
Depth: 61' - 10"
Foundation: Crawlspace, Slab

ORDER ONLINE @ EPLANS.COM

FIRST FLOOR

SECOND FLOOR

plan# HPK2000141

First Floor: 1,944 sq. ft.
Second Floor: 1,427 sq. ft.
Total: 3,371 sq. ft.
Bedrooms: 4
Bathrooms: 3½
Width: 52' - 0"
Depth: 84' - 0"
Foundation: Slab, Unfinished
Basement, Crawlspace

ORDER ONLINE @ EPLANS.COM

The dazzling exterior of this Southern estate is true to form with six magnificent columns creating an awe-inspiring facade. The foyer leads to the living room with its 15-foot ceiling and paired window walls. Access to both the rear covered porch and the side courtyard is gained from the living room. The angled kitchen is flanked by the sunny eating bay and the convenient utility room. The side-loading, two-car garage at the rear contains an expansive storage area. The second floor holds the game room, an ancillary kitchen and three bedrooms, while the master suite finds seclusion on the first floor. Note that Bedroom 4 includes a dressing area, a private bath, and access to the balcony.

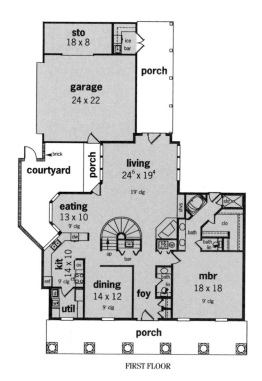

FIRST FLOOR

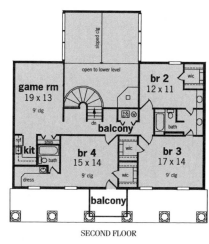

SECOND FLOOR

plan# HPK2000142

Square Footage: 4,038
Bedrooms: 4
Bathrooms: 4½
Width: 98' - 0"
Depth: 90' - 0"
Foundation: Unfinished Basement, Crawlspace, Slab

ORDER ONLINE @ EPLANS.COM

Reminiscent of the old Newport mansions, this luxury house has volume ceilings, a glamorous master suite with a hearth-warmed sitting area, a glassed-in sunroom, a home office, three porches with a deck, and a gourmet kitchen with a pantry. Graceful French doors are used for all the entrances and in the formal living and dining rooms. The magnificent kitchen boasts a large pantry. A centrally positioned family room is graced with a large fireplace and is accessed by the rear porch, living room, and dining room.

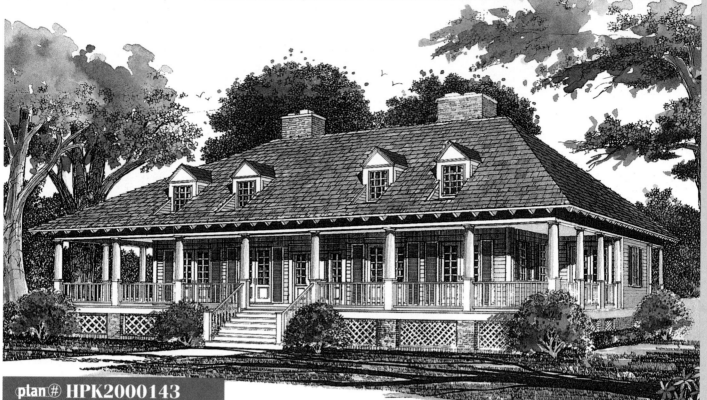

plan# HPK2000143

First Floor: 1,669 sq. ft.
Second Floor: 1,627 sq. ft.
Total: 3,296 sq. ft.
Bedrooms: 4
Bathrooms: 3½
Width: 64' - 0"
Depth: 46' - 0"
Foundation: Crawlspace

ORDER ONLINE @ EPLANS.COM

This home's massive hipped roof with two sets of twin dormers and exposed rafter tails provides immediate appeal. The central foyer—with a 10-foot ceiling—routes traffic efficiently to all zones. Formal living and dining rooms are located to the front of the plan with French doors opening to a covered porch. Informal living areas function with the rear covered porch for excellent indoor-outdoor relationships. The spacious family room has a 10-foot beam ceiling and a handy snack bar. The bedrooms are large, with good wardrobe storage and blank wall space for flexible and attractive furniture placement. The master bedroom features two walk-in closets, and the master bath has two wash basins, an ultra tub, and a stall shower.

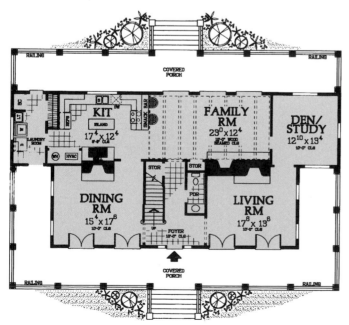

FIRST FLOOR

SECOND FLOOR

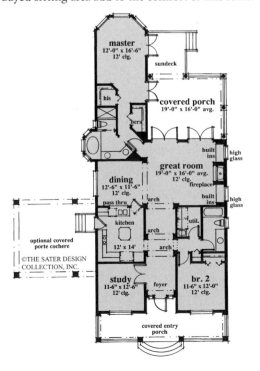

plan# HPK2000144

Square Footage: 1,792
Bedrooms: 2
Bathrooms: 2
Width: 32' - 0"
Depth: 82' - 0"
Foundation: Crawlspace

ORDER ONLINE @ EPLANS.COM

REAR EXTERIOR

A blend of Southern comfort and Gulf Coast style sets this home apart. Inside, decorative arches and columns mark the grand entrance to the living and dining areas, and the gourmet kitchen provides a pass-through to the dining room. On cold nights, a fireplace warms the great room, and on warm evenings, French doors to the covered porch let in cool breezes. At the rear of the plan, the master suite privately accesses a sundeck, and French doors open to the covered porch. Two walk-in closets, a garden tub, and a bayed sitting area add to the comfort of this suite.

plan# HPK2000145

Square Footage: 2,978
Bedrooms: 3
Bathrooms: 3½
Width: 84' - 0"
Depth: 90' - 0"
Foundation: Slab

ORDER ONLINE @ EPLANS.COM

This home is designed to be a dream come true. A formal living area opens from the gallery foyer through graceful arches and looks out to the veranda. The veranda hosts an outdoor grill and service counter—perfect for outdoor entertaining. The leisure room offers a private veranda, a cabana bath, and a wet bar just off the gourmet kitchen. Walls of windows and a bayed breakfast nook let in natural light and set a bright tone for this area. The master suite opens to the rear property through French doors and boasts a lavish bath with a corner whirlpool tub that overlooks a private garden. An art niche off the gallery hall, a private dressing area, and a secluded study complement the master suite. Two family bedrooms occupy the opposite wing of the plan and share a full bath and private hall.

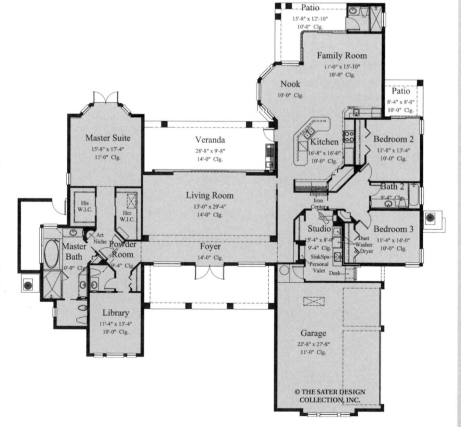

© THE SATER DESIGN COLLECTION, INC.

plan# HPK2000146

Square Footage: 2,061
Bedrooms: 3
Bathrooms: 2½
Width: 88' - 10"
Depth: 40' - 9"
Foundation: Slab, Crawlspace

ORDER ONLINE @ EPLANS.COM

This amazing home is detailed with sloped roofs, a stone facade, and muntin windows. Enjoy the stone fireplace whether relaxing in the great room or sipping a drink at the bar extended from the kitchen. Adjacent to the kitchen, a dining area includes sliding glass doors leading to a covered patio. A private patio area is available to the master bedroom, as well as a spacious private bath, which includes a double-bowl sink and a vast walk-in closet. Two family bedrooms each have double-door closets and share a full bath. A three-car garage resides to the far right of the plan, with an entryway opening to the utility room.

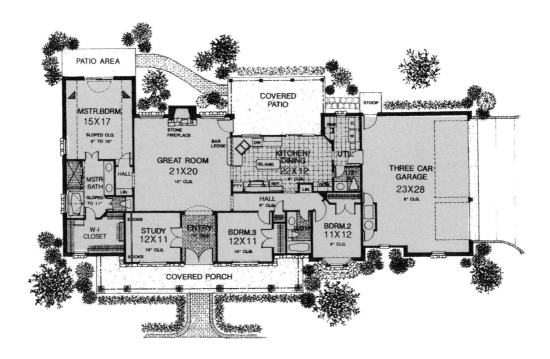

plan# HPK2000147

Square Footage: 1,704
Bedrooms: 3
Bathrooms: 2
Width: 47' - 0"
Depth: 66' - 0"
Foundation: Crawlspace, Slab

ORDER ONLINE @ EPLANS.COM

This Southern cottage provides spacious front and rear porches, along with many other amenities. The entry leads to the formal dining room on the right and a grand living space with a tray ceiling just beyond. The open kitchen and breakfast areas allow courtyard views and connect directly to the living areas. The large master suite features separate walk-in closets and a bath with two lavatories, a whirlpool tub, and a separate shower. Two family bedrooms share a full bath.

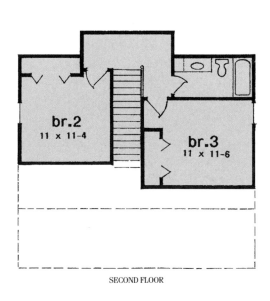

plan# HPK2000148

First Floor: 1,050 sq. ft.
Second Floor: 458 sq. ft.
Total: 1,508 sq. ft.
Bedrooms: 3
Bathrooms: 2½
Width: 35' - 6"
Depth: 39' - 9"
Foundation: Pier (same as Piling)

ORDER ONLINE @ EPLANS.COM

This adorable abode could serve as a vacation cottage, guest house, starter home, or in-law quarters. The side-gabled design allows for a front porch with a "down-South" feel. Despite the small size, this home is packed with all the necessities. The first-floor master suite has a large bathroom and a walk-in closet. An open, functional floor plan includes a powder room, a kitchen/breakfast nook area, and a family room with a corner fireplace. Upstairs, two additional bedrooms share a bath. One could be used as a home office.

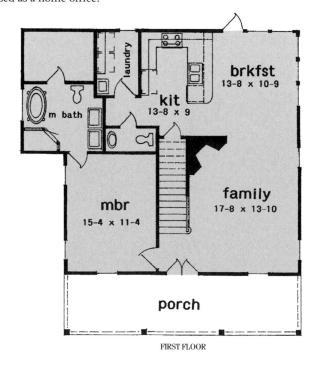

FIRST FLOOR

SECOND FLOOR

plan# HPK2000149

Square Footage: 2,648
Bonus Space: 266 sq. ft.
Bedrooms: 4
Bathrooms: 2
Width: 68' - 10"
Depth: 77' - 10"
Foundation: Crawlspace, Slab, Unfinished Basement

ORDER ONLINE @ EPLANS.COM

This charming Colonial Revival home with side-loading garage is perfect for a corner lot. The inviting porch opens to the foyer that is flanked by the formal dining room on the right and a flex room on the left. Twin arches announce the great room where the warming fireplace is framed by windows. The generous island kitchen is certain to please the gourmet of the family and the sunny breakfast nook offers a casual alternative to the formal dining room. The family bedrooms are situated on the left sharing a Jack-and-Jill bath. And on the far right, the master suite offers a pampering private bath that includes His and Hers walk-in closets and a delightful garden tub.

plan# HPK2000150

Square Footage: 1,997
Bedrooms: 4
Bathrooms: 2½
Width: 56' - 4"
Depth: 67' - 4"
Foundation: Crawlspace, Slab, Unfinished Basement

ORDER ONLINE @ EPLANS.COM

The wide front steps, columned porch, and symmetrical layout give this charming home a Georgian appeal. The large kitchen, with its walk-in pantry, island/snack bar, and breakfast nook, will gratify any cook. The central great room offers radiant French doors on both sides of the fireplace. Outside those doors is a comfortable covered porch with two skylights. To the left of the great room reside four bedrooms—three secondary bedrooms and a master bedroom. The master bedroom enjoys a walk-in closet, twin-vanity sinks, a separate shower and tub, and private access to the rear porch.

plan# HPK2000151

Square Footage: 1,688
Bedrooms: 3
Bathrooms: 2
Width: 70' - 1"
Depth: 48' - 0"
Foundation: Crawlspace, Slab,
Unfinished Basement

ORDER ONLINE @ EPLANS.COM

Dormers and columns decorate the exterior of this three-bedroom country home. Inside, the foyer has immediate access to one family bedroom and the formal dining area. Ahead is the great room with a warming fireplace and ribbon of windows for natural lighting. The master suite is set to the back of the plan and has a lavish bath with a garden tub, separate shower, and two vanities.

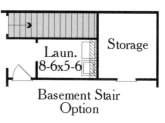

Basement Stair
Option

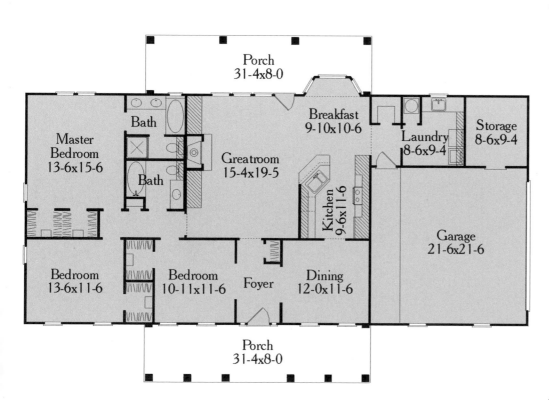

This rustic farmhouse has all of the charm of a country cottage, with the modern amenities found in today's luxury homes. Enter from a welcoming porch to the airy foyer. Columns and an archway announce the great room, with a fireplace for chilly nights and rear-porch access for those sunny summer days. The kitchen is designed for convenience and easily serves the vaulted sun room/breakfast area. Two generous suites are located on the left; the rear bedroom would make an excellent master suite and includes a splendid bath. Upstairs, two more suites (both with private baths) access a gathering room with a balcony, a great place for family fun.

plan# HPK2000152

First Floor: 2,507 sq. ft.
Second Floor: 1,165 sq. ft.
Total: 3,672 sq. ft.
Bedrooms: 4
Bathrooms: 4½
Width: 119' - 0"
Depth: 52' - 10"
Foundation: Crawlspace

ORDER ONLINE @ EPLANS.COM

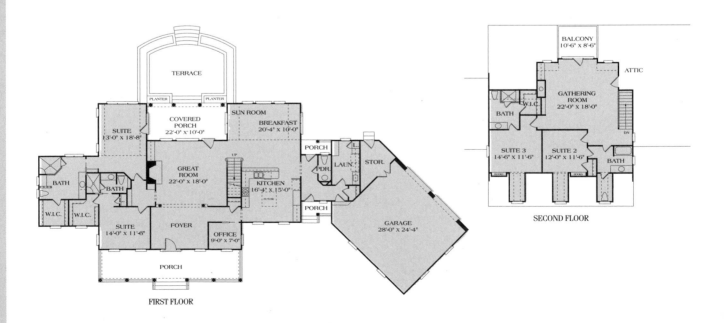

FIRST FLOOR

SECOND FLOOR

plan# HPK2000153

First Floor: 1,905 sq. ft.
Second Floor: 1,027 sq. ft.
Total: 2,932 sq. ft.
Bedrooms: 3
Bathrooms: 3½
Width: 66' - 10"
Depth: 61' - 2"
Foundation: Crawlspace

ORDER ONLINE @ EPLANS.COM

Six columns, a covered front porch and triple dormer windows give this home a special dignity and charm. Inside, the foyer opens to a formal dining room to the left and a study to the right; a powder room is also nearby. The gathering room, home to a fireplace, leads to a covered terrace that's perfect for outdoor entertaining. The master suite offers a walk-in closet and a well-appointed bath with a whirlpool tub and a compartmented toilet. A roomy kitchen, cozy breakfast room and convenient laundry room complete the first floor. On the second level, a recreation room adds to the fun. The two family bedrooms—each with a private bath—also include walk-in closets.

FIRST FLOOR

SECOND FLOOR

plan# HPK2000154

First Floor: 2,005 sq. ft.
Second Floor: 964 sq. ft.
Total: 2,969 sq. ft.
Bonus Space: 340 sq. ft.
Bedrooms: 3
Bathrooms: 2½
Width: 74' - 11"
Depth: 58' - 3"
Foundation: Crawlspace

ORDER ONLINE @ EPLANS.COM

With a strong Colonial presence and graceful Southern charm, this wonderful home will delight inside and out. Enter off the front porch to a foyer, which opens through French doors to the living room, or under an arch to the dining room. The family room is large enough to entertain in style, including a fireplace and deck access. Designed for both beauty and function, the kitchen efficiently serves the box-bay breakfast nook. The master suite resides in the entire left wing with a fantastic vaulted bath that soothes with a spa tub. Upstairs, two bedrooms and a full bath join almost limitless space for expansion, with a bonus room, future bedroom, unfinished space, and future bath. The plan is completed by a garage with ample storage.

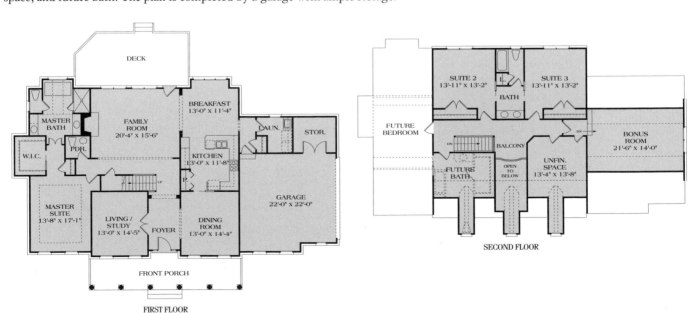

plan⊕ HPK2000155

First Floor: 2,008 sq. ft.
Second Floor: 1,027 sq. ft.
Total: 3,035 sq. ft.
Bedrooms: 4
Bathrooms: 3½
Width: 66' - 0"
Depth: 74' - 0"
Foundation: Unfinished Basement, Crawlspace, Slab

ORDER ONLINE @ EPLANS.COM

A porch with wood railings borders the facade of this plan, lending a farmhouse or country feel. The family room includes a fireplace and French doors to the porch, which open further to the deck area. The master bedroom is filled with luxuries from the walk-in closet with shelves, the full bath with a skylight, sloped ceiling, and vanity to the shower with a convenient seat. Three additional bedrooms upstairs share two full baths between them. A breezeway, placed between the garage and the house, leads easily to the deck area. Extras include a large utility room, pantry, half-bath downstairs, and two storage areas.

FIRST FLOOR

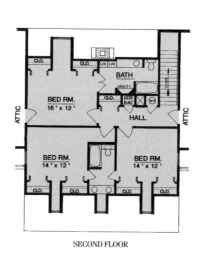

SECOND FLOOR

This three-bedroom home brings the past to life with Tuscan columns, dormers, and fanlight windows. The entrance is flanked by the dining room and study. The great room boasts cathedral ceilings and a fireplace, with an open design that connects to the kitchen area. The spacious kitchen adjoins a breakfast nook and accesses the rear covered veranda. The master bedroom enjoys a sitting area, access to the veranda, and a spacious bathroom. This home is complete with two family bedrooms.

plan# HPK2000156

Square Footage: 2,387
Bonus Space: 377 sq. ft.
Bedrooms: 3
Bathrooms: 2½
Width: 69' - 6"
Depth: 68' - 11"
Foundation: Slab, Crawlspace

ORDER ONLINE @ EPLANS.COM

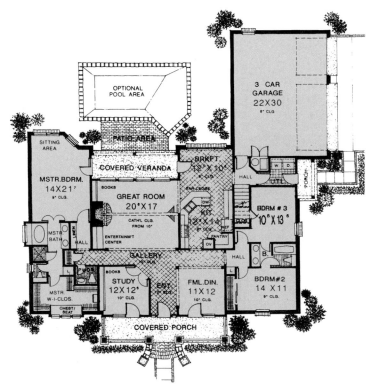

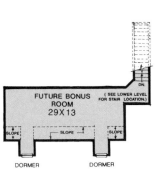

plan# HPK2000157

Square Footage: 2,078
Bedrooms: 4
Bathrooms: 2
Width: 75' - 0"
Depth: 47' - 10"
Foundation: Slab, Crawlspace

ORDER ONLINE @ EPLANS.COM

Colonial style meets farmhouse charm in this plan, furnishing old-fashioned charisma with a flourish. From the entry, double doors open to the country dining room and a large island kitchen. Nearby, the spacious great room takes center stage and is warmed by a fireplace flanked by large windows. Tucked behind the three-car garage, the secluded master suite features a vaulted ceiling. The master bath contains a relaxing tub, double-bowl vanity, separate shower, and compartmented toilet. Beyond the bath is a huge walk-in closet with two built-in chests. Three family bedrooms—one doubles as a study or home office—a full bath, and a utility room complete the plan.

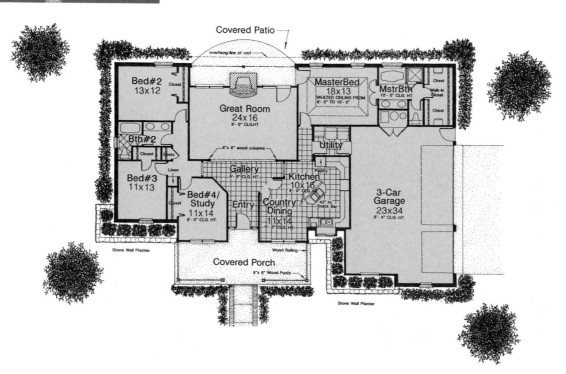

With three dormers and a welcoming front door accented by sidelights and a sunburst, this country cottage is sure to please. The dining room, immediately to the right from the foyer, is defined by decorative columns. In the great room, a volume ceiling heightens the space and showcases a fireplace and built-in bookshelves. The kitchen has plenty of work space and flows into the bayed breakfast nook. A considerate split-bedroom design places the plush master suite to the far left and two family bedrooms to the far right. A fourth bedroom and future space upstairs allow room to grow.

plan# HPK2000158

First Floor: 1,981 sq. ft.
Second Floor: 291 sq. ft.
Total: 2,272 sq. ft.
Bonus Space: 412 sq. ft.
Bedrooms: 4
Bathrooms: 3½
Width: 58' - 0"
Depth: 53' - 0"
Foundation: Crawlspace

ORDER ONLINE @ EPLANS.COM

FIRST FLOOR

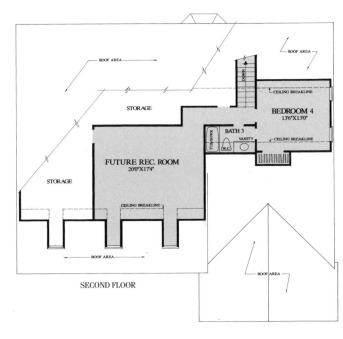

SECOND FLOOR

© William E. Poole Designs, Inc.

plan# HPK2000159

First Floor: 2,191 sq. ft.
Second Floor: 1,220 sq. ft.
Total: 3,411 sq. ft.
Bonus Space: 280 sq. ft.
Bedrooms: 4
Bathrooms: 3½
Width: 75' - 8"
Depth: 54' - 4"
Foundation: Crawlspace,
Unfinished Basement

ORDER ONLINE @ EPLANS.COM

This Colonial farmhouse will be the showpiece of your neighborhood. Come in from the wide front porch through French doors topped by a sunburst window. Continue past the formal dining and living rooms to a columned gallery and a large family room with a focal fireplace. The kitchen astounds with a unique layout, an island, and abundant counter and cabinet space. The master bath balances luxury with efficiency. Three upstairs bedrooms enjoy amenities such as dormer windows or walk-in closets. Bonus space is ready for expansion as your needs change.

SECOND FLOOR

FIRST FLOOR

© William E. Poole Designs, Inc.

Three petite dormers top a welcoming covered porch and add a touch of grace to an already beautiful home. Inside, the foyer opens to the left to a formal dining room, which in turn has easy access to the efficient kitchen. Here, a pantry and a snack bar in the breakfast area make meal preparations a delight. The nearby spacious family room features a fireplace, built-in bookshelves, and outdoor access. Located away from the master suite for privacy, two family bedrooms pamper with private baths and walk-in closets. On the other end of the home, the master suite provides luxury via a huge walk-in closet, whirlpool tub, and corner shower with a seat. An optional second floor features a fourth bedroom in private splendor with its own bath and access to a recreation room complete with a second fireplace.

plan# HPK2000160

Square Footage: 2,215
Bedrooms: 3
Bathrooms: 3
Width: 69' - 10"
Depth: 62' - 6"
Foundation: Crawlspace, Unfinished Basement

ORDER ONLINE @ EPLANS.COM

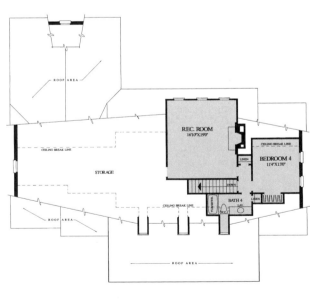

© William E. Poole Designs, Inc.

plan# HPK2000161

First Floor: 1,370 sq. ft.
Second Floor: 668 sq. ft.
Total: 2,038 sq. ft.
Bonus Space: 421 sq. ft.
Bedrooms: 3
Bathrooms: 2½
Width: 71' - 8"
Depth: 49' - 4"
Foundation: Crawlspace

ORDER ONLINE @ EPLANS.COM

This charming 1½-story home offers an inviting front porch and a rear screened porch, increasing the living space significantly. The foyer opens to the formal dining room and the great room, which in turn leads to the screened porch. The master suite is tucked away for privacy on the right—the sunny bedroom adjoins a luxurious private bath. The second-floor balcony, full bath, and lounge area separate the two family bedrooms.

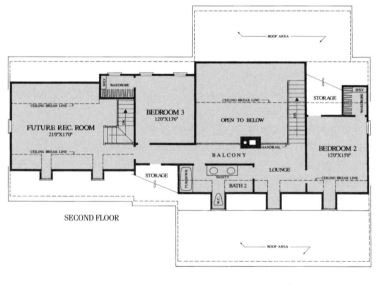

SECOND FLOOR

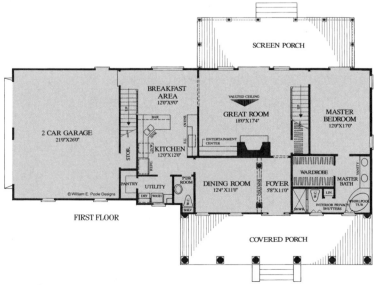

FIRST FLOOR

© William E. Poole Designs, Inc.

plan# HPK2000162

Square Footage: 2,096
Bonus Space: 374 sq. ft.
Bedrooms: 3
Bathrooms: 2
Width: 64' - 8"
Depth: 60' - 0"
Foundation: Crawlspace,
Unfinished Basement

ORDER ONLINE @ EPLANS.COM

Brick and siding, a long covered porch, and three petite dormers combine to give this home plenty of curb appeal. Inside, the layout is equally delightful. The formal dining room is defined from the foyer by graceful columns, and the great room features a fireplace, built-ins, and French doors to the backyard. The efficient kitchen offers a pantry, a corner sink, and a bayed breakfast area. Two family bedrooms and a full bath are located to the right side of the plan, and the master suite provides privacy, a walk-in closet, and a pampering bath to the left.

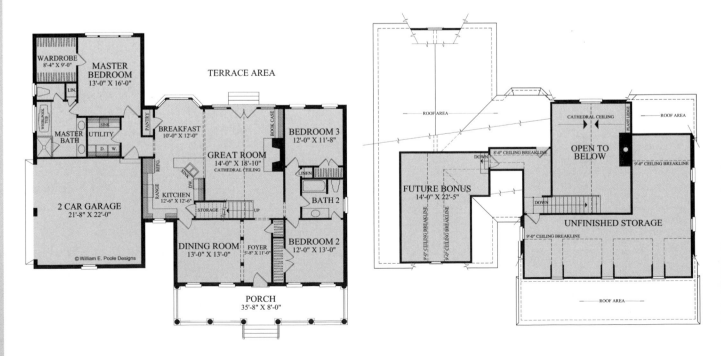

© WILLIAM E POOLE DESIGNS, INC.

plan# HPK2000163

Square Footage: 2,777
Bonus Space: 424 sq. ft.
Bedrooms: 3
Bathrooms: 2½
Width: 75' - 6"
Depth: 60' - 2"
Foundation: Crawlspace, Unfinished Basement

ORDER ONLINE @ EPLANS.COM

This home is an absolute dream when it comes to living space! Whether formal or casual, there's a room for every occasion. The foyer opens to the formal dining room on the left; straight ahead lies the magnificent hearth-warmed living room. The island kitchen opens not only to a breakfast nook, but to a huge family/sunroom surrounded by two walls of windows! The right wing of the plan holds the sleeping quarters—two family bedrooms sharing a bath, and a majestic master suite. The second floor holds an abundance of expandable space.

© William E. Poole Designs, Inc.

plan# HPK2000164

First Floor: 2,998 sq. ft.
Second Floor: 1,556 sq. ft.
Total: 4,554 sq. ft.
Bonus Space: 741 sq. ft.
Bedrooms: 4
Bathrooms: 4½
Width: 75' - 6"
Depth: 91' - 2"
Foundation: Crawlspace

ORDER ONLINE @ EPLANS.COM

The paired double-end chimneys, reminiscent of the Georgian style of architecture, set this design apart from the rest. The covered entry opens to the columned foyer with the dining room on the left and the living room on the right, each enjoying the warmth and charm of a fireplace. Beyond the grand staircase, the family room delights with a third fireplace and a window wall that opens to the terrace. The expansive kitchen and breakfast area sit on the far left; the master suite is secluded on the the right with its pampering private bath. The second floor holds three additional bedrooms (including a second master bedroom), three full baths, a computer room, and the future recreation room.

FIRST FLOOR

SECOND FLOOR

plan# HPK2000165

First Floor: 3,170 sq. ft.
Second Floor: 1,914 sq. ft.
Total: 5,084 sq. ft.
Bonus Space: 445 sq. ft.
Bedrooms: 4
Bathrooms: 3½
Width: 100' - 10"
Depth: 65' - 5"
Foundation: Crawlspace

ORDER ONLINE @ EPLANS.COM

This elegantly appointed home is a beauty inside and out. A centerpiece stair rises gracefully from the two-story grand foyer. The kitchen, breakfast room, and family room provide open space for the gathering of family and friends. The beam-ceilinged study and the dining room flank the grand foyer, and each includes a fireplace. The master bedroom features a cozy sitting area and a luxury master bath with His and Hers vanities and walk-in closets. Three large bedrooms and a game room complete the second floor. A large expandable area is available at the top of the rear stair.

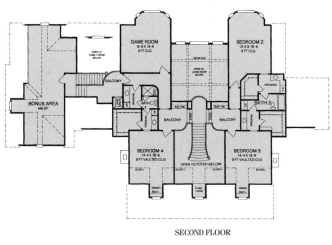

SECOND FLOOR

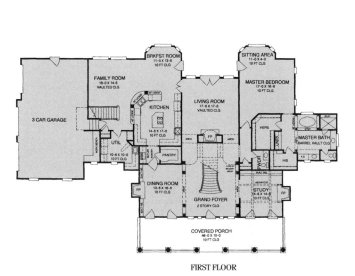

FIRST FLOOR

plan# HPK2000282

First Floor: 2,732 sq. ft.
Second Floor: 2,734 sq. ft.
Total: 5,466 sq. ft.
Bedrooms: 5
Bathrooms: 5½ + ½
Width: 85' - 0"
Depth: 85' - 6"
Foundation: Crawlspace, Slab,
Unfinished Walkout Basement

ORDER ONLINE @ EPLANS.COM

Down on the Farm

Contrary to the previous Colonial homes, Southern Farmhouses are noted for their asymmetrical designs. They range from the basic homes of farming families to the extravagant Victorian and Queen-Anne turrets of the upper class. Farmhouses were examples of what could be done with the newly available resources of the Industrial Revolution, through the convenience of the railroad, which could import higher-end materials. On the other hand, the working-class farmers designed the homes for efficiency, with central fireplaces and second-floor bedrooms to promote and take advantage of heat circulation. Broad porches are a staple of this design, a way for the family to enjoy outdoor living during the days before air conditioners.

In this particular home, gabled roofs of multiple heights and sizes add space and are in keeping with the asymmetrical characteristic. A long front porch precedes an impressive two-story foyer, a modern addition to this early 20th-century home. The room layout stays true to the original form, but doesn't forego any of the luxuries to which we've become accustomed. On either side of the entry are a traditional formal parlor and a dining room, while a grand room with expansive views and a fireplace lies beyond the curved staircase. An informal entry on the left side of the plan provides access near the home office for business clients or customers, as well as to the kitchen and hearth room for friends and family. Upstairs reside the bedrooms, where the master suite includes a bedroom and sitting area, adjoining a master bath and His and Hers closets. A clear sign of 21st-century influences: The master suite also has direct access to the 16-by-21-foot exercise room.

In conclusion, the farmhouse is not just for the farm anymore. It's still a place for family and friends, and it still uses top-notch design and materials, but by adding your own personal touches and luxuries, you can make it your own private country retreat.

PHOTOGRAPHY BY BRELAND-FARMER DESIGNERS. THIS HOME, AS SHOWN IN THE PHOTOGRAPH, MAY DIFFER FROM THE ACTUAL BLUEPRINTS. FOR MORE DETAILED INFORMATION, PLEASE CHECK THE FLOOR PLANS CAREFULLY.

FIRST FLOOR   SECOND FLOOR

Multiple cross-gabled and gambrel roofs add depth and dimension to the home's facade. The wraparound porch is a signature characteristic of farmhouse designs.

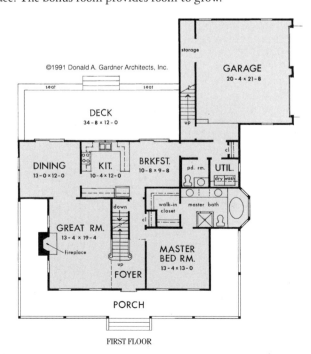

The welcoming charm of this country farmhouse is expressed by its many windows and its covered wraparound porch. A two-story foyer is enhanced by a Palladian window in a clerestory dormer above to let in natural lighting. The first-floor master suite allows privacy and accessibility. The master bath includes a whirlpool tub, separate shower, double-bowl vanity, and walk-in closet. The first floor features nine-foot ceilings throughout with the exception of the kitchen area, which sports an eight-foot ceiling. The second floor contains two additional bedrooms, a full bath, and plenty of storage space. The bonus room provides room to grow.

plan# HPK2000166

First Floor: 1,356 sq. ft.
Second Floor: 542 sq. ft.
Total: 1,898 sq. ft.
Bonus Space: 393 sq. ft.
Bedrooms: 3
Bathrooms: 2½
Width: 59' - 0"
Depth: 64' - 0"

ORDER ONLINE @ EPLANS.COM

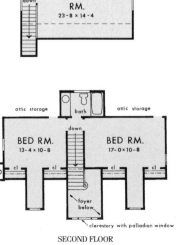

©1991 Donald A. Gardner Architects, Inc.

GARAGE
20-4 × 21-8

storage

DECK
34-8 × 12-0

seat   seat

DINING
13-0 × 12-0

KIT.
10-4 × 12-0

BRKFST.
10-8 × 9-8

pd. rm.

UTIL.

dry wash

walk-in closet

master bath

down

cl

GREAT RM.
13-4 × 19-4

fireplace

up

FOYER

MASTER BED RM.
13-4 × 13-0

PORCH

FIRST FLOOR

BONUS RM.
23-8 × 14-4

down

SECOND FLOOR

attic storage

bath

down

attic storage

BED RM.
13-4 × 10-8

BED RM.
17-0 × 10-8

cl   cl   cl   cl

foyer below

clerestory with palladian window

© 1991 DONALD A. GARDNER ARCHITECTS, INC., PHOTOGRAPHY COURTESY OF DONALD A. GARDNER ARCHITECTS, INC. THIS HOME, AS SHOWN IN THE PHOTOGRAPH, MAY DIFFER FROM THE ACTUAL BLUEPRINTS.

plan# HPK2000167

First Floor: 1,804 sq. ft.
Second Floor: 1,041 sq. ft.
Total: 2,845 sq. ft.
Bedrooms: 4
Bathrooms: 3½
Width: 57' - 3"
Depth: 71' - 0"
Foundation: Finished Walkout
Basement

ORDER ONLINE @ EPLANS.COM

There's a feeling of old Charleston in this stately home—particularly on the quiet side porch that wraps around the kitchen and breakfast room. The interior of this home revolves around a spacious great room with a welcoming fireplace. The left wing is dedicated to the master suite, which boasts wide views of the rear property. A corner kitchen easily serves planned events in the formal dining room, as well as family meals in the breakfast area. Three family bedrooms, one with a private bath and the others sharing a bath, are tucked upstairs.

REAR EXTERIOR

THIS HOME, AS SHOWN IN THE PHOTOGRAPH, MAY DIFFER FROM THE ACTUAL BLUEPRINTS. FOR MORE DETAILED INFORMATION, PLEASE CHECK THE FLOOR PLANS CAREFULLY.

FIRST FLOOR

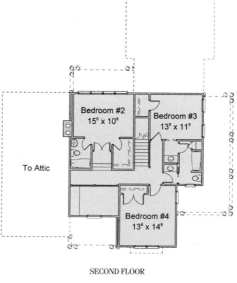

SECOND FLOOR

plan# HPK2000168

Country Victoriana embellishes this beautiful home. Perfect for a corner lot, this home begs for porch swings and lemonade. Inside, extra-high ceilings expand the space as a thoughtful floor plan invites family and friends. The two-story great room enjoys a warming fireplace and wonderful rear views. The country kitchen has a preparation island and easily serves the sunny bayed nook and the formal dining room. To the far left, a bedroom serves as a perfect guest room; to the far right, a turret houses a private den. Upstairs, two bedrooms (one in a turret) share a full bath and ample bonus space. The master suite opens through French doors to reveal a grand bedroom and a sumptuous bath with a bumped-out spa tub.

First Floor: 1,464 sq. ft.
Second Floor: 1,054 sq. ft.
Total: 2,518 sq. ft.
Bonus Space: 332 sq. ft.
Bedrooms: 4
Bathrooms: 3
Width: 59' - 0"
Depth: 51' - 6"
Foundation: Crawlspace

ORDER ONLINE @ EPLANS.COM

FIRST FLOOR

SECOND FLOOR

plan# HPK2000169

First Floor: 1,378 sq. ft.
Second Floor: 912 sq. ft.
Total: 2,290 sq. ft.
Bedrooms: 4
Bathrooms: 2½
Width: 74' - 0"
Depth: 46' - 0"
Foundation: Unfinished Basement

ORDER ONLINE @ EPLANS.COM

A beautiful country facade is just the beginning of what this design has to offer. Inside, the two-story foyer includes a large coat closet and decorative entry to the formal living room. The foyer also leads through a hall—with a convenient half-bath—to the formal dining room and family room with its three-sided fireplace. The angled family room opens to a gourmet kitchen, which features a snack bar, walk-in pantry and access to a two-car garage with a workshop/storage area. Located on the first floor for privacy, the master bedroom features a pampering bath with a separate tub and shower, individual sinks, and a walk-in closet. The second floor contains a multimedia loft, an ample laundry area and three bedrooms that share a full bath.

FIRST FLOOR

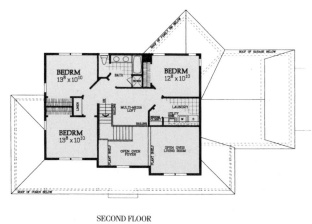

SECOND FLOOR

© William E. Poole Designs, Inc.

plan# HPK2000170

First Floor: 1,480 sq. ft.
Second Floor: 1,651 sq. ft.
Total: 3,131 sq. ft.
Bedrooms: 4
Bathrooms: 3½
Width: 67' - 5"
Depth: 61' - 5"
Foundation: Crawlspace

ORDER ONLINE @ EPLANS.COM

This design incorporates Victorian touches with the masterful use of a turret and a gazebo. With a wealth of windows, this home never lacks natural light. Inside, divergent room shapes offer an interesting appeal. The family room is centrally located with a fireplace on the left wall and a built-in entertainment system. The island kitchen features a built-in desk, abundant counter space, and a butler's pantry. A separate utility room houses the washer/dryer, fold down ironing board, and sink. The second floor houses the sleeping quarters, including the lavish master suite, complete with a private sitting area and fireplace, and three additional family bedrooms sharing two full baths.

FIRST FLOOR

SECOND FLOOR

© William E. Poole Designs, Inc.

plan# HPK2000171

First Floor: 1,047 sq. ft.
Second Floor: 976 sq. ft.
Total: 2,023 sq. ft.
Bonus Space: 318 sq. ft.
Bedrooms: 3
Bathrooms: 2½
Width: 58' - 0"
Depth: 37' - 4"
Foundation: Crawlspace,
Unfinished Basement

ORDER ONLINE @ EPLANS.COM

With all of the sleeping quarters located on the second floor, the first floor is ideal for family interaction and entertaining. The great room sits between the front and rear porches and opens to the adjacent breakfast area and kitchen. The bay-windowed dining room provides an option for formal meals. On the second floor, the master bedroom boasts a whirlpool tub, compartmented shower and toilet, dual-sink vanity, and His and Hers wardrobe. Two family bedrooms share a full bath. Future expansion space completes this plan.

SECOND FLOOR

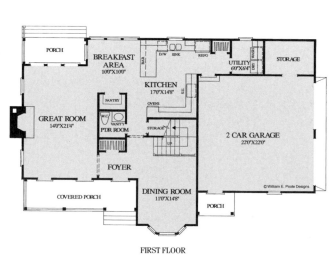

FIRST FLOOR

© William E. Poole Designs, Inc.

A porch wraps around two sides and joins a screened porch in the rear, giving this country-style plan a true down-home appeal. The great room, which soars two stories high, enjoys a fireplace and two entries to the screened porch. It also opens easily into the breakfast alcove and is conveniently tied to the kitchen by an angled counter. A formal dining room is just to the right of the foyer. The luxurious master suite pampers with a walk-in closet, twin-sink vanity, garden tub, and step-up shower. Upstairs, three bedrooms share two baths and a loft study. Ample room is available to add a recreation room. A side-loading garage offers lots of room for storage.

plan# HPK2000172

First Floor: 1,921 sq. ft.
Second Floor: 921 sq. ft.
Total: 2,842 sq. ft.
Bonus Space: 454 sq. ft.
Bedrooms: 4
Bathrooms: 3½
Width: 62' - 2"
Depth: 71' - 0"
Foundation: Crawlspace,
Unfinished Basement

ORDER ONLINE @ EPLANS.COM

FIRST FLOOR

SECOND FLOOR

© William E. Poole Designs, Inc.

plan# HPK2000173

First Floor: 1,913 sq. ft.
Second Floor: 997 sq. ft.
Total: 2,910 sq. ft.
Bonus Space: 377 sq. ft.
Bedrooms: 4
Bathrooms: 3½
Width: 63' - 0"
Depth: 59' - 4"
Foundation: Crawlspace,
Unfinished Basement

ORDER ONLINE @ EPLANS.COM

This enchanting farmhouse brings the past to life with plenty of modern amenities. An open-flow kitchen/breakfast area and family room combination is the heart of the home, opening up to the screened porch and enjoying the warmth of a fireplace. For more formal occasions, the foyer is flanked by a living room on the left and a dining room on the right. An elegant master bedroom, complete with a super-sized walk-in closet, is tucked away quietly behind the garage. Three more bedrooms reside upstairs, along with two full baths and a future recreation room.

FIRST FLOOR

SECOND FLOOR

plan# HPK2000174

First Floor: 1,671 sq. ft.
Second Floor: 980 sq. ft.
Total: 2,651 sq. ft.
Bedrooms: 5
Bathrooms: 2
Width: 72' - 0"
Depth: 58' - 0"
Foundation: Unfinished Basement, Crawlspace, Slab

ORDER ONLINE @ EPLANS.COM

Beautiful by the sea or out in the country, this wonderful home is designed for outdoor living. Three porches and a brick-paved courtyard are easily accessible for year-round relaxation and endless entertaining possibilities. Enter the home and turn to the left for an ample living room, warmed by a fireplace. Just ahead, the tiled kitchen offers a brilliant layout and an island serving bar, easily hosting the eating nook and dining room. At the rear, the master suite offers a bayed sitting area and a lavish bath with a spa tub. Upstairs, four generous bedrooms share a dual-vanity bath. The home is completed by a three-car garage and plenty of extra storage.

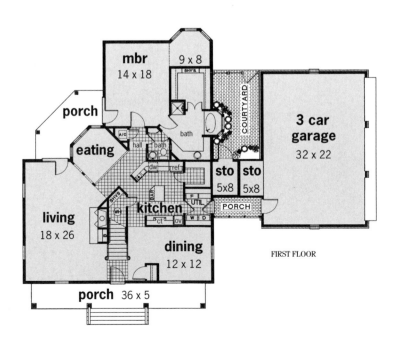

FIRST FLOOR

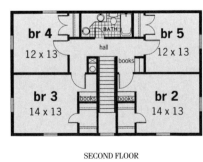

SECOND FLOOR

plan# HPK2000175

First Floor: 794 sq. ft.
Second Floor: 756 sq. ft.
Total: 1,550 sq. ft.
Bonus Space: 251 sq. ft.
Bedrooms: 3
Bathrooms: 2½
Width: 46' - 11"
Depth: 35' - 1"
Foundation: Slab

ORDER ONLINE @ EPLANS.COM

This classic Colonial-style home offers a taste of the past with its pedimented rooflines and shuttered windows. Through the entry is the elegantly columned dining room. The spacious family room features an optional warming hearth. The kitchen has plenty of counter space and convenient access to the breakfast area. Two family bedrooms and a master suite are located on the second floor, where a bonus room adds additional space.

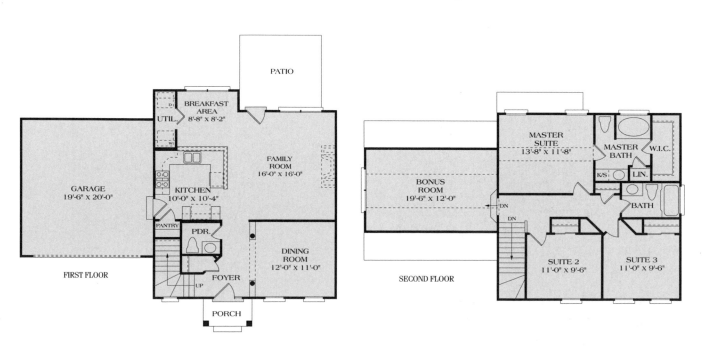

plan# HPK2000176

First Floor: 792 sq. ft.
Second Floor: 768 sq. ft.
Total: 1,560 sq. ft.
Bedrooms: 3
Bathrooms: 2½
Width: 43' - 4"
Depth: 42' - 6"
Foundation: Slab

ORDER ONLINE @ EPLANS.COM

Three solid pillars support the shed-like roof of this attractive bunga-low. Inside, formal and informal gatherings will be accommodated easily. For casual get-togethers, the spacious gathering room with its fireplace and rear-yard access is complemented by the nearby availability of the galley kitchen. Formal dinner parties will be a breeze in the dining room at the front of the house—or make it a formal living room if you have the need. Upstairs, two bedrooms share a full hall bath, while the master suite features a walk-in closet and a bath of its own.

plan⟨#⟩ HPK2000177

First Floor: 760 sq. ft.
Second Floor: 742 sq. ft.
Total: 1,502 sq. ft.
Bonus Space: 283 sq. ft.
Bedrooms: 3
Bathrooms: 2½
Width: 39' - 1"
Depth: 36' - 9"
Foundation: Slab

ORDER ONLINE @ EPLANS.COM

Made for a narrow footprint or in-fill lot, this home offers traditional lines with a farmhouse flavor. A welcoming porch ushers family and guests into the foyer. The large U-shaped kitchen is just to the right with a nearby laundry room for convenience. The dining area is found to the rear and enjoys rear views and porch access. The family room is perfect for a fireplace and entertaining guests or spending a quiet night at home. The master suite features a coffered ceiling, walk-in closets and a full bath. Two family suites share a full bath, and a bonus room is found just across the hall.

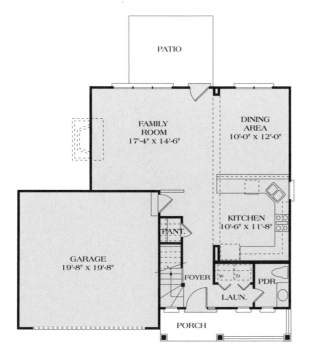

FIRST FLOOR

SECOND FLOOR

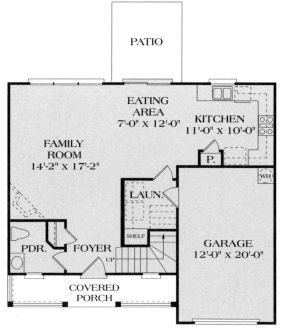

plan# **HPK2000178**

First Floor: 680 sq. ft.
Second Floor: 674 sq. ft.
Total: 1,354 sq. ft.
Bedrooms: 3
Bathrooms: 2½
Width: 34' - 5"
Depth: 31' - 3"
Foundation: Slab

ORDER ONLINE @ EPLANS.COM

At first glance you will notice something special about this otherwise traditional Colonial home: past the darling pedimented porch is a brick border running along the entire front facade! Inside, a family room with a corner fireplace awaits. To the right are the eating area and U-shaped, step-saving kitchen with pantry and a laundry room. Upstairs, the master suite has His and Hers closets and a private bath. Two more bedrooms and a full hall bath complete this plan.

FIRST FLOOR

SECOND FLOOR

plan# HPK2000179

First Floor: 1,169 sq. ft.
Second Floor: 1,034 sq. ft.
Total: 2,203 sq. ft.
Bonus Space: 347 sq. ft.
Bedrooms: 3
Bathrooms: 2½
Width: 55' - 4"
Depth: 52' - 0"
Foundation: Crawlspace

ORDER ONLINE @ EPLANS.COM

This fashionable farmhouse shows off the height of style, but never at the expense of comfort. Clapboard siding sets off a lighthearted symmetry on this country exterior that braces an Early American flavor with new spirit. Inside, formal rooms flank the foyer and lead to casual living space. An expansive family room with a focal-point fireplace opens to a wide-open breakfast area and gourmet kitchen. The rear covered porch invites enjoyment of the outdoors and adjoins an entertainment porch. Upstairs, the lavish master suite offers twin vanities and a generous walk-in closet. Two additional bedrooms share a hall bath. A sizable bonus room includes a walk-in closet.

FIRST FLOOR

SECOND FLOOR

plan# HPK2000180

First Floor: 1,670 sq. ft.
Second Floor: 763 sq. ft.
Total: 2,433 sq. ft.
Bedrooms: 3
Bathrooms: 2½
Width: 53' - 0"
Depth: 54' - 0"
Foundation: Crawlspace

ORDER ONLINE @ EPLANS.COM

Pillars line the front of a fine covered porch on this attractive two-story home. Craftsman architecture is represented by a smattering of shingles on the second story and the shelter of an overhanging roofline. Inside, a formal dining room has easy access to the efficient kitchen as well as to the front porch. A spacious gathering room features a fireplace, access to the rear patio/deck and shares a snack bar with the kitchen and breakfast room. Located on the first floor for privacy, the master suite is sure to please with its many amenities, which include a large walk-in closet, plenty of windows, a detailed ceiling, and a sumptuous bath. Upstairs, two suites share a full bath as well as a large loft—perfect for a study area, computer space, or play area. A two-car garage easily shelters the family fleet.

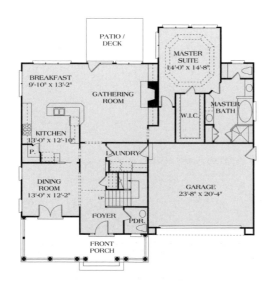

FIRST FLOOR

SECOND FLOOR

plan# HPK2000181

First Floor: 1,120 sq. ft.
Second Floor: 1,083 sq. ft.
Total: 2,203 sq. ft.
Bonus Space: 597 sq. ft.
Bedrooms: 3
Bathrooms: 2½
Width: 40' - 0"
Depth: 40' - 0"
Foundation: Unfinished Basement

ORDER ONLINE @ EPLANS.COM

Sweeping front and rear raised covered porches, delicately detailed railings, and an abundance of fireplaces give this farmhouse its character. Designed to accommodate a relatively narrow building site, the efficient floor plan delivers outstanding livability for the active family. Both the formal living room and dining room have corner fireplaces, as does the family room. The large, tiled country kitchen has an abundance of work space, a planning desk, and easy access to the utility room. On the second floor, the master retreat features a fireplace and an expansive bathing and dressing suite.

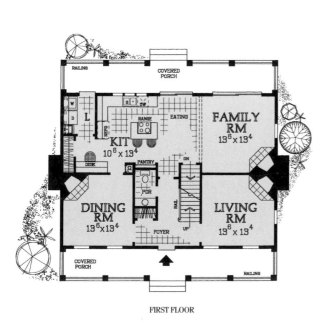

FIRST FLOOR

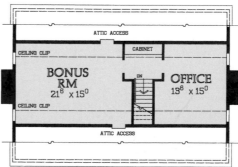

SECOND FLOOR

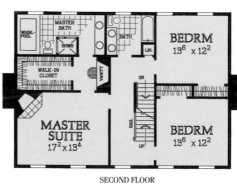

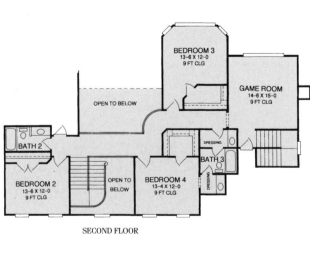

plan# HPK2000182

First Floor: 2,055 sq. ft.
Second Floor: 1,229 sq. ft.
Total: 3,284 sq. ft.
Bedrooms: 4
Bathrooms: 3½
Width: 65' - 0"
Depth: 60' - 10"
Foundation: Crawlspace, Slab

ORDER ONLINE @ EPLANS.COM

A pedimented entry, shingle accents, and shutters blend modern and traditional looks on this Southern design. The foyer features a two-story ceiling and opens to the formal dining room, which has a lovely tray ceiling. A gallery hall connects the formal living room with all areas of the home. French doors open the living space to the back property. The master wing includes two walk-in closets, an angled garden tub, a separate shower with a seat, and a knee-space vanity. Second-floor sleeping quarters are connected by a balcony hall that leads to a sizable game room.

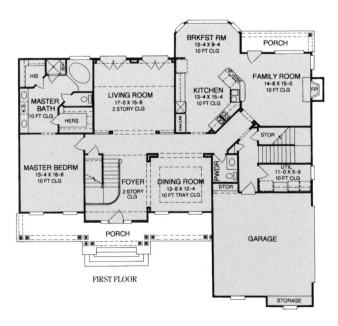

FIRST FLOOR

SECOND FLOOR

plan# HPK2000183

First Floor: 2,028 sq. ft.
Second Floor: 558 sq. ft.
Total: 2,586 sq. ft.
Bonus Space: 272 sq. ft.
Bedrooms: 4
Bathrooms: 3
Width: 64' - 10"
Depth: 61' - 0"
Foundation: Crawlspace, Slab,
Unfinished Basement

ORDER ONLINE @ EPLANS.COM

Double columns and an arch-top clerestory window create an inviting entry to this fresh interpretation of traditional style. Decorative columns and arches open to the formal dining room and to the octagonal great room, which has a 10-foot tray ceiling. The U-shaped kitchen looks over an angled counter to a breakfast bay that brings in the outdoors and shares a through-fireplace with the great room. A sitting area and a lavish bath set off the secluded master suite. A nearby secondary bedroom with its own bath could be used as a guest suite. Upstairs, two family bedrooms share a full bath and a hall that leads to an expandable area.

FIRST FLOOR

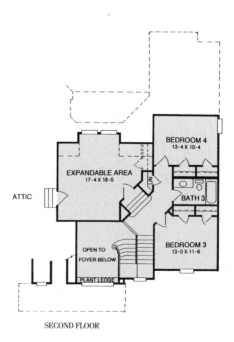

SECOND FLOOR

This home is unique because of its farmhouse styling and the multitude of windows—Palladian, decorative, and sunburst—that grace the exterior of the plan. A large front porch and flower box add even more charm. A rounded formal dining room looks out through windows to the front porch. The kitchen, with an island, leads to the dining area, which offers access to the patio. Upstairs, the master bedroom boasts a vaulted ceiling and a private sitting area, as well as a full bath and walk-in closet. Bedrooms 2 and 3 share a full bath.

plan# HPK2000184

First Floor: 1,447 sq. ft.
Second Floor: 1,008 sq. ft.
Total: 2,455 sq. ft.
Bonus Space: 352 sq. ft.
Bedrooms: 3
Bathrooms: 2½
Width: 65' - 0"
Depth: 37' - 11"
Foundation: Crawlspace, Slab, Unfinished Basement

ORDER ONLINE @ EPLANS.COM

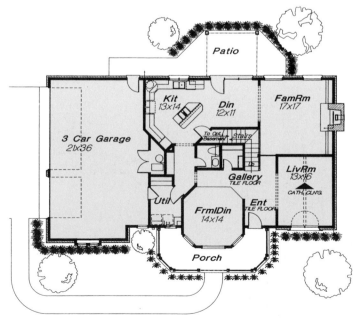

FIRST FLOOR

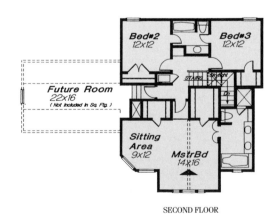

SECOND FLOOR

ptan# HPK2000185

First Floor: 1,572 sq. ft.
Second Floor: 700 sq. ft.
Total: 2,272 sq. ft.
Bonus Space: 212 sq. ft.
Bedrooms: 4
Bathrooms: 2½
Width: 70' - 0"
Depth: 38' - 5"
Foundation: Slab, Unfinished
Basement

ORDER ONLINE @ EPLANS.COM

Country and Victorian elements give this home a down-home feel. A charming porch wraps around the front of this farmhouse, whose entry opens to a formal dining room. The island kitchen and sun-filled breakfast area are located nearby. The family room is warmed by a fireplace flanked by windows. Located for privacy, the first-floor master bedroom features its own covered patio and a private bath designed for relaxation. The second floor contains three family bedrooms—each with walk-in closets—a full bath and a future bonus room.

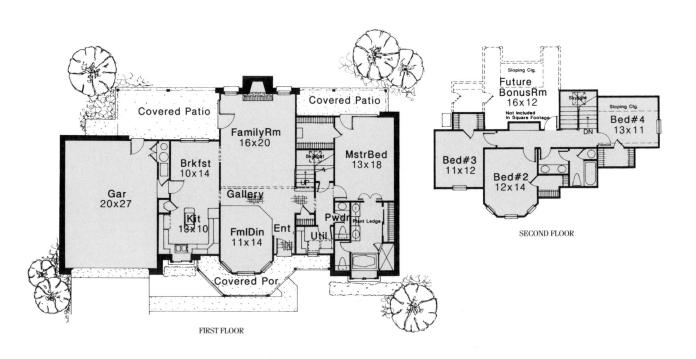

FIRST FLOOR

SECOND FLOOR

plan# **HPK2000186**

First Floor: 1,778 sq. ft.
Second Floor: 498 sq. ft.
Total: 2,276 sq. ft.
Bonus Space: 315 sq. ft.
Bedrooms: 4
Bathrooms: 3
Width: 54' - 8"
Depth: 53' - 2"

ORDER ONLINE @ EPLANS.COM

A metal roof tops the front porch, and columns and gables add to this classic farmhouse facade. Front and side stairs show the way to the porch, creating a warm, inviting welcome. Double doors lead into a versatile bedroom/study, and the dining room is connected to the kitchen by a butler's pantry. The great room is enhanced with a cathedral ceiling, built-in cabinetry, and a fireplace that faces the kitchen. A bay window extends the breakfast nook; French doors access the rear porch. The master suite features a cathedral ceiling, large walk-in closet, and elegant bath. Two additional bedrooms can be found on the second floor, along with a bonus room and a full bath.

FIRST FLOOR

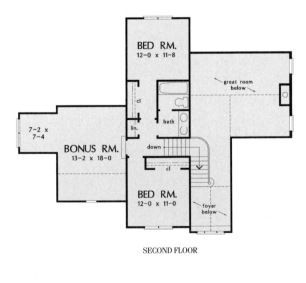

SECOND FLOOR

© 2001 Donald A. Gardner, Inc.

plan# HPK2000187

First Floor: 1,547 sq. ft.
Second Floor: 684 sq. ft.
Total: 2,231 sq. ft.
Bonus Space: 300 sq. ft.
Bedrooms: 3
Bathrooms: 2½
Width: 59' - 2"
Depth: 41' - 4"

ORDER ONLINE @ EPLANS.COM

Stone and siding create a stunning exterior, especially when combined with a sloped roofline and a decorative wood bracket. A metal roof embellishes the garage's box-bay window, and arches are seen in and above windows as well as the front entrance. The great room is filled with light from its many windows and French doors, and a glimpse of the fireplace can be seen from every gathering room. The master bedroom is topped by a cathedral ceiling and has a large walk-in closet. The loft makes a perfect sitting or study area that receives a lot of light from the open, two-story great room. The second floor bathroom includes twin lavatories, and the versatile bonus room is easily accessible.

FIRST FLOOR

SECOND FLOOR

© 2001 DONALD A. GARDNER
All rights reserved

© 2001 Donald A. Gardner, Inc.

Country accents and farmhouse style enhance the facade of this lovely two-story home. The first floor provides a formal dining room and great room warmed by a fireplace. The kitchen connects to a breakfast bay—perfect for casual morning meals. The first-floor master suite includes two walk-in closets and a private bath. Upstairs, a loft overlooks the two-story great room. Three second-floor bedrooms share a hall bath. The bonus room above the garage is great for a home office or guest suite.

plan# HPK2000188

First Floor: 1.667 sq. ft.
Second Floor: 803 sq. ft.
Total: 2,470 sq. ft.
Bonus Space: 318 sq. ft.
Bedrooms: 4
Bathrooms: 2½
Width: 52' - 4"
Depth: 57' - 0"

ORDER ONLINE @ EPLANS.COM

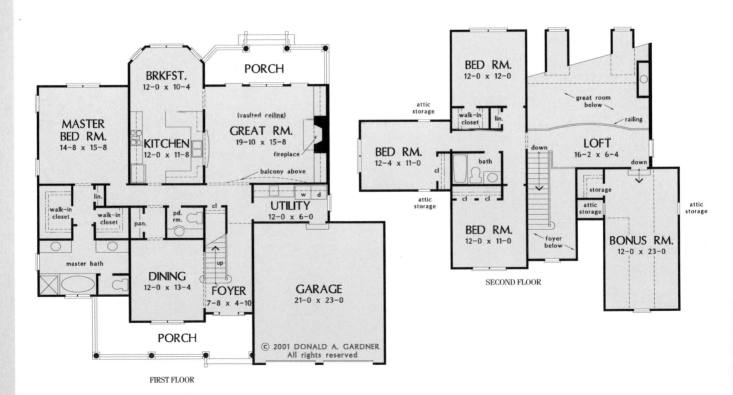

FIRST FLOOR

SECOND FLOOR

2003 Donald A. Gardner, Inc.

plan# HPK2000189

First Floor: 1,562 sq. ft.
Second Floor: 502 sq. ft.
Total: 2,064 sq. ft.
Bonus Space: 416 sq. ft.
Bedrooms: 3
Bathrooms: 2½
Width: 54' - 0"
Depth: 55' - 10"

ORDER ONLINE @ EPLANS.COM

Capturing the Heartland feel, this farmhouse is designed to make an impression. A welcoming front porch guides family and friends inside, where they're greeted by a two-story foyer. Columns mark the entry to the dining room. The great room features numerous windows, French doors, and a stunning fireplace. The kitchen is the hub of the home, servicing the great room through a pass-through. A cathedral ceiling visually expands the master suite, and a French door leads to the rear porch. The master bath features a double vanity, garden tub, shower with seat, and a compartmented toilet. Secondary bedrooms share a full bath with the bonus room.

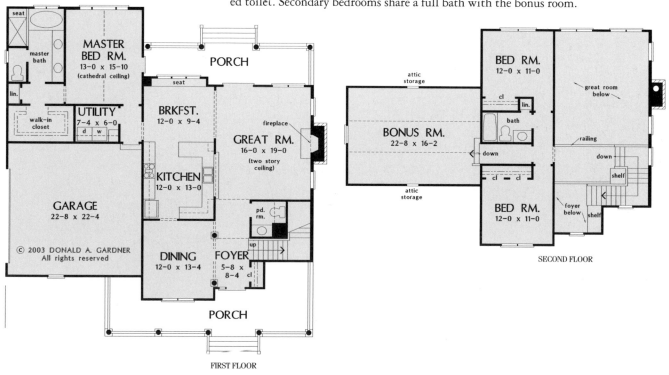

FIRST FLOOR

SECOND FLOOR

© 2002 Donald A. Gardner, Inc.

With spacious front and rear porches, twin gables, and an arched entrance, this home has charm and curb appeal. Columns make a grand impression both inside and outside, and transoms above French doors brighten both the front and rear of the floor plan. An angled counter separates the kitchen from the great room and breakfast area, and the mudroom/utility area is complete with a sink. A tray ceiling tops the master bedroom, and the formal living room/study and bonus room are flexible spaces, tailoring to family needs. A balcony overlooks the foyer and great room; an additional upstairs bedroom has its own bath and can be used as a guest suite.

plan# HPK2000190

First Floor: 1.798 sq. ft.
Second Floor: 723 sq. ft.
Total: 2,521 sq. ft.
Bonus Space: 349 sq. ft.
Bedrooms: 4
Bathrooms: 3½
Width: 66' - 8"
Depth: 49' - 8"

ORDER ONLINE @ EPLANS.COM

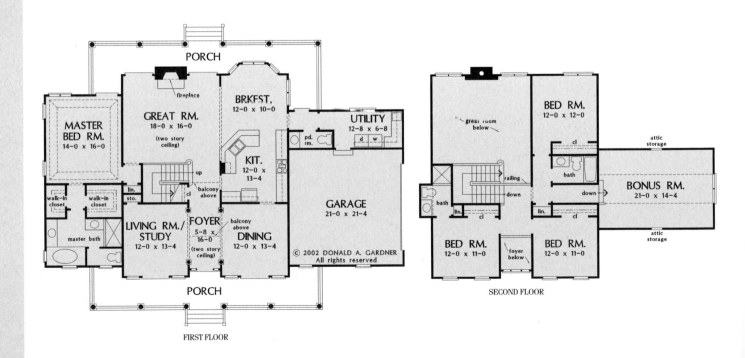

© 1999 Donald A. Gardner, Inc.

plan# HPK2000191

First Floor: 1,685 sq. ft.
Second Floor: 815 sq. ft.
Total: 2,500 sq. ft.
Bedrooms: 4
Bathrooms: 2½
Width: 52' - 8"
Depth: 72' - 4"

ORDER ONLINE @ EPLANS.COM

A prominent center gable and an inviting front porch create excellent curb appeal for this appealing two-story family home. An exciting balcony that overlooks the two-story foyer as well as the two-story great room provides an impressive welcome. Elegant columns mark entry to both the dining room and great room. The generously proportioned kitchen features a nearby pantry and is open to the breakfast room and great room for easy entertaining and family togetherness. Located on the first floor, the master bedroom enjoys a tray ceiling, back-porch access, a private bath, and ample closet space. Upstairs, three more bedrooms share a spacious bath.

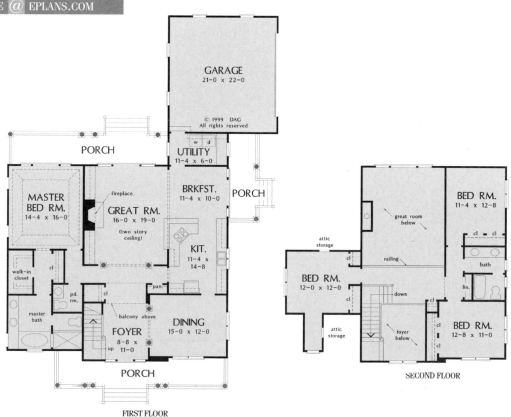

© 2003 Donald A. Gardner, Inc.

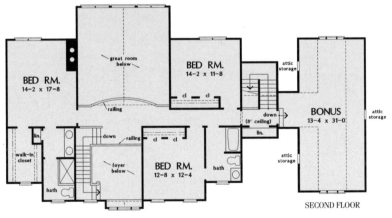

BED RM.
14-2 x 17-8

great room
below

BED RM.
14-2 x 11-8

attic
storage

walk-in
closet

down
(8' ceiling)

BONUS
13-4 x 31-0

attic
storage

foyer
below

BED RM.
12-8 x 12-4

bath

attic
storage

bath

SECOND FLOOR

plan# HPK2000192

First Floor: 2,237 sq. ft.
Second Floor: 1,182 sq. ft.
Total: 3,419 sq. ft.
Bonus Space: 475 sq. ft.
Bedrooms: 4
Bathrooms: 3½
Width: 85' - 4"
Depth: 56' - 4"

ORDER ONLINE @ EPLANS.COM

An elegant exterior with country and traditional flair surrounds a modern floor plan with the latest amenities and custom features. Two spacious porches promote outdoor entertaining. Columns define rooms without enclosing space, and a curved balcony separates the two-story foyer and great room. Built-in cabinetry and fireplaces complement the great room and master bedroom. The bright breakfast nook features a bay window, and is convenient to the kitchen, complete with a walk-in pantry and island. The spacious bonus room can be a large home theater or divided into a home office and gym.

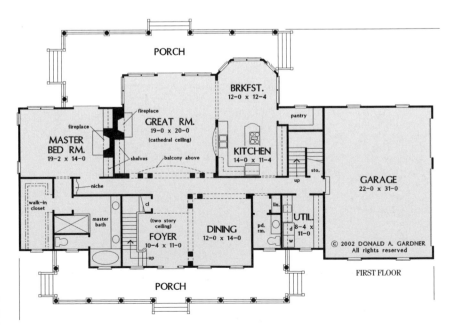

PORCH

BRKFST.
12-0 x 12-4

fireplace

GREAT RM.
19-0 x 20-0
(cathedral ceiling)

pantry

MASTER
BED RM.
19-2 x 14-0

fireplace

shelves

balcony above

KITCHEN
14-0 x 11-4

walk-in
closet

niche

GARAGE
22-0 x 31-0

master
bath

cl

(two story
ceiling)
FOYER
10-4 x 11-0

DINING
12-0 x 14-0

pd.
rm.

UTIL.
8-4 x
11-0

up

© 2002 DONALD A. GARDNER
All rights reserved

up

PORCH

FIRST FLOOR

© 2002 Donald A. Gardner, Inc.

plan# HPK2000193

First Floor: 1,633 sq. ft.
Second Floor: 751 sq. ft.
Total: 2,384 sq. ft.
Bonus Space: 359 sq. ft.
Bedrooms: 3
Bathrooms: 3½
Width: 69' - 8"
Depth: 44' - 0"

ORDER ONLINE @ EPLANS.COM

This farmhouse captures old-time ambiance with a large wraparound porch and vintage columns. A trio of gables and a side-entry garage add to the curb appeal. Filled with natural light by clerestory windows and French doors, this open floor plan is warm and welcoming. A two-story ceiling extends from the foyer into the great room; a balcony overlooks both areas. A counter separates the kitchen from the great room and breakfast nook. A fireplace, built-in cabinetry, and bay windows add custom style. The master suite is complete with a spacious master bath. Upstairs, two additional bedrooms and two full baths are separated by a loft. A short hall accesses the bonus room.

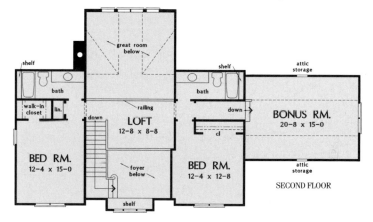

SECOND FLOOR

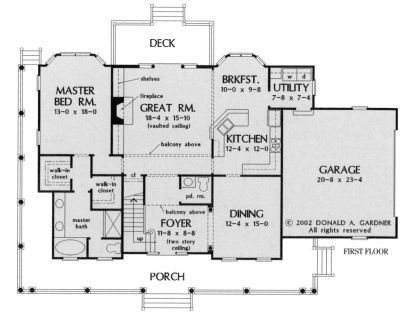

FIRST FLOOR

© 1990 Donald A. Gardner Architects, Inc.

B·NATHAN·

A wraparound covered porch and the open deck with a spa and seating provide this home with plenty of room for outside living. A central great room features a vaulted ceiling, fireplace, and clerestory windows above. The loft/study on the second floor overlooks this gathering area. Besides a formal dining room, kitchen, breakfast room, and sunroom on the first floor, there is also a generous master suite with a garden tub. Three second-floor bedrooms complete the sleeping accommodations.

ptan# HPK2000194

First Floor: 1,734 sq. ft.
Second Floor: 958 sq. ft.
Total: 2,692 sq. ft.
Bedrooms: 4
Bathrooms: 3½
Width: 55' - 0"
Depth: 59' - 10"

ORDER ONLINE @ EPLANS.COM

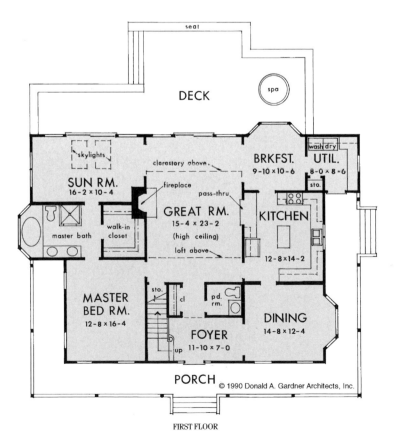

© 1990 Donald A. Gardner Architects, Inc.

FIRST FLOOR

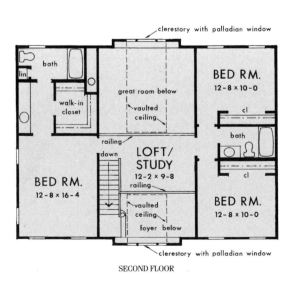

SECOND FLOOR

plan# HPK2000195

First Floor: 1,295 sq. ft.
Second Floor: 600 sq. ft.
Total: 1,895 sq. ft.
Bedrooms: 3
Bathrooms: 2½
Width: 50' - 0"
Depth: 55' - 3"
Foundation: Unfinished Basement

ORDER ONLINE @ EPLANS.COM

This Southern Country farmhouse extends a warm welcome with a wrap-around porch and a bayed entry. An unrestrained floor plan, replete with soaring, open space as well as sunny bays and charming niches, invites traditional festivities and cozy family gatherings. Colonial columns introduce the two-story great room, which boasts an extended-hearth fireplace and French doors to the wraparound porch, and opens through a wide arch to the tiled country kitchen with a cooktop island counter and snack bar. The first-floor master suite enjoys its own bay window, private access to the wraparound porch, and a sumptuous bath with a clawfoot tub and separate vanities. Upstairs, two family bedrooms share a full bath and a balcony hall that overlooks the great room and the entry.

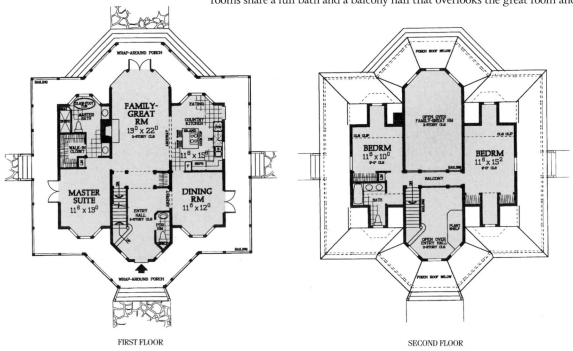

FIRST FLOOR

SECOND FLOOR

The appearance of this Early American home brings the past to mind with its wraparound porch, wood siding, and flower-box detailing. Inside, columns frame the great room and the dining room. Left of the foyer lies the living room with a warming fireplace. The angular kitchen joins a sunny breakfast nook. The master bedroom has a spacious private bath and a walk-in closet. Stairs to the second level lead from the breakfast area to an open landing overlooking the great room. Three family bedrooms—two with walk-in closets and all three with private access to a bath—complete this level.

plan# HPK2000196

First Floor: 1,840 sq. ft.
Second Floor: 950 sq. ft.
Total: 2,790 sq. ft.
Bedrooms: 4
Bathrooms: 3½
Width: 58' - 6"
Depth: 62' - 0"
Foundation: Finished Walkout Basement

ORDER ONLINE @ EPLANS.COM

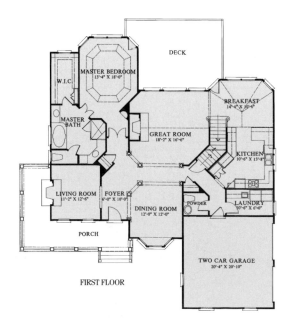

FIRST FLOOR

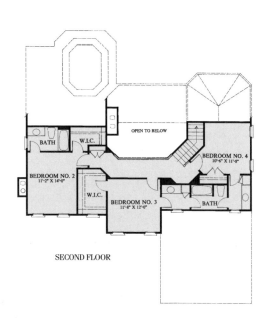

SECOND FLOOR

© 2004 Donald A. Gardner, Inc.

plan# HPK2000197

First Floor: 1,542 sq. ft.
Second Floor: 635 sq. ft.
Total: 2,177 sq. ft.
Bonus Space: 348 sq. ft.
Bedrooms: 3
Bathrooms: 2½
Width: 55' - 10"
Depth: 51' - 4"

ORDER ONLINE @ EPLANS.COM

An inviting porch framed by two sets of bold columns, siding and a brick chimney adorn the facade of this eye-catching traditional home. Gorgeous Palladian windows allow an abundance of natural light to enter, illuminating every inch of this beautiful home. The expansiveness of the great room is augmented by a cathedral ceiling, massive windows and an outlet to the rear porch. Tucked away in a corner is the master bedroom, from where you can relax and enjoy a spectacular view while lying in bed or soaking in the luxurious, angled bathtub. A full bath separates the secondary bedrooms, acting as a buffer to reduce noise. Convenience is highlighted with the thoughtful placement of the kitchen, which accesses the sunny dining room, the great room and the rear porch, making it easier to serve alfresco meals. The utility room, powder room, plenty of storage space, and built-in shelves, closets and a fireplace are just a few of the numerous amenities that accompany this family-efficient home. A bonus room above the two-car garage allows room to grow.

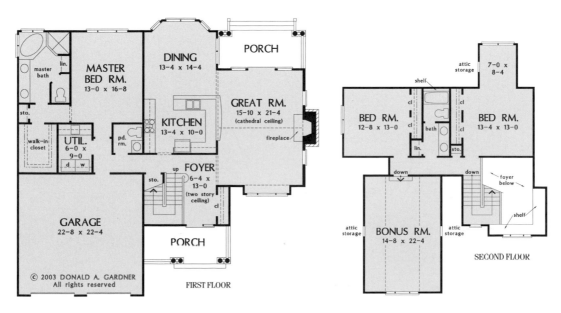

plan# **HPK2000005**

Square Footage: 2,497
Bonus Space: 966 sq. ft.
Bedrooms: 3
Bathrooms: 3½
Width: 87' - 0"
Depth: 57' - 3"
Foundation: Crawlspace, Slab,
Unfinished Basement

ORDER ONLINE @ EPLANS.COM

Southern Eclectic

The variety of style that exists in the South is celebrated in this section, which features key examples of homes made popular between the Civil War and World War II. As fashions in residential design shifted in favor of period styles, and advances in construction technology made solid masonry more affordable, even small homes began to take on the look of Old World architecture. The home featured here is a good example of the result: a modest, 2,500-square-foot home with a prominent, classically inspired columned entry and symmetrical layout. At the same time, a wide porch and decorative shutters allow the home to retain the warm, local charm of the region.

In complement to the exterior, the practically minded layout of the plan provides for comfort and utility. The two-car garage at the right of the plan loads at the side, preserving the integrity of the facade. This also allows private rooms to find quiet at the other end of the home, dominated by the master suite. The other bedrooms each benefit from their own baths-a decidedly modern convenience homeowners will appreciate.

For those looking to build an attractive, efficient home that fits their family just right, look to the small cottages and single-story designs collected in this section. Many feature extended living areas like patios, decks, and porches that add functional space to the home without significantly raising construction costs.

PHOTO BY KEN PURCELL.
THIS HOME, AS SHOWN IN THE PHOTOGRAPH, MAY DIFFER FROM THE ACTUAL BLUEPRINTS.
FOR MORE DETAILED INFORMATION, PLEASE CHECK THE FLOOR PLANS CAREFULLY

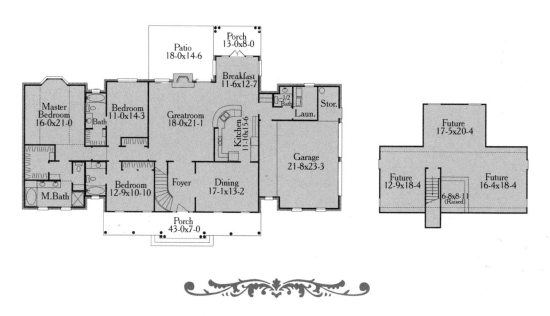

A columned front porch and gabled entry creates architectural interest at the front of the home. The result is a distinctive but neighborhood-friendly facade.

PHOTO COURTESY OF LIVING CONCEPTS HOME PLANNING
THIS HOME AS SHOWN IN THE PHOTOGRAPH MAY DIFFER FROM THE ACTUAL BLUEPRINTS.

plan# HPK2000198

First Floor: 1,824 sq. ft.
Second Floor: 842 sq. ft.
Total: 2,666 sq. ft.
Bonus Space: 267 sq. ft.
Bedrooms: 3
Bathrooms: 3½
Width: 59' - 0"
Depth: 53' - 6"
Foundation: Crawlspace

ORDER ONLINE @ EPLANS.COM

Horizontal siding, double-hung windows, and European gables

lend a special charm to this contemporary home. The formal dining room opens from the foyer and offers a wet bar and a box-bay window. The great room features a fireplace and opens to a golf porch as well as a charming side porch. A well-lit kitchen contains a cooktop island counter and two pantries. The first-floor master suite has a tray ceiling, a box-bay window, and a deluxe bath with a garden tub and an angled shower. Both of the upper-level bedrooms privately access a full bath.

REAR EXTERIOR

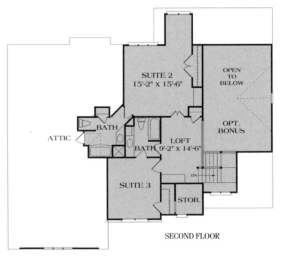

SECOND FLOOR

FIRST FLOOR

plan# HPK2000199

First Floor: 2,199 sq. ft.
Second Floor: 1,235 sq. ft.
Total: 3,434 sq. ft.
Bonus Space: 150 sq. ft.
Bedrooms: 4
Bathrooms: 4
Width: 62' - 6"
Depth: 54' - 3"
Foundation: Finished Walkout
Basement

ORDER ONLINE @ EPLANS.COM

The covered front porch of this home warmly welcomes family and visitors. To the right of the foyer is a versatile option room. On the other side is the formal dining room. A comfortable great room boasts French doors to a rear deck and easy access to a large breakfast area and sunroom. The adjacent kitchen includes a cooking island/breakfast bar. Secluded on the main level for privacy, the master suite features a lavish bath loaded with amenities. Just off the bedroom is a private deck. Three additional bedrooms and two baths occupy the second level.

FIRST FLOOR

SECOND FLOOR

THIS HOME, AS SHOWN IN THE PHOTOGRAPH, MAY DIFFER FROM THE ACTUAL BLUEPRINTS. FOR MORE DETAILED INFORMATION, PLEASE CHECK THE FLOOR PLANS CAREFULLY.

plan# **HPK2000200**

First Floor: 1,819 sq. ft.
Second Floor: 638 sq. ft.
Total: 2,457 sq. ft.
Bonus Space: 385 sq. ft.
Bedrooms: 3
Bathrooms: 2½
Width: 47' - 4"
Depth: 82' - 8"
Foundation: Crawlspace,
Unfinished Basement

ORDER ONLINE @ EPLANS.COM

Graceful dormers top a welcoming covered porch that is enhanced by Victorian details on this fine three-bedroom home. Inside, the foyer leads past the formal dining room back to the spacious two-story great room. Here, a fireplace, built-ins, and outdoor access make any gathering special. The nearby kitchen features a work island, a pantry, a serving bar, and an adjacent bayed breakfast area. Located on the first floor for privacy, the master suite is designed to pamper. Upstairs, two family bedrooms share a hall bath. Note the bonus space above the two-car garage.

FIRST FLOOR

SECOND FLOOR

PHOTO COURTESY OF: WILLIAM E. POOLE DESIGNS, INC. - ISLANDS OF BEAUFORT, BEAUFORT, SC
THIS HOME, AS SHOWN IN THE PHOTOGRAPH, MAY DIFFER FROM THE ACTUAL BLUEPRINTS.

© William E. Poole Designs, Inc.

plan# HPK2000201

First Floor: 1,970 sq. ft.
Second Floor: 660 sq. ft.
Total: 2,630 sq. ft.
Bonus Space: 424 sq. ft.
Bedrooms: 3
Bathrooms: 2½
Width: 62' - 6"
Depth: 79' - 10"
Foundation: Crawlspace,
Unfinished Basement

ORDER ONLINE @ EPLANS.COM

This wonderful cottage is flavored with elements of Greek Revival style and southern tradition. The columned portico is a sweet place to perch with a glass of lemonade on a summer afternoon. The breakfast area doubles as a sunroom for enjoying a cheerful cup of coffee every morning. The first-floor master suite is a relaxing haven complete with spa bath, and the upstairs bedrooms provide plenty of privacy for children and guests. Bonus space above the garage allows you to complete the home of your dreams.

FIRST FLOOR

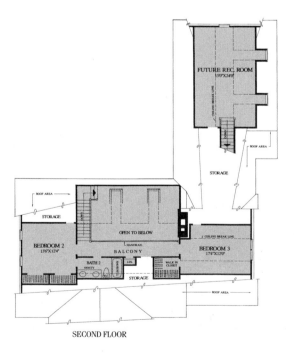

SECOND FLOOR

© William E. Poole Designs, Inc.

plan# HPK2000202

First Floor: 2,449 sq. ft.
Second Floor: 1,094 sq. ft.
Total: 3,543 sq. ft.
Bonus Space: 409 sq. ft.
Bedrooms: 4
Bathrooms: 3½
Width: 89' - 0"
Depth: 53' - 10"
Foundation: Crawlspace

ORDER ONLINE @ EPLANS.COM

An impressive front porch coupled with charming twin dormers makes this home a delightful addition to any neighborhood. The sunroom doubles as a cheerful area to enjoy meals, a view of the backyard, and gain access to the rear porch. The family room and living room/library each boast a private fireplace. Upstairs houses three additional bedrooms, two sharing a full bath with a dual-sink vanity and one with an attached full bath. Future expansion space and extra storage space complete the second floor.

FIRST FLOOR

SECOND FLOOR

© William E. Poole Designs, Inc.

plan# HPK2000203

First Floor: 1,694 sq. ft.
Second Floor: 874 sq. ft.
Total: 2,568 sq. ft.
Bonus Space: 440 sq. ft.
Bedrooms: 3
Bathrooms: 3½
Width: 74' - 2"
Depth: 46' - 8"
Foundation: Unfinished Basement, Crawlspace

ORDER ONLINE @ EPLANS.COM

A welcoming front porch lined by graceful columns introduces this fine farmhouse. Inside, the foyer leads through an elegant arch to the spacious great room, which features a fireplace and built-ins. The formal dining room and sunny breakfast room flank a highly efficient kitchen—complete with a pantry and a serving bar. Located on the first floor for privacy, the master suite is filled with pampering amenities. Upstairs, two large bedrooms have private baths and walk-in closets.

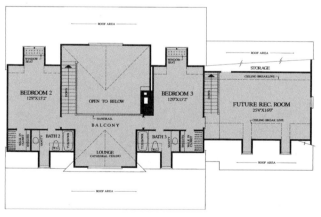

SECOND FLOOR

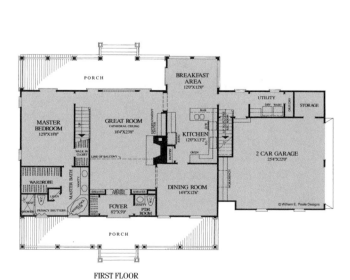

FIRST FLOOR

© William E. Poole Designs, Inc.

plan# **HPK2000204**

First Floor: 2,335 sq. ft.
Second Floor: 936 sq. ft.
Total: 3,271 sq. ft.
Bonus Space: 958 sq. ft.
Bedrooms: 3
Bathrooms: 3½
Width: 91' - 4"
Depth: 54' - 6"
Foundation: Unfinished Walkout Basement

ORDER ONLINE @ EPLANS.COM

Large rooms and a lack of hallways make practical use of the 3,000+ square feet used to create this plan. The majority of the living space is found on the first floor where a spacious family room is centered as the heart of the home. A snack bar in the U-shaped kitchen is ideal for informal meals. The screen porch, accessed from the breakfast area, makes outdoor entertaining a possibility. The master suite dominates the right side of the plan; the only first-floor bedroom. Upstairs houses two additional family bedrooms—each with a full bath. Future expansion space completes the second floor

FIRST FLOOR

SECOND FLOOR

© William E. Poole Designs, Inc.

plan# HPK2000205

First Floor: 2,746 sq. ft.
Second Floor: 992 sq. ft.
Total: 3,738 sq. ft.
Bonus Space: 453 sq. ft.
Bedrooms: 4
Bathrooms: 3½
Width: 80' - 0"
Depth: 58' - 6"
Foundation: Crawlspace

ORDER ONLINE @ EPLANS.COM

The columned entry of this Colonial home speaks for itself, but the inside actually seals the deal. The cooktop-island kitchen flows easily into the breakfast area and great room. The vaulted-ceiling sunroom accesses a rear covered porch perfect for outdoor entertaining. The master suite enjoys a private entrance to the rear porch, central His and Hers wardrobes, and a spacious bath. Upstairs, three family bedrooms share two full baths. Expansion space makes a future rec room an option. Extra storage space in the garage is an added convenience.

FIRST FLOOR

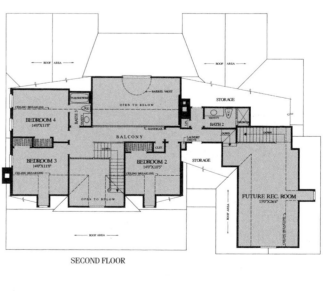

SECOND FLOOR

plan # HPK2000206

First Floor: 1,993 sq. ft.
Second Floor: 894 sq. ft.
Total: 2,887 sq. ft.
Bonus Space: 176 sq. ft.
Bedrooms: 3
Bathrooms: 2½
Width: 55' - 0"
Depth: 78' - 6"
Foundation: Crawlspace

ORDER ONLINE @ EPLANS.COM

Here's a country home that offers lots of down-home appeal but steps out with upscale style. The grand foyer leads to a spacious great room with an extended-hearth fireplace and access to the rear covered porch. Open planning allows the windowed breakfast nook to enjoy the glow of the fireplace, and the secluded formal dining room has its own hearth. The master suite offers private access to the rear covered porch, and a spacious bath that boasts two walk-in closets, twin vanities, and a windowed, whirlpool tub. Two upstairs bedrooms share a full bath in the balcony hall, which leads to a bonus room with a walk-in closet.

FIRST FLOOR

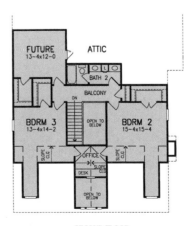

SECOND FLOOR

plan# HPK2000207

Square Footage: 2,402
Bonus Space: 294 sq. ft.
Bedrooms: 4
Bathrooms: 2½
Width: 56' - 6"
Depth: 82' - 0"
Foundation: Crawlspace, Slab, Unfinished Basement

ORDER ONLINE @ EPLANS.COM

Pillars and shuttered windows grace the facade of this handsome home. Space is well organized for casual and comfortable family living and for memorable social events. The formal dining room is just to the left as guests enter and is served from the kitchen through a butler's pantry. Straight ahead from the foyer the spacious great room enjoys a fireplace at one end and is connected to the kitchen by a counter/bar at the opposite end. The stylish breakfast bay projects out over the covered rear porch. Four bedrooms, including an unforgettable master suite, are also located on the first level.

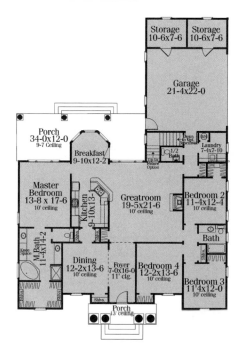

REAR EXTERIOR

plan# HPK2000208

Square Footage: 1,701
Bedrooms: 3
Bathrooms: 2
Width: 45' - 0"
Depth: 68' - 2"
Foundation: Slab

ORDER ONLINE @ EPLANS.COM

Don't let the bricks and classic columns fool you—this is one home that's fully prepared for the new age. A spacious great room offers an entertainment center, a massive fireplace and, best of all, access to a private side patio. Casual dining space opens to the kitchen, which features a walk-in pantry. Three tall windows and a vaulted ceiling enhance the master suite. Separate lavatories and a garden tub highlight the private bath.

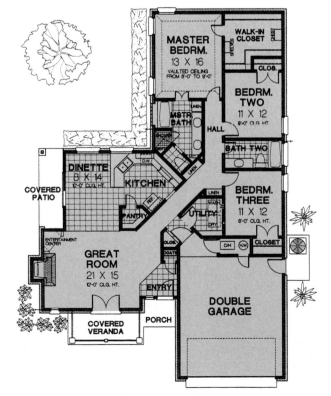

plan# HPK2000209

Square Footage: 2,172
Bedrooms: 3
Bathrooms: 2
Width: 79' - 0"
Depth: 47' - 0"
Foundation: Crawlspace, Slab

ORDER ONLINE @ EPLANS.COM

The simplicity of the ranch lifestyle is indicated in every detail of this charming country design. Front and rear verandas along with earthy materials combine to give the exterior of this home a true land-lover's look. A central fireplace warms the cathedral-enhanced space of the formal great room. The casual kitchen area features an island workstation overlooking the rear veranda. The master suite is a sumptuous retreat with a sitting area, private bath, and walk-in closet. Two additional bedrooms share a full hall bath.

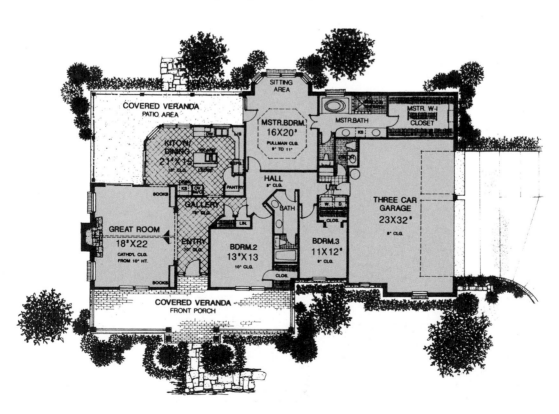

This utterly charming country house will be a welcome sight for sore eyes come day's end. Twin chimneys bedeck the roof line of the exterior. A great room and formal dining room are immediately accessible from the foyer. Two family bedrooms open off of the great room. Note the cathedral ceiling and expansive rear view. The kitchen area features snack bar and breakfast nook, from which you can reach the rear patio. A master suite, laundry, and side-load garage occupy the remainder of the interior. Unfinished attic space provides for various possibilities; plan to expand this area with an optional loft. A potential basement is also included with this design.

plan# HPK2000210

Square Footage: 2,286
Bonus Space: 443 sq. ft.
Bedrooms: 3
Bathrooms: 2½
Width: 76' - 10"
Depth: 55' - 6"
Foundation: Crawlspace, Slab, Unfinished Basement

ORDER ONLINE @ EPLANS.COM

plan# HPK2000211

Square Footage: 2,443
Bedrooms: 4
Bathrooms: 3½
Width: 74' - 4"
Depth: 61' - 10"
Foundation: Crawlspace, Slab,
Unfinished Basement

ORDER ONLINE @ EPLANS.COM

The Old South is revisited on this modern adaptation of the plantation home. Stucco and brick join the stately columns for a dignified look, softened by full-length multipane windows that frame the front door. Enter to a foyer that opens ahead to the hearth-warmed great room at the heart of the home. The spacious kitchen is centered between the breakfast nook and dining room for ultimate convenience. Bedrooms are separated, offering privacy to three secondary bedrooms and a lavish master suite. The garage provides extra storage, great for gardening equipment and seasonal toys.

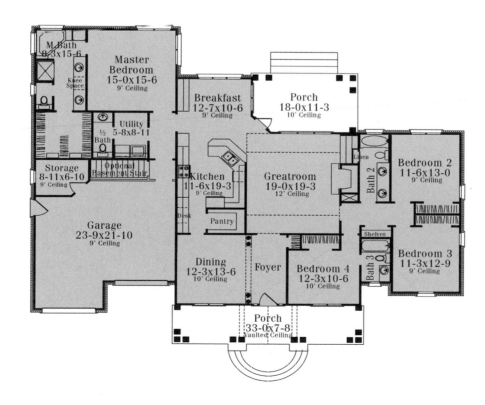

An arched entry is nicely accented by graceful columns on this attractive southern home. Inside, the foyer is flanked by a formal dining room and a bedroom/study. The spacious great room features a warming fireplace and access to the rear covered porch. An efficient kitchen is complete with an adjacent breakfast area and a nearby pantry. The master suite offers two walk-in closets, a double vanity, and a pampering bath with a separate tub and shower. Each of two family bedrooms has a walk-in closet.

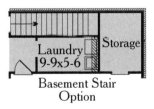

plan# HPK2000212

Square Footage: 1,867
Bedrooms: 3
Bathrooms: 2
Width: 70' - 6"
Depth: 51' - 0"
Foundation: Crawlspace, Slab, Unfinished Basement

ORDER ONLINE @ EPLANS.COM

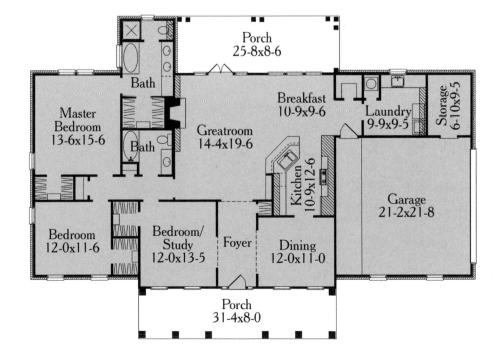

OPTIONAL LAYOUT

plan # HPK2000213

Square Footage: 2,062
Bedrooms: 3
Bathrooms: 2
Width: 68' - 0"
Depth: 49' - 5"
Foundation: Slab, Unfinished Basement, Crawlspace

ORDER ONLINE @ EPLANS.COM

An arch-topped columned porch offers an elegant entry to this home. The formal foyer provides two coat closets and access to the utility room. Straight ahead, the great room offers a built-in corner entertainment center and a fireplace flanked by French doors to the rear porch. A modified galley-style kitchen is just off the great room, serves the dining room with ease, and offers a walk-in pantry. Two bedrooms can be found, to the right of the floor plan, sharing a full bath. The master suite boasts an oversized walk-in closet and private bath.

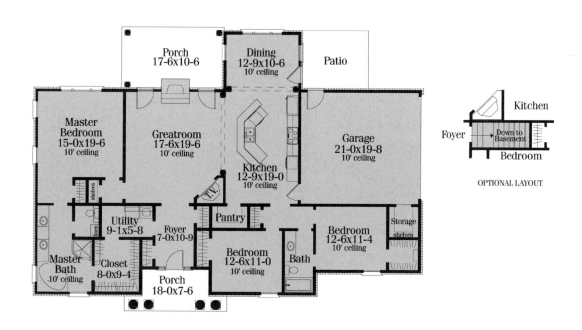

OPTIONAL LAYOUT

plan# HPK2000214

Shutters, multipane glass windows and a cross-hatched railing on the front porch make this a beautiful country cottage. To the left of the foyer is a spacious great room and a warming fireplace, framed by windows. To the right of the foyer, two family bedrooms feature walk-in closets and share a fully appointed bath. The efficient kitchen centers around a long island workstation and opens to the large dining/sitting room. The rear porch adds living space to view the outdoors. French doors, a fireplace and columns complete this three-bedroom design.

Square Footage: 2,053
Bedrooms: 3
Bathrooms: 2
Width: 57' - 8"
Depth: 71' - 10"
Foundation: Crawlspace, Slab,
Unfinished Basement

ORDER ONLINE @ EPLANS.COM

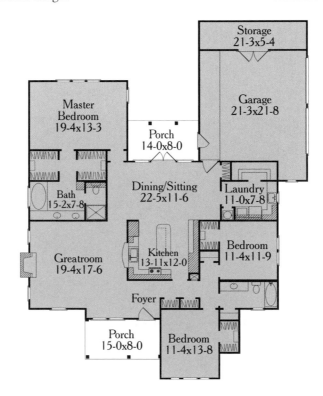

plan# HPK2000215

Square Footage: 1,727
Bonus Space: 563 sq. ft.
Bedrooms: 3
Bathrooms: 2
Width: 52' - 9"
Depth: 66' - 2"
Foundation: Slab, Crawlspace,
Unfinished Basement

ORDER ONLINE @ EPLANS.COM

This traditional country home features an array of family-friendly amenities. Triple dormers and a covered front porch enhance the exterior. The great room is warmed by a fireplace and is open to the dining area and kitchen. Three family bedrooms, including the master bedroom with a private bath and roomy walk-in closet, complete the main level, along with a rear porch and two-car garage. A bonus room is available for future use, perfect for a home office, fourth bedroom or attic storage. Please specify basement, crawlspace or slab foundation when ordering.

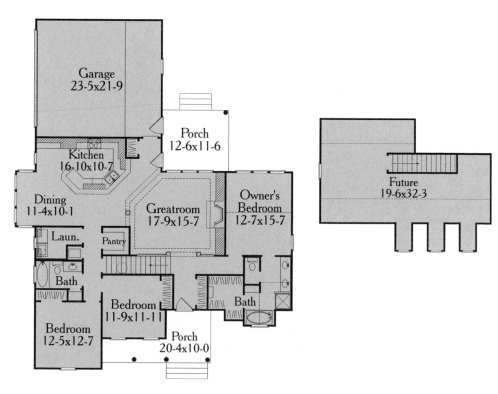

plan# HPK2000216

Square Footage: 1,543
Bedrooms: 3
Bathrooms: 2
Width: 51' - 5"
Depth: 66' - 6"
Foundation: Crawlspace, Slab

ORDER ONLINE @ EPLANS.COM

This lovely country cottage is sized just right for a family home and is perfect for anyone on a budget. A foyer with a coat closet begins the plan and leads to the hearth-warmed great room. Open planning expands the space visually, as the great room flows into the bayed dining room and island kitchen. Two bedrooms at the front of the home share a full bath, and the master suite is secluded for peace and quiet at the rear. Don't miss the patio and carport (with ample storage), located behind the home for extra security.

Storage
19-4 x 5-4

Carport
20-0 x 22-9

Patio

Owner's
Bedroom
17-9 x 13-8

Laun.
6-0 x 7-8

Desk

Porch
13-0 x 8-0

Dining
13-3 x 10-10

Greatroom
17-6 x 14-6

Bath

Bath

Kitchen
10-0 x 12-5

Foyer

Bath

Bedroom
10-7 x 11-4

Bedroom
11-2 x 12-0

Porch
18-0 x 6-0

plan# HPK2000217

Square Footage: 1,626
Bedrooms: 3
Bathrooms: 2
Width: 58' - 0"
Depth: 57' - 8"
Foundation: Unfinished Basement, Crawlspace, Slab

ORDER ONLINE @ EPLANS.COM

From any angle, this sweet country cottage is a dream come true for any family. From the foyer, either enter the sleeping area with two secondary bedrooms and a full bath, or veer to the right to the great room, graced with a cathedral ceiling and a fireplace. A U-shaped island kitchen flows effortlessly into the dining area. Porch access expands living space. The master bedroom has lots of light, a private bath, and a wonderful walk-in closet. Not to be missed: valuable storage space off the carport.

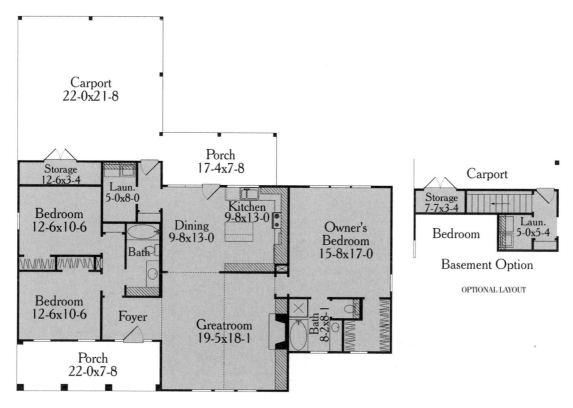

Carport
22-0x21-8

Porch
17-4x7-8

Storage
12-6x3-4

Laun.
5-0x8-0

Kitchen
9-8x13-0

Bedroom
12-6x10-6

Dining
9-8x13-0

Owner's
Bedroom
15-8x17-0

Bath

Bedroom
12-6x10-6

Foyer

Greatroom
19-5x18-1

Bath
8-2x8-1

Porch
22-0x7-8

Carport

Storage
7-7x3-4

Laun.
5-0x5-4

Bedroom

Basement Option

OPTIONAL LAYOUT

plan# HPK2000218

Square Footage: 1,539
Bedrooms: 3
Bathrooms: 2
Width: 51' - 5"
Depth: 66' - 6"
Foundation: Crawlspace, Slab

ORDER ONLINE @ EPLANS.COM

Looking for a lovely home with efficiency and attention to detail? Welcome home! An inviting porch and Palladian window create country ambiance. Inside, creative use of space means there is enough room for the whole family. The foyer, with coat closet, leads to an impressive great room with a focal-point fireplace and access to the rear patio. Or, if you prefer, enter through the rear door, past the laundry room, and into the L-shaped kitchen and the bayed dining room. Two bedrooms reside at the front of the plan; the master suite is nestled at the back. His and Hers closets and dual sinks in the pampering bath make the morning rush a distant memory.

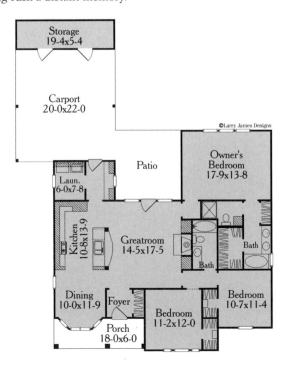

plan # HPK2000219

First Floor: 1,760 sq. ft.
Second Floor: 853 sq. ft.
Total: 2,613 sq. ft.
Bedrooms: 3
Bathrooms: 3½
Width: 56' - 0"
Depth: 46' - 6"
Foundation: Slab, Crawlspace,
Unfinished Basement

ORDER ONLINE @ EPLANS.COM

A covered front porch opens to a foyer that leads directly to the spacious great room, warmed by a country fireplace. A curved wall of windows invites nature indoors and overlooks the rear porch. The island kitchen is open to the formal dining room, also great for casual occasions. The first-floor master bedroom features a twin-vanity dressing area and a walk-in closet. Upstairs, a balcony overlooks the two-story great room. Two family bedrooms—each with private baths—share the second-floor study that opens to a petite front porch.

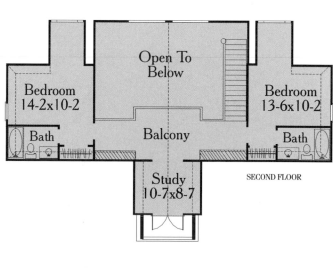

SECOND FLOOR

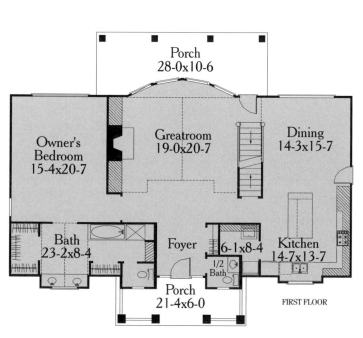

FIRST FLOOR

plan# HPK2000220

First Floor: 1,466 sq. ft.
Second Floor: 629 sq. ft.
Total: 2,095 sq. ft.
Bedrooms: 3
Bathrooms: 2½
Width: 32' - 0"
Depth: 59' - 0"
Foundation: Crawlspace

ORDER ONLINE @ EPLANS.COM

Designed for a narrow lot, this home's modest facade belies the functional, amenity-filled floor plan inside. You may enter through the front door to the dining area, but this casual home was meant to have family and friends come in through the back entrance. From here, the hearth-warmed gathering room opens to the sunny breakfast nook and angled serving-bar kitchen. A butler's pantry makes an elegant segue to the dining room. The master suite is located on this level and enjoys a splendid bath with dual amenities. Secondary bedrooms are upstairs and share a full bath with an optional twin sink. A two-car garage completes the plan, positioned at the rear to allow the home great curb appeal.

FIRST FLOOR

SECOND FLOOR

plan# HPK2000221

First Floor: 790 sq. ft.
Second Floor: 723 sq. ft.
Total: 1,513 sq. ft.
Bonus Space: 285 sq. ft.
Bedrooms: 3
Bathrooms: 2½
Width: 49' - 8"
Depth: 30' - 6"
Foundation: Unfinished Basement

ORDER ONLINE @ EPLANS.COM

The nostalgia of a more relaxed time, when neighbors visited and shared evening conversation, is provided with the exterior style of this delightful home. Large rooms and a clean, easy floor plan offer value and efficiency. Upgraded features include a first-floor utility room, a two-car garage, counter space with seating availability, a pantry, and a fireplace. The spacious second floor boasts a generously sized master bedroom including a private bath and roomy walk-in closet. Two additional bedrooms and a large bonus room that can be finished later complete this comfortable home.

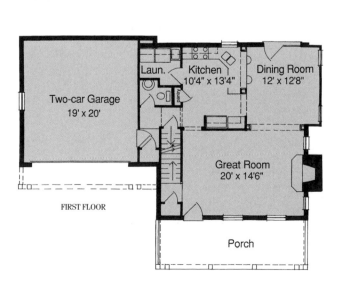

FIRST FLOOR

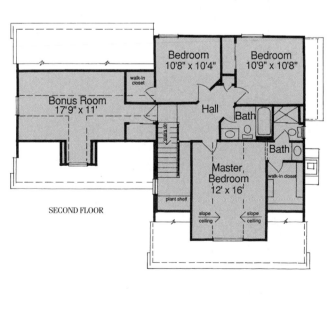

SECOND FLOOR

The covered front porch adds an element of Greek Revival to this Southern Country home. The dining room is defined by archways that open to the foyer and vaulted family room, where a fireplace offers warmth and a window wall offers beautiful views. The vaulted breakfast area adjoins the kitchen. The master wing is impressive with a bayed sitting area with a private fireplace. The lavish master bath features His and Hers walk-in closets. Two family bedrooms on the opposite side of the home share a hall bath. The formal living room converts to a fourth bedroom, providing flexible space.

plan # HPK2000222

Square Footage: 2,426
Bonus Space: 767 sq. ft.
Bedrooms: 4
Bathrooms: 2½
Width: 63' - 0"
Depth: 72' - 4"
Foundation: Crawlspace,
Unfinished Walkout Basement

ORDER ONLINE @ EPLANS.COM

OPT. SECOND FLOOR PLAN

plan# HPK2000223

Square Footage: 1,724
Bonus Space: 375 sq. ft.
Bedrooms: 3
Bathrooms: 2
Width: 53' - 6"
Depth: 58' - 6"
Foundation: Crawlspace,
Unfinished Walkout Basement, Slab

ORDER ONLINE @ EPLANS.COM

This down-home, one-story plan has all the comforts and necessities for solid family living. The vaulted family room, along with the adjoining country-style kitchen and breakfast nook, is at the center of the plan. The extended hearth fireplace flanked by radius windows will make this a cozy focus for family get-togethers and entertaining visitors. A formal dining room is marked off by decorative columns. The resplendent master suite assumes the entire right wing, where it is separated from two bedrooms located on the other side of the home. Built-in plant shelves in the master bath create a garden-like environment. Additional space is available for building another bedroom or study.

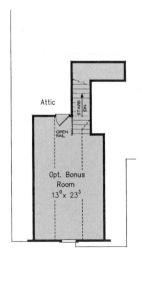

plan # HPK2000224

First Floor: 911 sq. ft.
Second Floor: 1,029 sq. ft.
Total: 1,940 sq. ft.
Bedrooms: 3
Bathrooms: 2½
Width: 20' - 10"
Depth: 75' - 10"
Foundation: Crawlspace

ORDER ONLINE @ EPLANS.COM

With irresistible charm and quiet curb appeal, this enchanting cottage conceals a sophisticated interior that's prepared for busy lifestyles. Built-in cabinetry in the great room frames a massive fireplace, which warms the area and complements the natural views. An open kitchen provides an island with a double sink and snack counter. Planned events are easily served in the formal dining room with French doors that lead to the veranda. On the upper level, a central hall with linen storage connects the sleeping quarters.

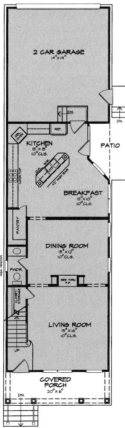

FIRST FLOOR

SECOND FLOOR

plan# HPK2000225

First Floor: 1,347 sq. ft.
Second Floor: 537 sq. ft.
Total: 1,884 sq. ft.
Bedrooms: 3
Bathrooms: 2½
Width: 32' - 10"
Depth: 70' - 10"
Foundation: Crawlspace

ORDER ONLINE @ EPLANS.COM

This old-fashioned townhouse design features an attractive two-story floor plan. Two front covered porches enhance the traditional facade. Inside, the foyer introduces an island kitchen that overlooks the dining room. A formal two-story living room, located at the rear of the plan, is warmed by a fireplace. The first-floor master suite enjoys a private bath and huge walk-in closet. A powder room, laundry room, and two-car garage complete the first floor. Upstairs, two secondary bedrooms—one with a walk-in closet—share a full hall bath. Bedroom 3 features a private balcony overlooking the front property. Optional storage is available on the second floor.

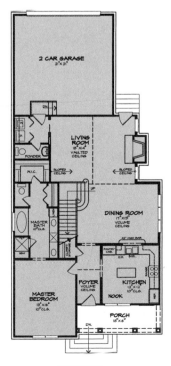

FIRST FLOOR

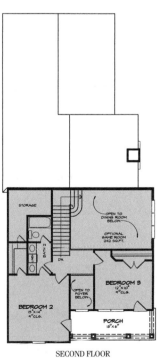

SECOND FLOOR

plan# **HPK2000226**

First Floor: 1,078 sq. ft.
Second Floor: 921 sq. ft.
Total: 1,999 sq. ft.
Bedrooms: 3
Bathrooms: 3
Width: 24' - 11"
Depth: 73' - 10"
Foundation: Crawlspace

ORDER ONLINE @ EPLANS.COM

This charming clapboard home is loaded with character and is perfect for a narrow lot. Columns and connecting arches separate the great room and the dining room. The efficient U-shaped kitchen features a corner sink with a window view and a bayed breakfast area with access to the rear porch. A bedroom and a bath are conveniently located for guests on the first floor. Upstairs, the master suite features a vaulted ceiling and a luxurious bath with dual vanities, a whirlpool tub and a separate shower.

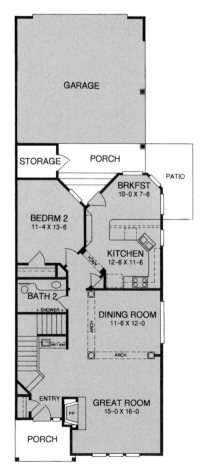

FIRST FLOOR

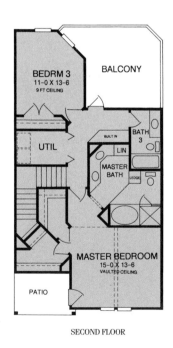

SECOND FLOOR

plan# HPK2000227

First Floor: 904 sq. ft.
Second Floor: 1,058 sq. ft.
Total: 1,962 sq. ft.
Bedrooms: 3
Bathrooms: 2½
Width: 22' - 0"
Depth: 74' - 0"
Foundation: Slab, Crawlspace

ORDER ONLINE @ EPLANS.COM

Reminiscent of the popular townhouses of the past, this fine clapboard home is perfect for urban or riverfront living. Two balconies grace the second floor—one at the front and one on the side. A two-way fireplace between the formal living and dining rooms provides visual impact. A passthrough from the kitchen to the dining room simplifies serving, and a walk-in pantry provides storage. On the second floor, the master bedroom opens to a large balcony, and the relaxing master bath is designed with a separate shower and an angled whirlpool tub.

FIRST FLOOR

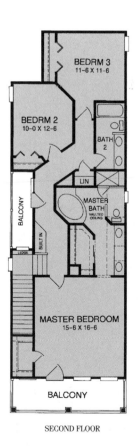

SECOND FLOOR

plan# HPK2000228

A charming elevation gives this home its curbside appeal. Inside, the two-story foyer opens through archways to the living and dining rooms. Clerestory windows flood the living room with natural light. The kitchen and breakfast room are nearby. An angled sink, with a serving ledge and pass-through, opens the kitchen to the living room beyond. An old-time side porch off the kitchen enhances the look of the home and provides convenient access to the outside. The master bath has all the frills and includes roomy His and Hers walk-in closets. Two bedrooms and a bath are located upstairs. A lovely balcony is located off Bedroom 2. This plan includes a two-car detached garage.

First Floor: 1,482 sq. ft.
Second Floor: 631 sq. ft.
Total: 2,113 sq. ft.
Bedrooms: 3
Bathrooms: 2½
Width: 41' - 10"
Depth: 56' - 5"
Foundation: Crawlspace, Slab

ORDER ONLINE @ EPLANS.COM

FIRST FLOOR

SECOND FLOOR

plan# HPK2000229

Square Footage: 2,733
Bedrooms: 4
Bathrooms: 2½
Width: 88' - 0"
Depth: 54' - 2"
Foundation: Slab, Crawlspace

ORDER ONLINE @ EPLANS.COM

The favorite gathering place of this beautiful home is certain to be its sun-filled breakfast and keeping room complemented by the full kitchen. Thoughtful placement of the kitchen provides easy service to both formal and informal eating areas. A large living room enjoys two sets of double French doors that open to outdoor living areas. French doors open onto the spacious master suite and its elegant master bath. Here, a soothing whirlpool tub takes center stage. Three other bedrooms, or two bedrooms and a study, are positioned at the opposite end of the house for privacy. Bedrooms 2 and 3 have their own walk-in closets.

This hipped-roof cottage has a special appeal that is perfect for an established neighborhood. The floor plan works around the great room featuring a fireplace and rear-porch access. To the left is the kitchen and dining area with a convenient laundry closet. To the right of the plan are the family bedrooms, which both have walk-in closets and share a full bath. The master suite is complemented by a private bath featuring a separate shower and tub and dual vanities.

plan# **HPK2000230**

Square Footage: 1,464
Bedrooms: 3
Bathrooms: 2
Width: 56' - 2"
Depth: 45' - 2"
Foundation: Crawlspace, Slab

ORDER ONLINE @ EPLANS.COM

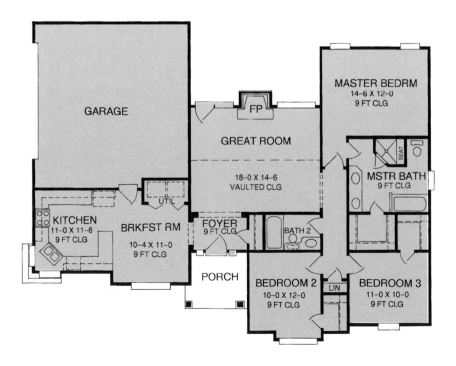

plan# HPK2000231

First Floor: 2,469 sq. ft.
Second Floor: 1,025 sq. ft.
Total: 3,494 sq. ft.
Bonus Space: 320 sq. ft.
Bedrooms: 4
Bathrooms: 3½
Width: 67' - 8"
Depth: 74' - 2"
Foundation: Unfinished Basement, Crawlspace, Slab

ORDER ONLINE @ EPLANS.COM

A lovely double arch gives this European-style home a commanding presence. Once inside, a two-story foyer provides an open view directly through the formal living room to the rear grounds beyond. The spacious kitchen with a work island and the bayed breakfast area share space with the family room. The private master suite features dual sinks, twin walk-in closets, a corner garden tub, and a separate shower. A large game room completes this wonderful family home.

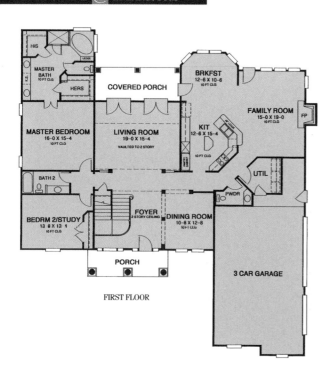

FIRST FLOOR

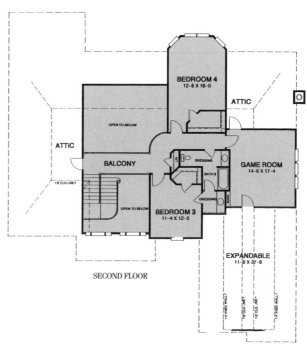

SECOND FLOOR

© William E. Poole Designs, Inc.

A smattering of architectual styles blend effortlessly to create this delightful two-story home. The foyer is flanked by the formal dining room and the living room. To the rear, the island kitchen and breakfast area enjoy a beamed ceiling, bringing a bit of the rustic exterior inside. The family room offers a cozy space for informal gatherings with its warming fireplace. The master suite sits on the far right; Bedroom 2, on the far left, would double easily as a guest room, giving adequate privacy. Two additional bedrooms, each with a private bath, reside on the second floor, as does space for a future rec room.

plan# HPK2000232

First Floor: 2,568 sq. ft.
Second Floor: 981 sq. ft.
Total: 3,549 sq. ft.
Bonus Space: 345 sq. ft.
Bedrooms: 4
Bathrooms: 4½
Width: 66' - 8"
Depth: 71' - 0"
Foundation: Unfinished Basement

ORDER ONLINE @ EPLANS.COM

FIRST FLOOR

SECOND FLOOR

plan# HPK2000233

First Floor: 1,627 sq. ft.
Second Floor: 783 sq. ft.
Total: 2,410 sq. ft.
Bonus Space: 418 sq. ft.
Bedrooms: 4
Bathrooms: 2½
Width: 46' - 0"
Depth: 58' - 6"
Foundation: Crawlspace

ORDER ONLINE @ EPLANS.COM

© William E. Poole Designs, Inc.

This "little jewel" of a home emanates a warmth and joy not soon forgotten. The two-story foyer leads to the formal living room, defined by graceful columns. A formal dining room opens from the living room, making entertaining a breeze. A family room at the back features a fireplace and works well with the kitchen and breakfast areas. A lavish master suite is secluded on the first floor; three family bedrooms reside upstairs.

FIRST FLOOR

SECOND FLOOR

© William E. Poole Designs, Inc.

plan# **HPK2000234**

Square Footage: 2,717
Bonus Space: 1,133 sq. ft.
Bedrooms: 3
Bathrooms: 2½
Width: 68' - 6"
Depth: 79' - 10"
Foundation: Crawlspace,
Unfinished Basement

ORDER ONLINE @ EPLANS.COM

French influence is highly evident on this fine three-bedroom home. From the hipped rooflines to the delicate detailing on the dormers and around the door, this house is full of class. Inside, the foyer introduces the formal living room, which opens to the formal dining room just off the kitchen. The beamed-ceiling family room offers a fireplace, built-ins, and a wonderful view of the backyard. Two family bedrooms, sharing a bath, and a lavish master suite with a private bath complete this floor. Upstairs is all bonus space, perfect for future expansion.

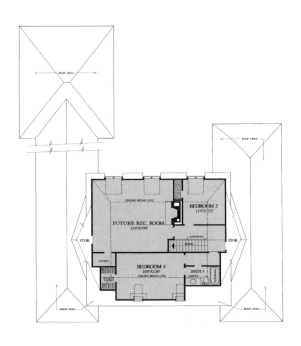

©William E. Poole Designs, Inc.

plan# HPK2000235

Square Footage: 3,049
Bonus Space: 868 sq. ft.
Bedrooms: 3
Bathrooms: 2½
Width: 72' - 6"
Depth: 78' - 10"
Foundation: Unfinished Basement, Crawlspace

ORDER ONLINE @ EPLANS.COM

This charming home, with its brick exterior and Old World accents, seems to have been plucked from the English countryside. The arched entry opens to the two-story foyer with a balcony overlook. The formal dining room sits on the left, and the living room is on the right. Beyond the elegant staircase, the family room offers a magnificent view of the backyard. Off to the left is the sunny breakfast alcove and the adjoining kitchen. A split-bedroom design places the master suite on the left and two family bedrooms on the right. An optional second floor allows for two more bedrooms, two additional baths, and a recreation room.

This narrow-lot plan has all the appeal and romance of a European cottage. The front porch welcomes you to a charming set of double doors. Two family bedrooms, a hall bath, a laundry room, and the two-car garage with storage are located at the front of the plan. The island kitchen easily serves the dining room, which accesses a private garden and the casual breakfast room. The spacious family room offers a warming fireplace, built-ins, and back-porch access. The plan is completed by the master suite, which features a private bath and walk-in closet.

plan# HPK2000236

Square Footage: 1,964
Bedrooms: 3
Bathrooms: 2
Width: 38' - 10"
Depth: 90' - 1"
Foundation: Slab

ORDER ONLINE @ EPLANS.COM

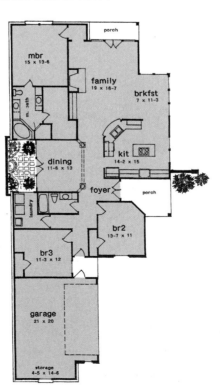

plan# HPK2000237

Square Footage: 1,760
Bedrooms: 3
Bathrooms: 2
Width: 42' - 6"
Depth: 56' - 11"
Foundation: Slab

ORDER ONLINE @ EPLANS.COM

French influences preside upon the facade of this enchanting cottage that enjoys an abundance of windows in the rear. The front courtyard gives shelter to the French-door entry. The two family bedrooms rest on the left with a conveniently placed full bath. The foyer leads to the family room at the rear with its window wall and fireplace flanked by built-ins. The adjoining breakfast nook sits in a sunny location with access to the rear porch. The island kitchen offers a pantry and plenty of counter space. The master suite is on the right, behind the garage, with an enormous walk-in closet and lavish private bath.

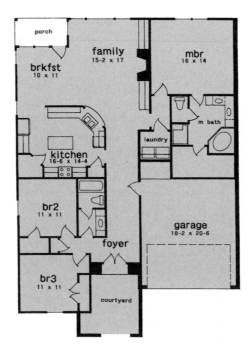

plan# HPK2000238

Square Footage: 2,757
Bedrooms: 4
Bathrooms: 2½
Width: 69' - 6"
Depth: 68' - 8"
Foundation: Unfinished Basement,
Slab, Crawlspace

ORDER ONLINE @ EPLANS.COM

French Country appointments lend an elegant Old World look to this design. The foyer opens to the well-proportioned dining room, which boasts a 12-foot ceiling. Two sets of French doors with transoms open off the living room to the rear porch. The kitchen, breakfast room, and family room are open to one another. The fireplace is visible from all these areas and provides a lovely focal point for the room. The master suite features a tray ceiling and a luxury master bath.

plan# HPK2000239

First Floor: 1,652 sq. ft.
Second Floor: 543 sq. ft.
Total: 2,195 sq. ft.
Bedrooms: 4
Bathrooms: 3½
Width: 46' - 0"
Depth: 72' - 0"
Foundation: Unfinished Walkout Basement

ORDER ONLINE @ EPLANS.COM

With brick and siding, a hipped roofline, a covered porch accented by columns, and two fireplaces, this three-bedroom home is a perfect example of Old World class. Inside, the foyer is flanked by a formal dining room and a cozy study. Directly ahead is the family room, complete with a fireplace, built-ins and French doors to the rear deck. Nearby, the elegant kitchen is full of amenities, including a snack bar, a pantry and the adjacent bayed breakfast area. Sleeping quarters consist of two family bedrooms that share a bath and a deluxe master bedroom.

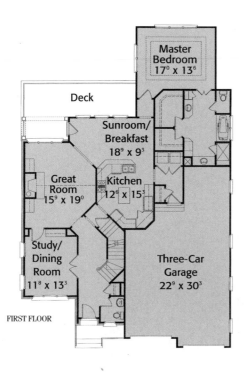

FIRST FLOOR

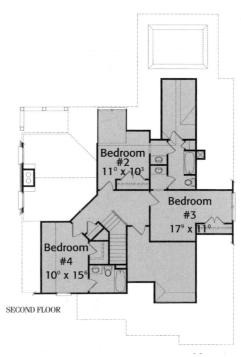

SECOND FLOOR

plan# HPK2000240

This spacious one-story home easily accommodates a large family, providing all the luxuries and necessities for gracious living. For formal occasions, a grand dining room sits just off the entry foyer and features a vaulted ceiling. The great room offers a beautiful ceiling treatment and access to the rear deck. For more casual times, the kitchen, breakfast nook, and adjoining keeping room with a fireplace fill the bill. The master suite is spacious and filled with amenities that include a sitting room, walk-in closet, and access to the rear deck. Two family bedrooms share a full bath. Each of these bedrooms provides its own lavatory.

Square Footage: 2,935
Bedrooms: 3
Bathrooms: 2½
Width: 71' - 0"
Depth: 66' - 0"
Foundation: Finished Walkout Basement

ORDER ONLINE @ EPLANS.COM

plan# HPK2000241

Square Footage: 2,170
Bedrooms: 4
Bathrooms: 3
Width: 62' - 0"
Depth: 61' - 6"
Foundation: Finished Walkout Basement

ORDER ONLINE @ EPLANS.COM

This classic cottage boasts a stone-and-wood exterior with a welcoming arch-top entry that leads to a columned foyer. An extended-hearth fireplace is the focal point of the family room, and a nearby sunroom with covered porch access opens up the living area to the outdoors. The gourmet island kitchen opens through double doors from the living area; the breakfast area looks out to a porch. Sleeping quarters include a master wing with a spacious, angled bath, and a sitting room or den that has its own full bath—perfect for a guest suite. On the opposite side of the plan, two family bedrooms share a full bath.

© 2004 Donald A. Gardner, Inc.

Choose an attractive lot for this plan, which enables rear views from all common rooms. Such views are an attractive backdrop for the spacious great room, which features a fireplace and decorative ceilings. The room's open access to the adjoining kitchen and foyer enable a balanced use of spaces. By contrast, the floor plan reserves the master suite for homeowners. With separate walk-in closets and vanities, a compartmented toilet, shower, and window-side tub, the master bath aspires to pamper and rejuvenate. The remaining bedrooms reside at the opposite side of the plan, sharing a common bath. The extended utility/mudroom near the garage is a useful working space.

plan# HPK2000242

Square Footage: 2,021
Bonus Space: 471 sq. ft.
Bedrooms: 3
Bathrooms: 2
Width: 60' - 3"
Depth: 58' - 10"

ORDER ONLINE @ EPLANS.COM

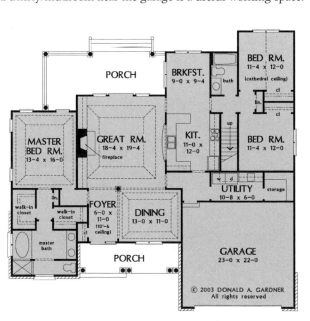

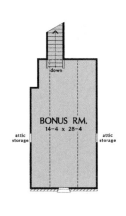

© 2003 DONALD A. GARDNER
All rights reserved

© 2004 Donald A. Gardner, Inc.

plan# HPK2000243

Square Footage: 2,304
Bonus Space: 361 sq. ft.
Bedrooms: 4
Bathrooms: 3
Width: 58' - 4"
Depth: 69' - 8"

ORDER ONLINE @ EPLANS.COM

A judicious mix of board-and-batten siding and stone creates a distinguished facade. Small architectural details, such as the paired dormer windows, box-bay window, and rooftop turret, add more interest to the exterior. The layout poses an efficient strategy for balancing shared, flexible areas with well-defined retreat spaces. The multifunctional great room takes in natural light from the center of the plan. The breakfast nook serves doubly as a dining area and buffer for the bedrooms on the right side of the home. The bedroom/study at the bottom left of the plan serves also to shield the master suite from street-side noise. The extended foyer is a refining touch.

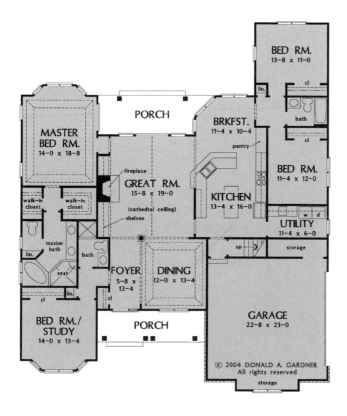

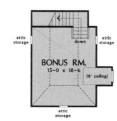

© 2002 Donald A. Gardner, Inc.

This quaint farmhouse lacks nothing—not even a bonus room to accommodate expansion needs. With its welcoming front porch, Palladian windows, and siding, this home brings curb appeal to any streetscape. Columns and a tray ceiling define the dining room. Columns also make a grand entrance to the great room, which features built-ins, a fireplace, a kitchen pass-through, and French doors leading to the deck. A breakfast room off the kitchen makes the perfect place to enjoy a cup of coffee. Designed for privacy, the master suite has a tray ceiling in the bedroom, a spacious walk-in closet, and a master bath equipped with a double vanity, private privy, large shower, and garden tub. The utility/mudroom is complete with a sink.

plan# HPK2000244

Square Footage: 1,827
Bonus Space: 384 sq. ft.
Bedrooms: 3
Bathrooms: 2
Width: 61' - 8"
Depth: 62' - 8"

ORDER ONLINE @ EPLANS.COM

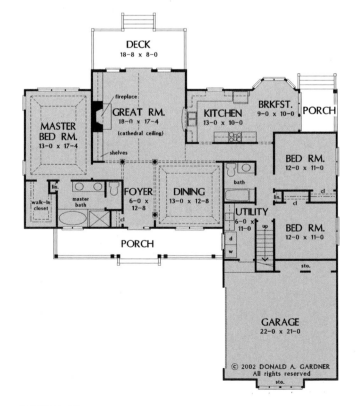

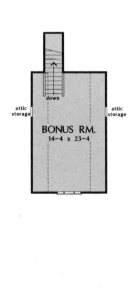

© 2004 Donald A. Gardner, Inc.

plan# HPK2000245

Square Footage: 1,921
Bonus Space: 449 sq. ft.
Bedrooms: 3
Bathrooms: 2
Width: 62' - 6"
Depth: 49' - 8"

ORDER ONLINE @ EPLANS.COM

Brick and siding blend to form a classic facade for this elegant yet economical home. Two sets of twin columns accent the front door, while each set frames striking double-hung windows. The front-entry garage allows the home to fit on a small or narrow lot, cutting costs. Off the foyer, double doors lead to the flexible bedroom/study, and across the hall a tray ceiling highlights the dining room. A coffered ceiling adds architectural interest to the great room, while a cathedral ceiling tops the master bedroom. An open island kitchen has views of the breakfast area and great room, which also has built-in shelves flanking the fireplace. In the master bath, a privy and dual vanity sinks conveniently help coordinate morning routines. As a covered porch off the great room provides space for outdoor relaxation and entertaining, the bonus room above the garage offers expansion possibilities.

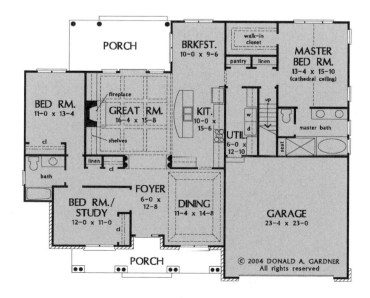

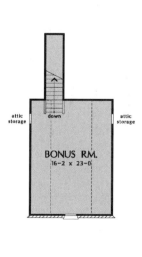

© 2004 DONALD A. GARDNER
All rights reserved

© 1994 Donald A. Gardner Architects, Inc.

plan⊕ HPK2000246

First Floor: 1,841 sq. ft.
Second Floor: 594 sq. ft.
Total: 2,435 sq. ft.
Bonus Space: 391 sq. ft.
Bedrooms: 4
Bathrooms: 3
Width: 82' - 2"
Depth: 48' - 10"

ORDER ONLINE @ EPLANS.COM

Spaciousness and lots of amenities earmark this design as a family favorite. The front wraparound porch leads to the foyer and in turn to a bedroom/study and dining room. The central great room presents a warming fireplace, a two-story cathedral ceiling, and access to the rear porch. The kitchen features an island food-prep counter and opens to a bayed breakfast area, which conveniently accesses the garage through a side utility room. In the master suite, a private bath with a bumped-out tub and a walk-in closet are extra enhancements. Upstairs, two bedrooms flank a full bath. A bonus room over the garage allows for future expansion.

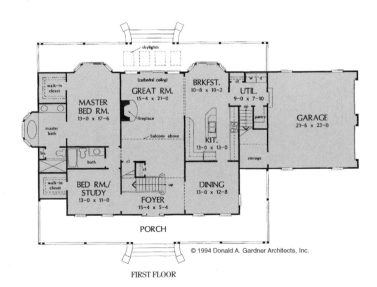

© 1994 Donald A. Gardner Architects, Inc.

FIRST FLOOR

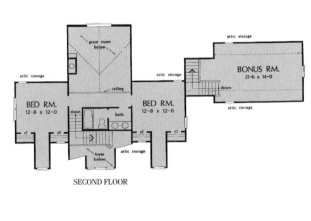

SECOND FLOOR

© 2004 Donald A. Gardner, Inc.

plan# HPK2000247

First Floor: 1,575 sq. ft.
Second Floor: 776 sq. ft.
Total: 2,351 sq. ft.
Bonus Space: 394 sq. ft.
Bedrooms: 3
Bathrooms: 2½
Width: 45' - 0"
Depth: 54' - 0"

ORDER ONLINE @ EPLANS.COM

The quaint pleasures of country living abound in this charming cottage. Attractive gables crown each door of the two-bay garage. The home's front entrance leads from the covered porch almost directly to the great room, where a fireplace and built-in cabinets create a stunning focal point. In the kitchen, a breakfast bar doubles as a serving counter to the dining room and a coffered ceiling tops the adjacent sun room. The master suite sits tucked away from daily activity and contains such luxuries as a tray ceiling, expansive windows, and a walk-in closet, plus a shower with bench and two vanity sinks in the master bath. Upstairs, two extra bedrooms and one bath provide space for children or guests, a bonus room offers expansion options, and a loft/study overlooks the great room below. The rear covered porch off the dining and sun rooms adds the finishing touch to this pleasing design.

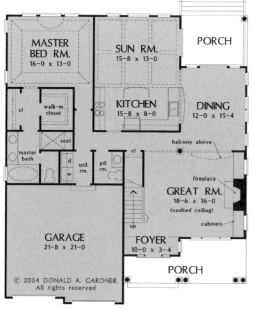

FIRST FLOOR

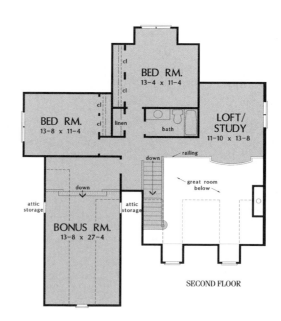

SECOND FLOOR

© 2004 Donald A. Gardner, Inc.

This home is deceptively large, with most of its living space tucked at the back, far from street noise. The vaulted foyer opens to a formal dining room with an elegant tray ceiling. A central kitchen with yards of counter space makes service a breeze to the dining room or the breakfast nook beyond. The back porch is tucked into an L between the nook and the great room, where a fireplace flanked by built-in cabinets will become a favorite gathering spot. Two bedrooms and the master suite open from a hallway behind the great room. Note the separate entrance to the front bedroom. Upstairs, a spacious bonus room waits to be finished as needed.

plan # HPK2000248

Square Footage: 2,036
Bonus Space: 506 sq. ft.
Bedrooms: 3
Bathrooms: 2
Width: 52' - 0"
Depth: 72' - 8"

ORDER ONLINE @ EPLANS.COM

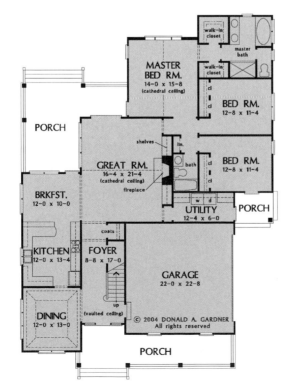

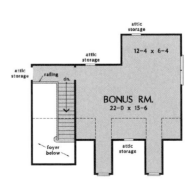

© 2004 Donald A. Gardner, Inc.

plan# HPK2000249

Square Footage: 1,886
Bonus Space: 588 sq. ft.
Bedrooms: 3
Bathrooms: 2
Width: 51' - 6"
Depth: 65' - 8"

ORDER ONLINE @ EPLANS.COM

A standing-seam metal roof highlights the facade of this charming farmhouse. Modest in appearance, it provides lots of space within. Porches front and back are accessed by French doors from the high-ceilinged great room, whose fireplace can be enjoyed from the open kitchen as well. Dining options include a casual snack bar at the kitchen's island, a sunny breakfast nook, or the tray-ceilinged formal dining room. Down a hallway, past the walk-in pantry, lies the master suite and stair to a loft and bonus space. Two family bedrooms occupy the front corner of the home, along with a full bath and mudroom-style entry from the garage.

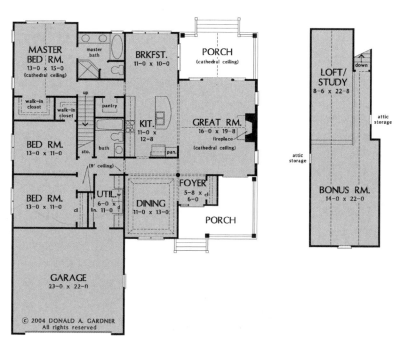

plan # HPK2000250

First Floor: 1,728 sq. ft.
Second Floor: 1,413 sq. ft.
Total: 3,141 sq. ft.
Bedrooms: 4
Bathrooms: 3½
Width: 47' - 2"
Depth: 65' - 5"
Foundation: Finished Basement

ORDER ONLINE @ EPLANS.COM

Designed for a sloping lot, but adaptable to suit your needs, this Southern Colonial favorite is full of the amenities you ask for most. From the two-story foyer you'll discover a powder room and dramatic staircase to the left and the dining room to the right. Ahead, the family room features a soaring ceiling, warming fireplace and lanai access. The bayed breakfast area flows into the kitchen, complete with an island cooktop. A staircase here gives family access to the upper level. The first-floor master suite is private and plush, with lanai access, sweeping views and a luxurious bath. Upstairs, three bedroom suites share a bonus room and two full baths.

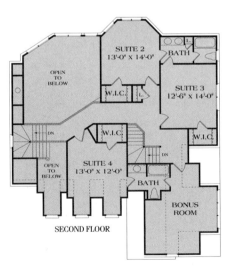

SECOND FLOOR

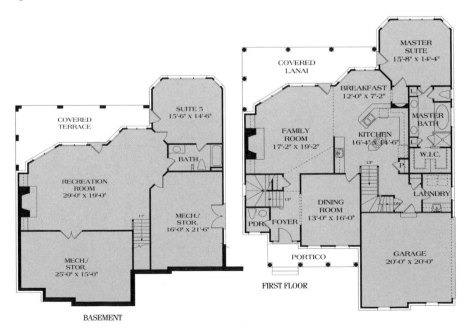

BASEMENT

FIRST FLOOR

plan# HPK2000251

Square Footage: 2,439
Bonus Space: 390 sq. ft.
Bedrooms: 3
Bathrooms: 2½
Width: 77' - 0"
Depth: 59' - 1"
Foundation: Crawlspace, Slab

ORDER ONLINE @ EPLANS.COM

This charmer is constructed with shingle and stone facade. Fronted with rustic columns and an august Tudor-style chimney, the exterior evokes images of a country farmhouse. The dormer windows allow for a brightened entry way on sunny days. On your left lies the great room with a vaulted ceiling. The gallery, suitable for a private collection of art, faces you. The kitchen is located to the left, joining forces with the breakfast area (the kitchen's best secret is a corner pantry). From here you can also access the covered patio. A formal dining room—also convertible to a study—opens off the gallery through an archway. After passing two hall closets and a family bedroom on your right, you will come to the bonus staircase for an upstairs attic or loft, and the master suite. A third bedroom and utility area also occupy this part of the floor.

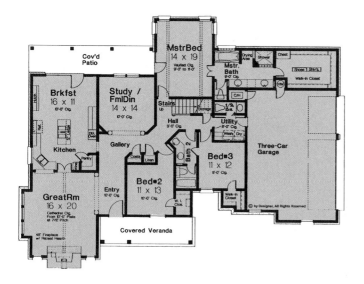

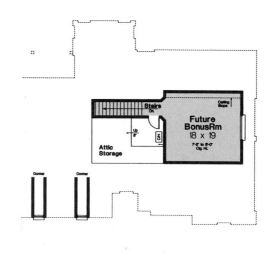

© 2004 Donald A. Gardner, Inc.

plan# HPK2000252

Columns, arched openings, and stone accents provide an abundance of curb appeal. Siding provides a low-maintenance exterior, freeing up time for family and fun. A courtyard entrance to the garage helps make the most of a smaller lot. Inside, the gathering rooms are open to each other, creating a natural traffic flow. A cathedral ceiling, fireplace, and built-in cabinetry highlight the great room, while a counter separates the kitchen from the breakfast nook. At the end of a private hallway, a niche featuring favorite art announces the entrance to an elegant master suite. Secondary bedrooms are found at the opposite end of the house, along with a stair to the bonus room above the garage.

Square Footage: 1,956
Bonus Space: 358 sq. ft.
Bedrooms: 3
Bathrooms: 2
Width: 57' - 0"
Depth: 66' - 8"

ORDER ONLINE @ EPLANS.COM

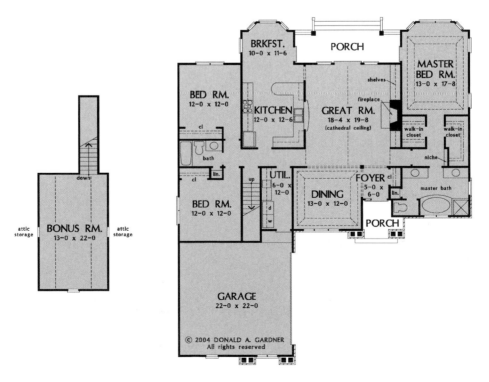

© 2004 DONALD A. GARDNER
All rights reserved

plan# HPK2000253

Square Footage: 1,932
Bedrooms: 3
Bathrooms: 2
Width: 65' - 10"
Depth: 53' - 5"
Foundation: Slab, Crawlspace

ORDER ONLINE @ EPLANS.COM

Enter this beautiful home through graceful archways and columns. The foyer, dining room, and living room are one open space, defined by a creative room arrangement. The living room opens to the breakfast room and porch. The bedrooms are off a small hall reached through an archway. Two family bedrooms share a bath, and the master bedroom enjoys a private bath with a double-bowl vanity. A garage with storage and a utility room complete the floor plan.

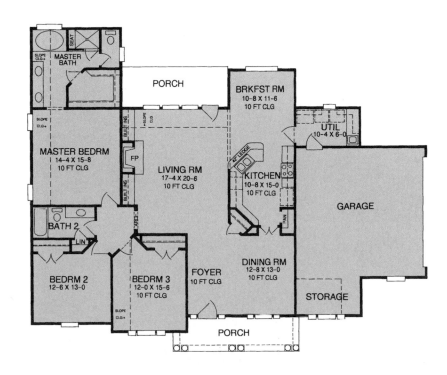

plan# HPK2000003

First Floor: 2,853 sq. ft.
Second Floor: 627 sq. ft.
Total: 3,480 sq. ft.
Bedrooms: 3
Bathrooms: 2½
Width: 80' - 0"
Depth: 96' - 0"
Foundation: Slab

ORDER ONLINE @ EPLANS.COM

©LAURENCE-TAYLOR PHOTOGRAPHY COURTESY OF SATER DESIGN COLLECTION / THIS HOME, AS SHOWN IN THE PHOTOGRAPH, MAY DIFFER FROM THE ACTUAL BLUEPRINTS. FOR MORE DETAILED INFORMATION, PLEASE CHECK THE FLOOR PLANS CAREFULLY.

Open Spaces

The modern Floridian home draws its influence from the architecture and lifestyle of the Mediterranean coast. For instance, the traditional placement of a central courtyard has been retained in this design, helping to cool the interior of the home and to maintain a connection to the surrounding landscape. This home, like others in this section, also shares the Mediterranean preference for bright, saturated colors, tiled roofs and details, and arched windows and doorways.

But where tradition ends, innovation begins, and the modern Floridian home includes some undeniably New World pleasures. For instance, the kitchen is still central to the communal life of the home. But gone are the low ceilings and molded-in surfaces, in favor of vertical freedom and clean lines. Likewise, the Mediterranean ethic of pampering visitors has been preserved in the accommodating guest rooms, often with private full baths. But what's good for the guest is even better for the owners, who will appreciate how well they can treat themselves in their gratifying suite. Finally, many of the homes in this section include expansive rear lanais accompanying the courtyard and pool areas. Protecting outdoor spaces from the elements and unwanted visitors with an atrium enclosure will let you enjoy long, Mediterranean-inspired evenings with full peace of mind.

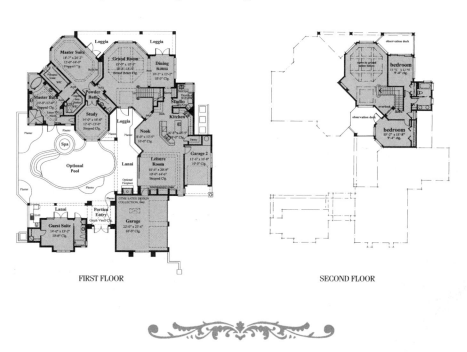

FIRST FLOOR   SECOND FLOOR

Outdoor entertaining opportunities abound in the courtyard oasis. Sliding glass walls and doors make indoor areas more seasonal and functional.

Low rooflines and grand arches lend a Mediterranean flavor to this contemporary estate. Lovely glass-paneled doors lead to an open interior defined by decorative columns, stone arches, and solid coffered ceilings. A formal living room boasts a fireplace, access to the veranda, and oversized windows for amazing views. Leisure space near the kitchen invites casual gatherings and allows the family to relax in front of a built-in entertainment center. A favorite feature, the outdoor kitchen encourages dining alfresco. A secluded master suite—with a sitting area, splendid bath, and access to the veranda—stretches across the left wing, which includes a quiet study with a vintage high-beamed ceiling. Among the four additional bedroom suites, one boasts a morning kitchen; two have access to a private deck or veranda.

plan# HPK2000254

First Floor: 4,385 sq. ft.
Second Floor: 1,431 sq. ft.
Total: 5,816 sq. ft.
Bedrooms: 5
Bathrooms: 6
Width: 88' - 0"
Depth: 110' - 1"
Foundation: Slab

ORDER ONLINE @ EPLANS.COM

FIRST FLOOR

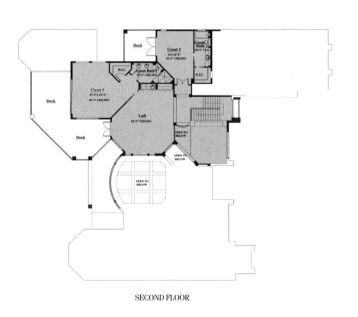

SECOND FLOOR

© LAURENCE TAYLOR PHOTOGRAPHYCOURTESY OF SATER DESIGN COLLECTION
THIS HOME, AS SHOWN IN THE PHOTOGRAPH, MAY DIFFER FROM THE ACTUAL BLUEPRINTS.

plan# HPK2000255

Square Footage: 4,604
Bonus Space: 565 sq. ft.
Bedrooms: 3
Bathrooms: 4½
Width: 98' - 5"
Depth: 126' - 11"
Foundation: Slab

ORDER ONLINE @ EPLANS.COM

Stunning with texture, style, and grace, this Floridian home amazes at first sight. The entry is bordered by twin carousel bays and opens to an elegant floor plan. Intricate ceiling treatments in the dining room and study lend an extra touch of glamour. The living room is ahead, complete with a fireplace and sliding glass walls that allow the outdoors in. The right wing is entirely devoted to the master suite, presenting a sunny sitting area, French doors to the lanai, and views of the master garden out of the exquisite bath. On the left side of the plan, light streams into the gourmet kitchen from the family room and breakfast nook. A courtyard at the rear features a fireplace and outdoor kitchen.

REAR EXTERIOR

THIS HOME, AS SHOWN IN THE PHOTOGRAPH, MAY DIFFER FROM THE ACTUAL BLUEPRINTS. FOR MORE DETAILED INFORMATION, PLEASE CHECK THE FLOOR PLANS CAREFULLY.

Make dreams come true with this fine sunny design. An octagonal study provides a nice focal point both inside and out. The living areas remain open to each other and access outdoor areas. A wet bar makes entertaining a breeze, especially with a window pass-through to a grill area on the lanai. The kitchen enjoys shared space with a lovely breakfast nook and a bright leisure room. Two bedrooms are located near the family living center. In the master bedroom suite, luxury abounds with a two-way fireplace, a morning kitchen, two walk-in closets, and a compartmented bath. Another full bath accommodates a pool area.

plan# HPK2000256

Square Footage: 3,477
Bedrooms: 3
Bathrooms: 3½
Width: 95' - 0"
Depth: 88' - 8"
Foundation: Slab

ORDER ONLINE @ EPLANS.COM

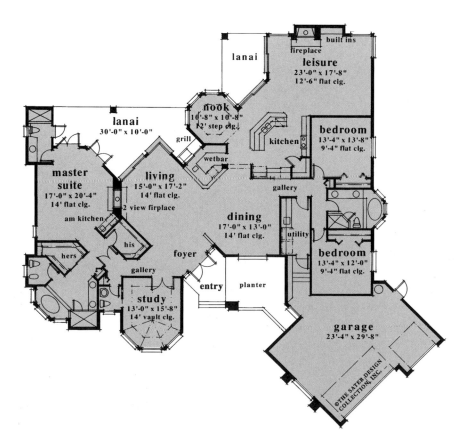

COURTESY OF SATER DESIGN COLLECTION
THIS HOME, AS SHOWN IN THE PHOTOGRAPH, MAY DIFFER FROM THE ACTUAL BLUEPRINTS.

plan # HPK2000257

Square Footage: 1,576
Bedrooms: 3
Bathrooms: 2
Width: 40' - 0"
Depth: 67' - 8"
Foundation: Slab

ORDER ONLINE @ EPLANS.COM

Though modest in size, this home boasts an interior courtyard with a solarium. The luxurious master suite surrounds the solarium and opens with double doors to the large open family room. The elegant dining room shares a volume ceiling with this space and connects via a serving bar to the gourmet kitchen. Besides the fireplace in the family room, there is also a sliding glass door to a covered patio. Two family bedrooms are to the rear of the plan and share a full bath. The utility area just off the foyer and breakfast nook with bright multi-pane windows lends convenience to the plan. Plans include three exterior choices!

HOME DESIGN SERVICES
THIS HOME, AS SHOWN IN THE PHOTOGRAPH, MAY DIFFER FROM THE ACTUAL BLUEPRINTS.
FOR MORE DETAILED INFORMATION, PLEASE CHECK THE FLOOR PLANS CAREFULLY.

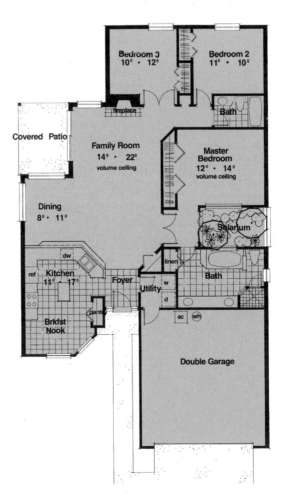

This charming stucco home would be perfect for a couple of empty-nesters who expect frequent visitors! An efficient arrangement of rooms is enhanced by beveled corners, elegant ceiling treatments, and built-in conveniences. A formal living room, with a spectacular view of the rear property beyond the covered patio, occupies the center of the home. The more casual gathering areas, including a spacious kitchen, breakfast nook, and family room, cluster in the left corner. A bedroom, bath, and laundry facilites are also here. The master suite and an additional bedroom lie on the opposite side.

plan# HPK2000258

Square Footage: 2,144
Bedrooms: 3
Bathrooms: 2
Width: 61' - 10"
Depth: 60' - 0"
Foundation: Unfinished Basement

ORDER ONLINE @ EPLANS.COM

PHOTO BY TARYN HANNAFORD
THIS HOME, AS SHOWN IN THE PHOTOGRAPH, MAY DIFFER FROM THE ACTUAL BLUEPRINTS.

plan# HPK2000259

Square Footage: 2,293
Bonus Space: 509 sq. ft.
Bedrooms: 3
Bathrooms: 2
Width: 51' - 0"
Depth: 79' - 4"
Foundation: Slab

ORDER ONLINE @ EPLANS.COM

Multiple rooflines, shutters, and a charming vaulted entry lend interest and depth to the exterior of this well-designed three-bedroom home. Inside, double doors to the left open to a cozy den. The dining room, open to the family room and foyer, features a stunning ceiling design. A fireplace and patio access and view adorn the family room. Two family bedrooms share a double-sink bathroom to the right, and the master bedroom resides to the left. Note the private patio access, two walk-in closets, and luxurious bath that ensure a restful retreat for the homeowner.

REAR EXTERIOR

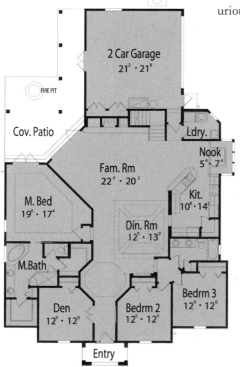

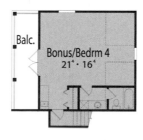

THIS HOME, AS SHOWN IN THE PHOTOGRAPH, MAY DIFFER FROM THE ACTUAL BLUEPRINTS. FOR MORE DETAILED INFORMATION, PLEASE CHECK THE FLOOR PLANS CAREFULLY.

plan# HPK2000260

Square Footage: 1,736
Bedrooms: 3
Bathrooms: 2
Width: 62' - 0"
Depth: 43' - 0"
Foundation: Unfinished Basement

ORDER ONLINE @ EPLANS.COM

This Florida dream home has a unique floor plan...The curving walls of the entry hall open like a tulip to the living and dining areas, where endless windows offer a panorama of the rear garden. An open kitchen ensures easy interaction while entertaining or simply going about daily tasks. A quiet hallway angles away from the center of the home, leading to the master suite and two additional bedrooms. A full bath is located at the head of the hallway for convenience.

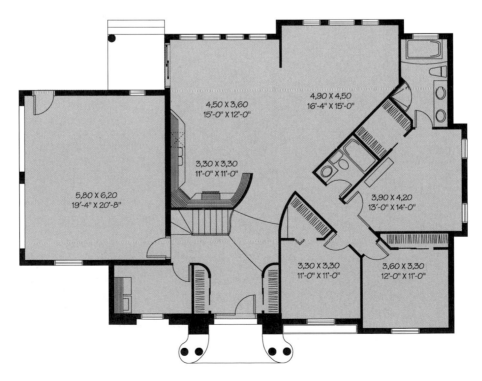

plan# HPK2000261

Square Footage: 1,712
Bedrooms: 3
Bathrooms: 2½
Width: 67' - 0"
Depth: 42' - 4"
Foundation: Crawlspace

ORDER ONLINE @ EPLANS.COM

A stylish stucco exterior enhances this home's curb appeal. A sunken great room offers a corner fireplace flanked by wide patio doors. A well-designed kitchen features an ideal view of the great room and fireplace through the breakfast-bar opening. The rear patio offers plenty of outdoor entertaining and relaxing space. The master suite features a private bath and walk-in closet. The master bath contains dual vanities, while the two family bedrooms each access a bath. A spacious two-car garage completes this plan.

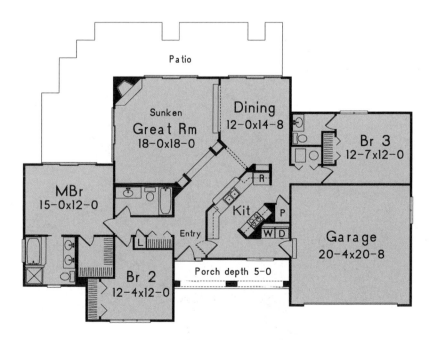

plan# HPK2000262

First Floor: 2,058 sq. ft.
Second Floor: 712 sq. ft.
Total: 2,770 sq. ft.
Bedrooms: 3
Bathrooms: 2½
Width: 57' - 3"
Depth: 81' - 3"
Foundation: Crawlspace

ORDER ONLINE @ EPLANS.COM

If you've always dreamed of owning a villa, we invite you to experience this European lifestyle—on a perfectly manageable scale. This home offers the best of traditional formality and casual elegance. The foyer leads to the great room, with a bold but stylish fireplace and three French doors to the rear terrace—sure to be left open during fair weather. The large kitchen opens gracefully to a private dining room that has access to a covered outdoor patio. The master suite combines great views and a sumptuous bath to complete this winning design. Upstairs, a balcony hall overlooking the great room leads to two family bedrooms that share a full hall bath.

REAR EXTERIOR

FIRST FLOOR

SECOND FLOOR

plan# HPK2000263

Square Footage: 2,259
Bedrooms: 4
Bathrooms: 3
Width: 59' - 8"
Depth: 54' - 4"
Foundation: Slab

ORDER ONLINE @ EPLANS.COM

This over 2,200-square-foot house offers four bedrooms, three full baths, and ample space for living and entertaining. Bring the outdoors in with access to the lanai from the great room, fourth bedroom, and breakfast area. The large, gourmet kitchen offers a snack bar—ideal for casual meals. Retreat to the master suite after a hard day to relax in a spacious bath with huge corner shower, dual sinks, and corner garden tub.

plan# **HPK2000264**

Square Footage: 2,581
Bedrooms: 4
Bathrooms: 3
Width: 60' - 0"
Depth: 75' - 0"
Foundation: Slab

ORDER ONLINE @ EPLANS.COM

Four bedrooms and three full baths are included in this economical floor plan. Enjoy open views to the outdoors from the master suite, living room, breakfast area, and family room. In addition to a private study, there is a separate dining area adjacent to the living room creating a great entertainment space. The pool bath is accessible from the interior and exterior of the house. Another full bath is located next to the larger bedroom. The master suite offers access to the lanai and the luxurious master bath has dual sinks, a huge corner shower, and corner garden tub. Carefree, easy living is the standard in this delightful Mediterranean-style home.

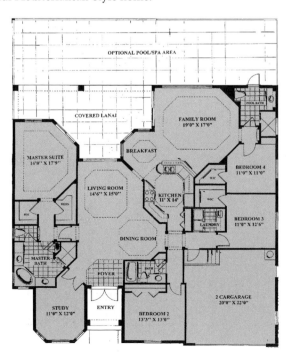

plan # HPK2000265

Square Footage: 2,948
Bedrooms: 3
Bathrooms: 3
Width: 54' - 8"
Depth: 99' - 8"
Foundation: Slab

ORDER ONLINE @ EPLANS.COM

This is definitely sun country—with an expansive lanai garnished with your own private pool! Venture beneath the historic red-tiled roof, stucco, and arched, Palladian windows to glimpse how they really live in the Sunshine State. If you can tear yourself away from the central attraction, view the family room with tray ceilings on your left, and take a peak into the guest suite with its private bath. We've also hid here a utility room for wet bathing suits. Visit the kitchen area, with functional wraparound counter and dinette. Access the dining room, which forms a larger room with the conventional living room. Directly across, a foyer opens onto the lanai through french doors, and gives way to the master suite—with study and private access to the lanai—on the left. This plan also provides for an optional outdoor kitchen on the lanai, a pool bath, spa and cabana.

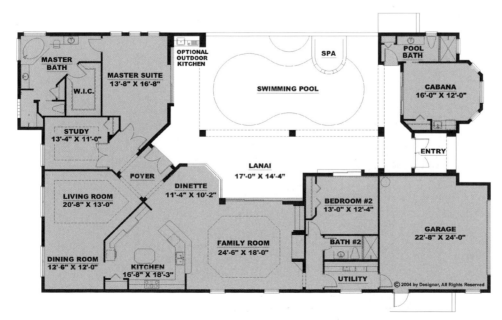

A Mediterranean dream—amenities abound throughout this three-bedroom home. With large rooms and spacious outdoor living areas, this home is great for entertaining. A summer kitchen on the covered lanai and a full pool bath invite the possibility of warm weather fun. The lavish master suite sits to the right of the first floor, equipped with a sitting area, His & Hers walk-in closets, and a dual-sink vanity. Upstairs houses two additional family bedrooms—both with full baths—a loft area, and a large study. A three-car garage completes this plan.

plan# HPK2000266

First Floor: 2,114 sq. ft.
Second Floor: 924 sq. ft.
Total: 3,038 sq. ft.
Bedrooms: 3
Bathrooms: 4
Width: 60' - 0"
Depth: 62' - 8"
Foundation: Slab

ORDER ONLINE @ EPLANS.COM

FIRST FLOOR

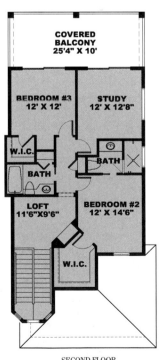

SECOND FLOOR

plan# HPK2000267

First Floor: 1,899 sq. ft.
Second Floor: 1,152 sq. ft.
Total: 3,051 sq. ft.
Bedrooms: 4
Bathrooms: 3½
Width: 67' - 8"
Depth: 59' - 8"
Foundation: Slab

ORDER ONLINE @ EPLANS.COM

The neutral tones of the stucco facade and characteristic red tiled roof emote the Mediterranean influence of this two-story home. An elegant entry speaks to the amenities that await inside. Upgraded ceiling treatments throughout the first floor bring a custom feel to interior spaces. The open layout is spacious and flows seamlessly. Outdoor living areas are accessed through sliding doors in the great room. The master suite boasts His and Hers amenities. On the second floor, a guest suite is attended by a private bath, and two additional bedrooms share a Jack-and-Jill bath. The loft offers an overhead view of the great room below.

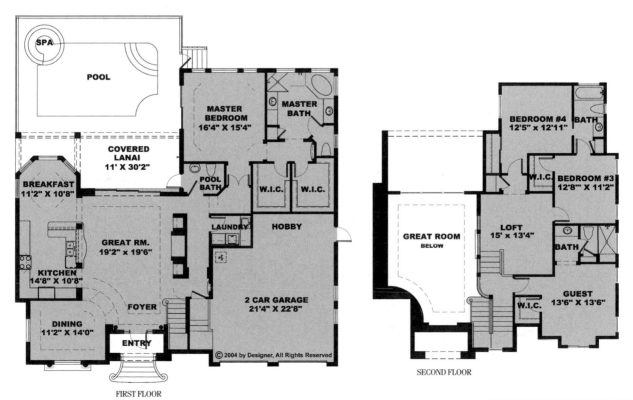

FIRST FLOOR

SECOND FLOOR

© 2004 by Designer, All Rights Reserved

The spectacular interior of this Floridian-style home will amaze you and your guests! Mediterranean accents and bay windows lend character to the stucco exterior. Inside, the formal parlor and dining room are enhanced by decorative ceiling treatments and built-in cabinetry. An elegant arch leads to the casual areas of this home, which include the kitchen, nook, and leisure room. Almost every room, including the master suite and a guest suite, offers access to the rear veranda, making it easy to gather outside for meals prepared in the outdoor kitchen.

plan# HPK2000268

Square Footage: 2,227
Bedrooms: 3
Bathrooms: 3½
Width: 65' - 0"
Depth: 77' - 0"
Foundation: Slab

ORDER ONLINE @ EPLANS.COM

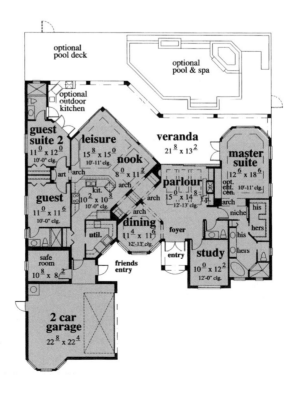

plan# HPK2000269

Square Footage: 3,265
Bedrooms: 4
Bathrooms: 3½
Width: 80' - 0"
Depth: 103' - 8"
Foundation: Slab

ORDER ONLINE @ EPLANS.COM

A turret study and a raised entry add elegance to this marvelous stucco home. The master suite has its own foyer with a window seat overlooking a private garden and fountain area; the private master bath holds dual closets, a garden tub, and a curved-glass shower. Diverse living space is the key to this plan's appeal: entertain in the living and dining rooms, enjoy family time in the leisure room, and get some privacy in the study. A guest suite includes a full bath, porch access, and a private garden entry, making it perfect for use as an in-law suite. Secondary bedrooms share a full bath.

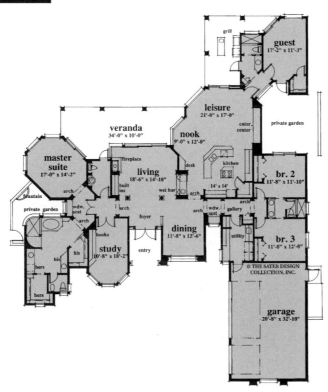

© THE SATER DESIGN COLLECTION, INC.

plan# HPK2000270

Square Footage: 3,866
Bedrooms: 3
Bathrooms: 3½
Width: 120' - 0"
Depth: 89' - 0"
Foundation: Crawlspace

ORDER ONLINE @ EPLANS.COM

This modern home adds a contemporary twist to the typical ranch-style plan. The turret study and bayed dining room add a sensuous look from the streetscape. The main living areas open up to the lanai and offer broad views to the rear through large expanses of glass and doors. The family kitchen, nook and leisure room focus on the lanai, the entertainment center and an ale bar. The guest suites have separate baths and also access the lanai. The master bath features a curved-glass shower, whirlpool tub, and private toilet and bidet room. Dual walk-in closets and an abundance of light further the appeal of this suite.

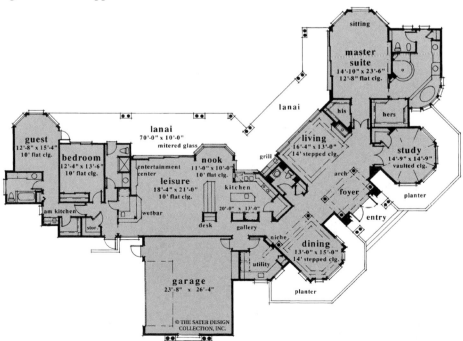

plan# HPK2000271

Square Footage: 2,582
Bedrooms: 3
Bathrooms: 2½
Width: 70' - 0"
Depth: 64' - 0"
Foundation: Slab

ORDER ONLINE @ EPLANS.COM

Double arches and tapered columns grace the raised entryway of this home. The large formal living and dining areas are located directly off the foyer. An archway leads to the informal living space and the bedrooms. The kitchen features a cooktop island, a pantry, a desk, a wet bar with pass-through to the dining room, and access to the utility room. The bayed study and master wing are opposite the informal living areas. The master bedroom features a tray ceiling, His and Hers walk-in closets and vanity sinks in the bath. A garden tub, private water closet and walk-in shower round out this plan.

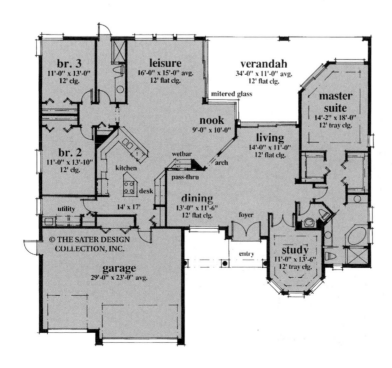

plan# HPK2000272

The dramatic entry with an arched opening leads to the comfortable interior of this delightful one-story home. Volume ceilings highlight the main living areas, which include a formal dining room and a great room with access to one of the verandas. In the turreted study, quiet time is assured. The master suite features a bath with a double-bowl vanity and a bumped-out whirlpool tub. The secondary bedrooms reside on the other side of the house.

Square Footage: 2,214
Bedrooms: 3
Bathrooms: 2
Width: 63' - 0"
Depth: 72' - 0"
Foundation: Slab

ORDER ONLINE @ EPLANS.COM

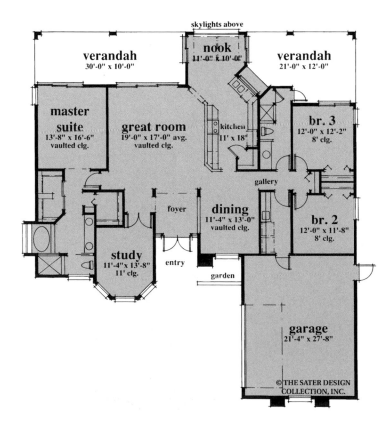

plan# HPK2000273

Square Footage: 1,487
Bedrooms: 3
Bathrooms: 2
Width: 58' - 0"
Depth: 58' - 0"
Foundation: Slab

ORDER ONLINE @ EPLANS.COM

Stucco styling, elegant arches, and a wealth of modern livability is presented in this compact one-story home. Inside, a great room with a vaulted ceiling opens to the lanai, offering wonderful options for either formal or informal entertaining. Step out onto the lanai and savor the outdoors from the delightful kitchen with its bay-windowed breakfast nook. Two secondary bedrooms (each with its own walk-in closet) share a full bath. Finally, enjoy the lanai from the calming master suite, which includes a pampering bath with a corner tub, separate shower, and large walk-in closet.

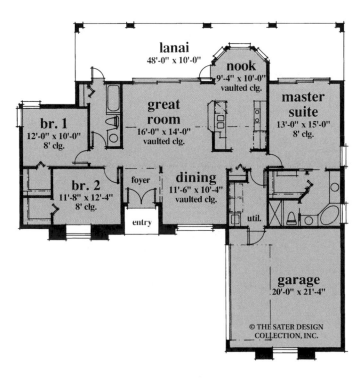

This sun country vacation home, with stucco, vertical siding, and elegant arches, boasts an exotic Key West-style influence, perfect for the Floridian coast. The lovely arched-exterior theme introduces a grand foyer, which leads to the living room and formal dining room and is complete with lofty 11-foot ceilings and stately columns. The peninsula kitchen, with a walk-in pantry and counter space galore, overlooks the breakfast nook and family room with a fireplace. French doors lead to a deck off the family room. The private master suite is secluded on the left side of the home and boasts 10-foot ceilings, dual vanities, a soaking tub, and His and Hers walk-in closets. Two additional bedrooms on the opposite side of the home from the master suite, share a full hall bath. A den or optional fourth bedroom/guest suite offers flexibility in living space.

plan# HPK2000274

Square Footage: 2,710
Bedrooms: 3
Bathrooms: 2½
Width: 64' - 0"
Depth: 80' - 0"
Foundation: Unfinished Walkout Basement

ORDER ONLINE @ EPLANS.COM

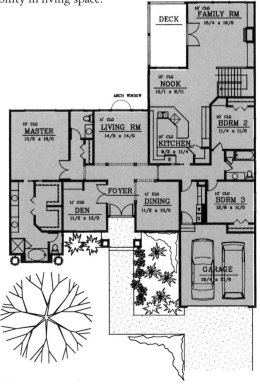

plan# HPK2000275

Square Footage: 2,111
Bedrooms: 3
Bathrooms: 2
Width: 49' - 0"
Depth: 74' - 0"
Foundation: Crawlspace, Slab

ORDER ONLINE @ EPLANS.COM

Perfect on the greens or by the beach, this beautiful Mediterranean home will win you over. A sizable porch greets family and guests and enters into the foyer. Down the hallway—great for hanging art or family photographs—you'll find built-in bookshelves, a niche for your collectibles and the angled dining room. The kitchen has a unique galley shape, with a serving bar and easy access to an octagonal informal eating area. The family room, with built-in bookshelves, a sunken fireplace and a sloped ceiling, accesses the screened porch for lazy days and warm, tropical nights. The master suite will wow you with its enormous bath and tons of counter space. Two more bedrooms—one with a walk-in closet—complete the plan.

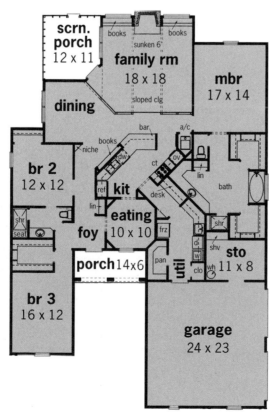

Perfect proportions and attention to detail make this Mediterranean home one in a million. Enter from the courtyards to the tiled foyer and continue to the massive great room. A two-way fireplace shares its glow with the hearth room. The well-planned kitchen enjoys light from a rear bay and sliding glass doors and easily serves the intricately adorned dining room. Two bedrooms (or make one a den) share a skylit bath on the far left. The master suite provides privacy and relishes a lovely ceiling treatment, skylit whirlpool bath, and access to the rear courtyard, which accommodates a soothing hot tub.

plan# HPK2000276

Square Footage: 1,970
Bedrooms: 3
Bathrooms: 2
Width: 57' - 8"
Depth: 58' - 0"

ORDER ONLINE @ EPLANS.COM

plan# HPK2000277

Square Footage: 2,052
Bedrooms: 3
Bathrooms: 3
Width: 60' - 0"
Depth: 50' - 0"
Foundation: Slab

ORDER ONLINE @ EPLANS.COM

A sensational Sun Country design, beautifully symmetrical and with a well-planned layout, this home is sure to please. Three bedrooms and three full baths serve the family well. Secluded to the left are the two family bedrooms and baths and tucked to the back right is the master suite, complete with a walk-in closet. Sliding glass doors from the great room—don't miss the corner hearth!—and nook offer access to the covered rear patio. Note the walk-in pantry in the island kitchen. A den/living room and dining room flank the entry foyer, and the plan is finished with a convenient laundry room.

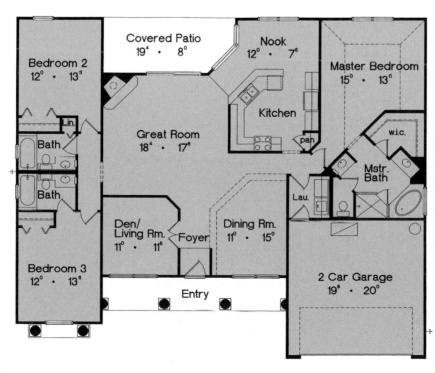

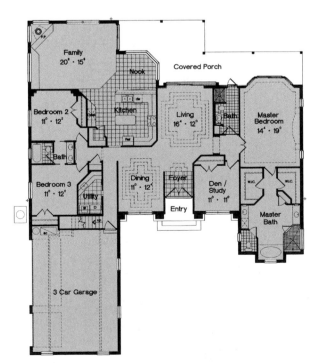

plan# HPK2000278

The perfect symmetry of the three arches at the entry to this home will please the purist and impress your guests. Double doors lead to the master suite, just past the den, which can easily access the pool bath. The master suite enjoys ceiling and built-in wall designs as a setting for the bed. The symmetry continues with a well-appointed master bath, complete with His and Hers everything! The family wing of this home provides generously designed kitchen space with an island, which overlooks the large nook with mitered glass. The family room's built-in fireplace/media wall is dramatic and functional. Two bedrooms share a private bath; an optional bonus space is over the garage for the future home theater.

Square Footage: 2,713
Bonus Space: 440 sq. ft.
Bedrooms: 3
Bathrooms: 3
Width: 66' - 4"
Depth: 80' - 8"
Foundation: Slab

ORDER ONLINE @ EPLANS.COM

plan# HPK2000279

Square Footage: 1,697
Bedrooms: 3
Bathrooms: 2
Width: 45' - 0"
Depth: 68' - 4"
Foundation: Slab

ORDER ONLINE @ EPLANS.COM

This innovative plan features a fabulous central living area with a volume ceiling. It includes a dining area with kitchen access, a great room with a built-in media center, and access to the rear covered patio. The bayed breakfast area with another volume ceiling shares natural light with the tiled kitchen. A plush master suite opens from the great room through a privacy door and offers vistas to the rear and side grounds. The traditional feel of the exterior and the up-to-date interior make this home a perfect design for today.

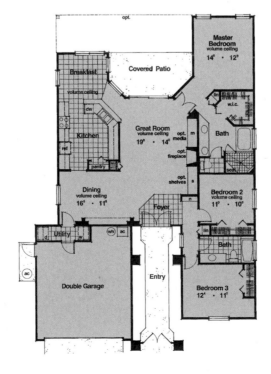

Circle-top windows are beautifully showcased in this magnificent home. The double-door entry leads into the foyer and welcomes guests into a formal living and dining room area with wonderful views. As you approach the entrance to the master suite, you pass the den/study, which can easily become a guest or bedroom suite. A gently bowed soffit and stepped ceiling treatments add excitement to the master bedroom, with floor-length windows framing the bed. The bay-window sitting area further enhances the opulence of the suite. The master bath comes complete with a double vanity, a make-up area, and a soaking tub balanced by the large shower and private toilet chamber. The walk-in closet caps off this well-appointed space with ample hanging and built-in areas.

plan# HPK2000280

Square Footage: 2,660
Bedrooms: 4
Bathrooms: 3
Width: 66' - 4"
Depth: 74' - 4"
Foundation: Slab

ORDER ONLINE @ EPLANS.COM

PHOTOGRAPHY BY MARK ENGLUND / HOMESTORE PLANS & PUBLICATIONS.
THIS HOME, AS SHOWN IN THE PHOTOGRAPH, MAY DIFFER FROM THE ACTUAL BLUEPRINTS.

plan# HPK2000281

Square Footage: 2,348
Bedrooms: 4
Bathrooms: 3
Width: 61' - 4"
Depth: 65' - 0"
Foundation: Slab

ORDER ONLINE @ EPLANS.COM

This home boasts great curb appeal with its Mediterranean influences—glass block and muntin windows, impressive pillars, and a stucco facade. The family side of this home abounds with thoughtful design features, like the island in the kitchen, the media/fireplace wall in the family room, and the mitered glass breakfast nook. A dramatic arched entry into the master suite leads to a gently curving wall of glass block, a double vanity, extra large shower, compartmented toilet, and large walk-in closet. Also special is the design of the three secondary bedrooms, which share private bath facilities

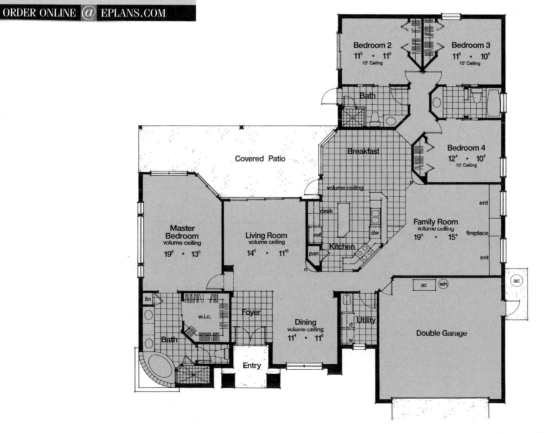

Turn Your *Dream Home* Into A Reality

Our home styles collection offers distinctive design coupled with plans to match every wallet. If you are looking to build your new home, look to Hanley Wood first.

Pick up a Copy Today!

Arts & Crafts Home Plans

This title showcases 85 home plans in the Craftsman, Prairie, and Bungalow homestyles.

$14.95 U.S.
ISBN 1-931131-26-0
128 full-color pages

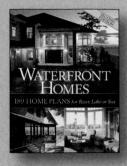

Waterfront Homes, 2nd Ed.

A collection of gorgeous homes for those who dream of life on the water's edge—this title features open floor plans with expansive views.

$10.95 U.S.
ISBN 1-931131-28-7
208 pages (32 full-color)

Finding the right new home to fit

- Your style
- Your budget
- Your life

Has never been easier.

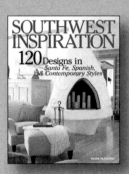

Southwest Inspiration

This title features 120 designs in Santa Fe, Spanish and Contemporary styles.

$14.95 U.S.
ISBN 1-931131-19-8
192 pages (76 full-color)

Mediterranean Inspiration

Bring home the timeless beauty of the Mediterranean with the gorgeous plans featured in this popular title.

$14.95 U.S.
ISBN 1-931131-09-0
192 pages (64 full-color)

American Collection: Craftsman

Celebrate the fine details and modest proportions of the Craftsman style with this beautiful collection of 165 homes.

$10.95 U.S.
ISBN 1-931131-54-6
192 full-color pages

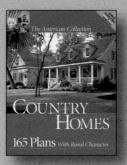

American Collection: Country

The American Collection: Country is a must-have if you're looking to build a country home or if you want to bring the relaxed country spirit into your current home.

$10.95 U.S.
ISBN 1-931131-35-X
192 full-color pages

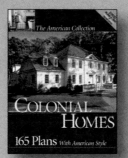

American Collection: Colonial

This beautiful collection features distinctly American home styles—find everything from Colonial, Cape Cod, Georgian, Farmhouse or Saltbox.

$10.95 U.S.
ISBN 1-931131-40-6
192 full-color pages

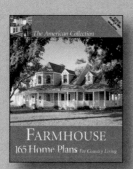

American Collection: Farmhouse

Homes with gabled roofs, wood, stone or glass themes, wrap-around porches and open floor-plans make up this wonderful assortment of farmhouse plans.

$10.95 U.S.
ISBN 1-931131-55-4
192 full-color pages

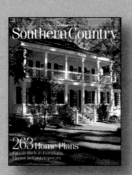

Southern Country, 2nd Ed.

Southern Country Home Plans showcases 300 plans from Historic Colonials to Contemporary Coastals.

$13.95 U.S.
ISBN-10 1-931131-56-2
320 full-color pages

Provençal Inspiration

This title features home plans, landscapes and interior plans that evoke the French Country spirit.

$14.95 U.S.
ISBN 1-881955-89-3
192 full-color pages

Hanley Wood provides the largest selection of plans from the nation's top designers and architects. Our special home styles collection offers designs to suit any taste.

Hanley Wood

One Thomas Circle, NW | Suite 600 | Washington, DC 20005
877.477.5450 | www.hanleywoodbooks.com

hanley▲wood
SELECTION, CONVENIENCE, SERVICE!

With more than 50 years of experience in the industry and millions of blueprints sold, Hanley Wood is a trusted source of high-quality, high-value pre-drawn home plans.

Using pre-drawn home plans is a **reliable, cost-effective way** to build your dream home, and our vast selection of plans is second-to-none. The nation's finest designers craft these plans that builders know they can trust. Meanwhile, our friendly, knowledgeable customer service representatives can help you every step of the way.

WHAT YOU'LL GET WITH YOUR ORDER

The contents of each designer's blueprint package is unique, but all contain detailed, high-quality working drawings. You can expect to find the following standard elements in most sets of plans:

I. FRONT PERSPECTIVE

This artist's sketch of the exterior of the house gives you an idea of how the house will look when built and landscaped.

2. FOUNDATION AND BASEMENT PLANS

This sheet shows the foundation layout including concrete walls, footings, pads, posts, beams, bearing walls, and foundation notes. If the home features a basement, the first-floor framing details may also be included on this plan. If your plan features slab construction rather than a basement, the plan shows footings and details for a monolithic slab. This page, or another in the set, may include a sample plot plan for locating your house on a building site. Additional sheets focus on foundation cross-sections and other details.

3. DETAILED FLOOR PLANS

These plans show the layout of each floor of the house. Rooms and interior spaces are carefully dimensioned, doors and windows located, and keys are given for cross-section details provided elsewhere in the plans.

4. HOUSE AND DETAIL CROSS-SECTIONS

Large-scale views show sections or cutaways of the foundation, interior walls, exterior walls, floors, stairways, and roof details. Additional cross-sections may show important changes in floor, ceiling, or roof heights, or the relationship of one level to another. These sections show exactly how the various parts of the house fit together and are extremely valuable during construction. Additional sheets may include enlarged wall, floor, and roof construction details.

5. FLOOR STRUCTURAL SUPPORTS

The floor framing plans provide detail for these crucial elements of your home. Each includes floor joist, ceiling joist, spacing, direction, span, and specifications. Beam and window headers, along with necessary details for framing connections, stairways, or dormers are also included.

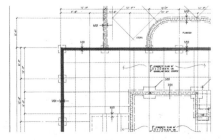

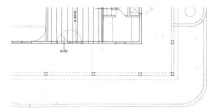

6. ELECTRICAL PLAN

The electrical plan offers suggested locations with notes for all lighting, outlets, switches, and circuits. A layout is provided for each level, as well as basements, garages, or other structures. This plan does not contain diagrams detailing how all wiring should be run, or how circuits should be engineered. These details should be designed by your electrician.

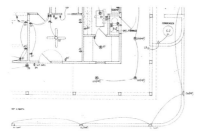

7. EXTERIOR ELEVATIONS

In addition to the front exterior, your blueprint set will include drawings of the rear and sides of your house as well. These drawings give notes on exterior materials and finishes. Particular attention is given to cornice detail, brick and stone accents, or other finish items that make your home unique.

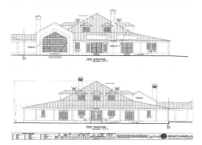

ROOF FRAMING PLANS — PLEASE READ

Some plans contain roof framing plans; however because of the wide variation in local requirements, many plans do not. If you buy a plan without a roof framing plan, you will need an engineer familiar with local building codes to create a plan to build your roof. Even if your plan does contain a roof framing plan, we recommend that a local engineer review the plan to verify that it will meet local codes.

BEFORE YOU CALL

You are making a terrific decision to use a pre-drawn house plan—it is one you can make with confidence, knowing that your blueprints are crafted by national-award-winning certified residential designers and architects, and trusted by builders.

Once you've selected the plan you want—or even if you have questions along the way—our experienced customer service representatives are available 24 hours a day, seven days a week to help you navigate the home-building process. To help them provide you with even better service, please consider the following questions before you call:

■ Have you chosen or purchased your lot?
If so, please review the building setback requirements of your local building authority before you call. You don't need to have a lot before ordering plans, but if you own land already, please have the width and depth dimensions handy when you call.

■ Have you chosen a builder?
Involving your builder in the plan selection and evaluation process may be beneficial. Luckily, builders know they can have confidence with pre-drawn plans because they've been designed for livability, functionality, and typically are builder-proven at successful home sites across the country.

■ Do you need a construction loan?
Construction loans are unique because they involve determining the value of something that is not yet constructed. Several lenders offer convenient contstruction-to-permanent loans. It is important to choose a good lending partner—one who will help guide you through the application and appraisal process. Most will even help you evaluate your contractor to ensure reliability and credit worthiness. Our partnership with IndyMac Bank, a nationwide leader in construction loans, can help you save on your loan, if needed (see the next page for details).

■ How many sets of plans do you need?
Building a home can typically require a number of sets of blueprints—one for yourself, two or three for the builder and subcontractors, two for the local building department, and one or

more for your lender. For this reason, we offer 5- and 8-set plan packages, but your best value is the Reproducible Plan Package. Reproducible plans are accompanied by a license to make modifications and typically up to 12 duplicates of the plan so you have enough copies of the plan for everyone involved in the financing and construction of your home.

■ Do you want to make any changes to the plan?
We understand that it is difficult to find blueprints for a home that will meet all of your needs. That is why Hanley Wood is glad to offer plan Customization Services. We will work with you to design the modifications you'd like to see and to adjust your blueprint plans accordingly—anything from changing the foundation; adding square footage, redesigning baths, kitchens, or bedrooms; or most other modifications. This simple, cost-effective service saves you from hiring an outside architect to make alterations. Modifications may only be made to Reproducible Plan Packages that include the license to modify.

■ Do you have to make any changes to meet local building codes?
While all of our plans are drawn to meet national building codes at the time they were created, many areas required that plans be stamped by a local engineer to certify that they meet local building codes. Building codes are updated frequently and can vary by state, county, city, or municipality. Contact your local building inspection department, office of planning and zoning, or department of permits to determine how your local codes will affect your construction project. The best way to assure that you can make changes to your plan, if necessary, is to purchase a Reproducible Plan Package.

■ Has everyone—from family members to contractors—been involved in selecting the plan?
Building a new home is an exciting process, and using pre-drawn plans is a great way to realize your dreams. Make sure that everyone involved has had an opportunity to review the plan you've selected. While Hanley Wood is the only plans provider with an exchange policy, it's best to be sure all parties agree on your selection before you buy.

CALL TOLL-FREE 1-800-521-6797

Source Key
HPK20

CUSTOMIZE YOUR PLAN – HANLEY WOOD CUSTOMIZATION SERVICES

Creating custom home plans has never been easier and more directly accessible. Using state-of-the-art technology and top-performing architectural expertise, Hanley Wood delivers on a long-standing customer commitment to provide world-class home-plans and customization services. Our valued customers—professional home builders and individual home owners—appreciate the convenience and accessibility of this interactive, consultative service.

With the Hanley Wood Customization Service you can:

■ Save valuable time by avoiding drawn-out and frequently repetitive face-to-face design meetings

■ Communicate design and home-plan changes faster and more efficiently

■ Speed-up project turn-around time

■ Build on a budget without sacrificing quality

■ Transform master home plans to suit your design needs and unique personal style

All of our design options and prices are impressively affordable. A detailed quote is available for a $50 consultation fee. Plan modification is an interactive service. Our skilled team of designers will guide you through the customization process from start to finish making recommendations, offering ideas, and determining the feasibility of your changes. This level of service is offered to ensure the final modified plan meets your expectations. If you use our service the $50 fee will be applied to the cost of the modifications.

You may purchase the customization consultation before or after purchasing a plan. In either case, it is necessary to purchase the Reproducible Plan Package and complete the accompanying license to modify the plan before we can begin customization.

Customization Consultation **$50**

TOOLS TO WORK WITH YOUR BUILDER

Two Reverse Options For Your Convenience – Mirror and Right-Reading Reverse (as available)

Mirror reverse plans simply flip the design 180 degrees—keep in mind, the text will also be flipped. For a minimal fee you can have one or all of your plans shipped mirror reverse, although we recommend having at least one regular set handy. Right-reading reverse plans show the design flipped 180 degrees but the text reads normally. When you choose this option, we ship each set of purchased blueprints in this format.

Mirror Reverse Fee (indicate the number of sets when ordering) $55
Right Reading Reverse Fee (all sets are reversed) $175

A Shopping List Exclusively for Your Home – Materials List

A customized Materials List helps you plan and estimate the cost of your new home, outlining the quantity, type, and size of materials needed to build your house (with the exception of mechanical system items). Included are framing lumber, windows and doors, kitchen and bath cabinetry, rough and finished hardware, and much more.

Materials List . . . .**$85 each**
Additional Materials Lists (at original time of purchase only)$20 each

Plan Your Home-Building Process – Specification Outline

Work with your builder on this step-by-step chronicle of 166 stages or items crucial to the building process. It provides a comprehensive review of the construction process and helps you choose materials.
Specification Outline . . . .**$10 each**

Get Accurate Cost Estimates for Your Home – Quote One® Cost Reports

The Summary Cost Report, the first element in the Quote One® package, breaks down the cost of your home into various categories based on building materials, labor, and installation, and includes three grades of construction: Budget, Standard, and Custom. Make even more informed decisions about your project with the second element of our package, the Material Cost Report. The material and installation cost is shown for each of more than 1,000 line items provided in the standard-grade Materials List, which is included with this tool. Additional space is included for estimates from contractors and subcontractors, such as for mechanical materials, which are not included in our packages.

Quote One® Summary Cost Report **$35**
Quote One® Detailed Material Cost Report **$140***
*****Detailed material cost report includes the Materials List**

Learn the Basics of Building – Electrical, Pluming, Mechanical, Construction Detail Sheets

If you want to know more about building techniques—and deal more confidently with your subcontractors—we offer four useful detail sheets. These sheets provide non-plan-specific general information, but are excellent tools that will add to your understanding of Plumbing Details, Electrical Details, Construction Details, and Mechanical Details.

Electrical Detail Sheet **$14.95**
Plumbing Detail Sheet **$14.95**
Mechanical Detail Sheet **$14.95**
Construction Detail Sheet **$14.95**
SUPER VALUE SETS:
Buy any 2: $26.95; Buy any 3: $34.95; Buy All 4: $39.95

Best Value

GETTY IMAGES (2)

hanley▲wood
DREAM HOME SOLUTIONS

MAKE YOUR HOME TECH-READY – HOME AUTOMATION UPGRADE

Building a new home provides a unique opportunity to wire it with a plan for future needs. A Home Automation-Ready (HA-Ready) home contains the wiring substructure of tomorrow's connected home. It means that every room—from the front porch to the backyard, and from the attic to the basement—is wired for security, lighting, telecommunications, climate control, home computer networking, whole-house audio, home theater, shade control, video surveillance, entry access control, and yes, video gaming electronic solutions.

Along with the conveniences HA-Ready homes provide, they also have a higher resale value. The Consumer Electronics Association (CEA), in conjunction with the Custom Electronic Design and Installation Association (CEDIA), have developed a TechHome™ Rating system that quantifies the value of HA-Ready homes. The rating system is gaining widespread recognition in the real estate industry.

Developed by CEDIA-certified installers, our Home Automation Upgrade package includes everything you need to work with an installer during the construction of your home. It provides a short explanation of the various subsystems, a wiring floor plan for each level of your home, a detailed materials list with estimated costs, and a list of CEDIA-certified installers in your local area.
Home Automation Upgrade $250

GET YOUR HOME PLANS PAID FOR!

IndyMac Bank, in partnership with Hanley Wood, will reimburse you up to $600 toward the cost of your home plans simply by financing the construction of your new home with IndyMac Bank Home Construction Lending.

IndyMac's construction and permanent loan is a one-time close loan, meaning that one application—and one set of closing fees—provides all the financing you need.

Apply today at www.indymacbank.com, call toll free at 1-866-237-3478, or ask a Hanley Wood customer service representative for details.

DESIGN YOUR HOME – INTERIOR AND EXTERIOR FINISHING TOUCHES

Be Your Own Interior Designer! – Home Furniture Planner

Effectively plan the space in your home using our Hands-On Home Furniture Planner. It's fun and easy—no more moving heavy pieces of furniture to see how the room will go together. The kit includes reusable peel-and-stick furniture templates that fit on a 12"x18" laminated layout board—enough space to lay out every room in your house.
Home Furniture Planning Kit **$15.95**

Enjoy the Outdoors! – Deck Plans

Many of our homes have a corresponding deck plan, sold separately, which includes a Deck Plan Frontal Sheet, Deck Framing and Floor Plans, Deck Elevations, and a Deck Materials List. A Standard Deck Details Package, also available, provides all the how-to information necessary for building any deck. Get both the Deck Plan and the Standard Deck Details Package for one low price in our Complete Deck Building Package. See the price tier chart below and call for deck plan availability.
Deck Details (only) **$14.95**
Deck Building Package . . . . **Plan price + $14.95**

Create a Professionally Designed Landscape – Landscape Plans

Many of our homes have a front-yard Landscape Plan that is complementary in design to the house plan. These comprehensive Landscape Blueprint Packages include a Frontal Sheet, Plan View, Regionalized Plant & Materials List, a sheet on Planting and Maintaining Your Landscape, Zone Maps, and a Plant Size and Description Guide. Each set of blueprints is a full 18" x 24" with clear, complete instructions in easy-to-read type. Our Landscape Plans are available with a Plant & Materials List adapted by horticultural experts to eight regions of the country. Please specify your region when ordering your plan—see region map below. Call for more information about landscape plan availability and applicable regions.

LANDSCAPE & DECK PRICE SCHEDULE

PRICE TIERS	1-SET STUDY PACKAGE	5-SET BUILDING PACKAGE	8-SET BUILDING PACKAGE	1-SET REPRODUCIBLE*
P1	$25	$55	$95	$145
P2	$45	$75	$115	$165
P3	$75	$105	$145	$195
P4	$105	$135	$175	$225
P5	$175	$205	$305	$405
P6	$215	$245	$345	$445

PRICES SUBJECT TO CHANGE   * REQUIRES A FAX NUMBER

TERMS & CONDITIONS

OUR 90-DAY EXCHANGE POLICY

BUY WITH CONFIDENCE!

Hanley Wood is committed to ensuring your satisfaction with your blueprint order, which is why we offer a 90-day exchange policy. With the exception of Reproducible Plan Package orders, we will exchange your entire first order for an equal or greater number of blueprints from our plan collection within 90 days of the original order. The entire content of your original order must be returned before an exchange will be processed. Please call our customer service department at 1-888-690-1116 for your return authorization number and shipping instructions. If the returned blueprints look used, redlined, or copied, we will not honor your exchange. Fees for exchanging your blueprints are as follows: 20% of the amount of the original order, plus the difference in cost if exchanging for a design in a higher price bracket or less the difference in cost if exchanging for a design in a lower price bracket. (Because they can be copied, Reproducible blueprints are not exchangeable or refundable.) Please call for current postage and handling prices. Shipping and handling charges are not refundable.

ARCHITECTURAL AND ENGINEERING SEALS

Some cities and states now require that a licensed architect or engineer review and "seal" a blueprint, or officially approve it, prior to construction. Prior to application for a building permit or the start of actual construction, we strongly advise that you consult your local building official who can tell you if such a review is required.

LOCAL BUILDING CODES AND ZONING REQUIREMENTS

Each plan was designed to meet or exceed the requirements of a nationally recognized model building code in effect at the time and place the plan was drawn. Typically plans designed after the year 2000 conform to the International Residential Building Code (IRC 2000 or 2003). The IRC is comprised of portions of the three major codes below. Plans drawn before 2000 conform to one of the three recognized building codes in effect at the time: Building Officials and Code Administrators (BOCA) International, Inc.;

the Southern Building Code Congress International, (SBCCI) Inc.; the International Conference of Building Officials (ICBO); or the Council of American Building Officials (CABO).

Because of the great differences in geography and climate throughout the United States and Canada, each state, county, and municipality has its own building codes, zone requirements, ordinances, and building regulations. Your plan may need to be modified to comply with local requirements. In addition, you may need to obtain permits or inspections from local governments before and in the course of construction. We authorize the use of the blueprints on the express condition that you consult a local licensed architect or engineer of your choice prior to beginning construction and strictly comply with all local building codes, zoning requirements, and other applicable laws, regulations, ordinances, and requirements. Notice: Plans for homes to be built in Nevada must be redrawn by a Nevada-registered professional. Consult your local building official for more information on this subject.

TERMS AND CONDITIONS

These designs are protected under the terms of United States Copyright Law and may not be copied or reproduced in any way, by

any means, unless you have purchased a Reproducible Plan Package and signed the accompanying license to modify and copy the plan, which clearly indicates your right to modify, copy, or reproduce. We authorize the use of your chosen design as an aid in the construction of ONE (1) single- or multifamily home only. You may not use this design to build a second dwelling or multiple dwellings without purchasing another blueprint or blueprints or paying additional design fees. Multi-use fees vary by designer—please call one of experienced sales representatives for a quote.

DISCLAIMER

The designers we work with have put substantial care and effort into the creation of their blueprints. However, because we cannot provide on-site consultation, supervision, and control over actual construction, and because of the great variance in local building requirements, building practices, and soil, seismic, weather, and other conditions, WE MAKE NO WARRANTY OF ANY KIND, EXPRESS OR IMPLIED, WITH RESPECT TO THE CONTENT OR USE OF THE BLUEPRINTS, INCLUDING BUT NOT LIMITED TO ANY WARRANTY OF MERCHANTABILITY OR OF FITNESS FOR A PARTICULAR PURPOSE. ITEMS, PRICES, TERMS, AND CONDITIONS ARE SUBJECT TO CHANGE WITHOUT NOTICE.

**CALL TOLL-FREE
1-800-521-6797
OR VISIT
EPLANS.COM**

IMPORTANT COPYRIGHT NOTICE

From the Council of Publishing Home Designers

Blueprints for residential construction (or working drawings, as they are often called in the industry) are copyrighted intellectual property, protected under the terms of the United States Copyright Law and, therefore, cannot be copied legally for use in building. The following are some guidelines to help you get what you need to build your home, without violating copyright law:

1. HOME PLANS ARE COPYRIGHTED
Just like books, movies, and songs, home plans receive protection under the federal copyright laws. The copyright laws prevent anyone, other than the copyright owner, from reproducing, modifying, or reusing the plans or design without permission of the copyright owner.

2. DO NOT COPY DESIGNS OR FLOOR PLANS FROM ANY PUBLICATION, ELECTRONIC MEDIA, OR EXISTING HOME
It is illegal to copy, change, or redraw home designs found in a plan book, CDROM or on the Internet. The right to modify plans is one of the exclusive rights of copyright. It is also illegal to copy or redraw a constructed home that is protected by copyright, even if you have never seen the plans for the home. If you find a plan or home that you like, you must purchase a set of plans from an authorized source. The plans may not be lent, given away, or sold by the purchaser.

3. DO NOT USE PLANS TO BUILD MORE THAN ONE HOUSE
The original purchaser of house plans is typically licensed to build a single home from the plans. Building more than one home from the plans without permission is an infringement of the home designer's copyright. The purchase of a multiple-set package of plans is for the construction of a single home only. The purchase of additional sets of plans does not grant the right to construct more than one home.

4. HOUSE PLANS IN THE FORM OF BLUEPRINTS OR BLACKLINES CANNOT BE COPIED OR REPRODUCED
Plans, blueprints, or blacklines, unless they are reproducibles, cannot be copied or reproduced without prior written consent of the copyright owner. Copy shops and blueprinters are prohibited from making copies of these plans without the copyright release letter you receive with reproducible plans.

5. HOUSE PLANS IN THE FORM OF BLUEPRINTS OR BLACKLINES CANNOT BE REDRAWN
Plans cannot be modified or redrawn without first obtaining the copyright owner's permission. With your purchase of plans, you are licensed to make non-structural changes by "red-lining" the purchased plans. If you need to make structural changes or need to redraw the plans for any reason, you must purchase a reproducible set of plans (see topic 6) which includes a license to modify the plans. Blueprints do not come with a license to make structural changes or to redraw the plans. You may not reuse or sell the modified design.

6. REPRODUCIBILE HOME PLANS
Reproducible plans (for example sepias, mylars, CAD files, electronic files, and vellums) come with a license to make modifications to the plans. Once modified, the plans can be taken to a local copy shop or blueprinter to make up to 10 or 12 copies of the plans to use in the construction of a single home. Only one home can be constructed from any single purchased set of reproducible plans either in original form or as modified. The license to modify and copy must be completed and returned before the plan will be shipped.

7. MODIFIED DESIGNS CANNOT BE REUSED
Even if you are licensed to make modifications to a copyrighted design, the modified design is not free from the original designer's copyright. The sale or reuse of the modified design is prohibited. Also, be aware that any modification to plans relieves the original designer from liability for design defects and voids all warranties expressed or implied.

8. WHO IS RESPONSIBLE FOR COPYRIGHT INFRINGEMENT?
Any party who participates in a copyright violation may be responsible including the purchaser, designers, architects, engineers, drafters, homeowners, builders, contractors, sub-contractors, copy shops, blueprinters, developers, and real estate agencies. It does not matter whether or not the individual knows that a violation is being committed. Ignorance of the law is not a valid defense.

9. PLEASE RESPECT HOME DESIGN COPYRIGHTS
In the event of any suspected violation of a copyright, or if there is any uncertainty about the plans purchased, the publisher, architect, designer, or the Council of Publishing Home Designers (www.cphd.org) should be contacted before proceeding. Awards are sometimes offered for information about home design copyright infringement.

10. PENALTIES FOR INFRINGEMENT
Penalties for violating a copyright may be severe. The responsible parties are required to pay actual damages caused by the infringement (which may be substantial), plus any profits made by the infringer commissions to include all profits from the sale of any home built from an infringing design. The copyright law also allows for the recovery of statutory damages, which may be as high as $150,000 for each infringement. Finally, the infringer may be required to pay legal fees which often exceed the damages.

BLUEPRINT PRICE SCHEDULE

PRICE TIERS	1-SET STUDY PACKAGE	5-SET BUILDING PACKAGE	8-SET BUILDING PACKAGE	1-SET REPRODUCIBLE*
A1	$465	$515	$570	$695
A2	$505	$560	$615	$755
A3	$570	$625	$685	$860
A4	$615	$680	$745	$925
C1	$660	$735	$800	$990
C2	$710	$785	$845	$1,055
C3	$775	$835	$900	$1,135
C4	$830	$905	$960	$1,215
L1	$920	$1,020	$1,105	$1,375
L2	$1,000	$1,095	$1,185	$1,500
L3	$1,105	$1,210	$1,310	$1,650
L4	$1,220	$1,335	$1,425	$1,830
SQ1				.40/SQ. FT.
SQ3				.55/SQ. FT.
SQ5				.80/SQ. FT.

PRICES SUBJECT TO CHANGE

* REQUIRES A FAX NUMBER

PLAN #	PRICE TIER	PAGE	MATERIALS LIST	QUOTE ONE®	DECK	DECK PRICE	LANDSCAPE	LANDSCAPE PRICE	REGIONS
HPK2000004	SQ1	6	Y						
HPK2000006	SQ1	8	Y	Y					
HPK2000007	C3	9							
HPK2000008	SQ1	10	Y						
HPK2000009	SQ1	11							
HPK2000283	SQ1	12							
HPK2000284	L2	13							
HPK2000010	C1	14	Y		ODA015	P2	OLA007	P4	1234568
HPK2000011	L1	15							
HPK2000012	C3	16							
HPK2000285	C3	17	Y	Y					
HPK2000286	C1	18							
IIPK2000013	C4	19							
HPK2000014	L2	20							
HPK2000015	C4	21							
HPK2000016	C2	22							
HPK2000017	C4	23							
HPK2000018	C4	24							
HPK2000019	L1	25							
HPK2000020	C2	26							
HPK2000021	C1	27							
HPK2000022	C2	28							
HPK2000023	C4	29							
HPK2000024	L2	30							
HPK2000025	L1	31							
HPK2000026	C3	32	Y						
HPK2000027	C4	33	Y						
HPK2000028	C4	34	Y						
HPK2000029	C3	35	Y						
HPK2000030	L1	36	Y						

PLAN #	PRICE TIER	PAGE	MATERIALS LIST	QUOTE ONE®	DECK	DECK PRICE	LANDSCAPE	LANDSCAPE PRICE	REGIONS
HPK2000031	C4	37							
HPK2000287	SQ1	38	Y				OLA017	P3	123568
HPK2000288	C2	39							
HPK2000032	L1	40							
HPK2000033	C2	41	Y	Y					
HPK2000289	A4	42							
HPK2000290	L1	43							
HPK2000034	C3	44							
HPK2000035	C3	45							
HPK2000036	C2	46							
HPK2000037	C2	47							
HPK2000291	C4	48							
HPK2000292	C3	49	Y						
HPK2000038	C2	50							
HPK2000039	C1	51							
HPK2000040	SQ1	52	Y	Y					
HPK2000041	L2	53							
HPK2000042	L3	54							
HPK2000043	C3	55							
HPK2000044	C4	56							
HPK2000045	C4	57							
HPK2000046	C3	58							
HPK2000047	C3	59							
HPK2000048	C2	60							
HPK2000049	L1	61							
HPK2000050	A3	62	Y						
HPK2000051	A4	63	Y						
HPK2000293	C2	64	Y						
HPK2000294	SQ1	65	Y						
HPK2000052	A4	66							

PLAN #	PRICE TIER	PAGE	MATERIALS LIST	QUOTE ONE®	DECK	DECK PRICE	LANDSCAPE	LANDSCAPE PRICE	REGIONS
HPK2000295	A3	67							
HPK2000296	L2	68	Y	Y					
HPK2000053	C4	69	Y						
HPK2000001	SQ3	70							
HPK2000054	L2	72							
HPK2000055	L1	73	Y	Y	ODA008	P3	OLA016	P4	1234568
HPK2000056	SQ1	74							
HPK2000057	SQ3	75							
HPK2000058	C2	76							
HPK2000059	SQ3	77							
HPK2000060	C4	78							
HPK2000061	SQ1	79	Y	Y					
HPK2000062	C1	80							
HPK2000063	C1	81							
HPK2000064	A4	82							
HPK2000065	C3	83							
HPK2000066	C2	84							
HPK2000067	C2	85							
HPK2000068	C3	86							
HPK2000069	C2	87							
HPK2000070	L1	88							
HPK2000071	C4	89							
HPK2000072	C4	90							
HPK2000073	L1	91							
HPK2000074	C3	92	Y						
HPK2000075	C3	93	Y						
HPK2000076	C2	94							
HPK2000077	C2	95							
HPK2000078	C2	96							
HPK2000079	SQ1	97							
HPK2000080	SQ1	98							
IIPK2000081	L2	99							
HPK2000082	L2	100							
HPK2000083	SQ1	101							
HPK2000084	SQ1	102							
HPK2000085	L2	103							
HPK2000086	C4	104							
HPK2000087	C2	105							
HPK2000088	C3	106							
HPK2000089	L1	107							
HPK2000090	L1	108							
HPK2000091	SQ1	109							
HPK2000092	L1	110							
HPK2000093	C2	111							
HPK2000094	L2	112							
HPK2000095	C3	113	Y						
HPK2000096	C1	114	Y						
HPK2000097	C4	115							
HPK2000098	L1	116	Y						
HPK2000099	L2	117	Y				OLA015	P4	123568
HPK2000100	C1	118	Y	Y			OLA015	P4	123568
HPK2000101	L1	119							
HPK2000102	L3	120							
HPK2000103	L4	121							
HPK2000104	C4	122							
HPK2000105	C4	123	Y						

PLAN #	PRICE TIER	PAGE	MATERIALS LIST	QUOTE ONE®	DECK	DECK PRICE	LANDSCAPE	LANDSCAPE PRICE	REGIONS
HPK2000106	SQ1	124							
HPK2000107	SQ1	125							
HPK2000002	C2	126							
HPK2000108	C2	128							
HPK2000109	C3	129							
HPK2000110	SQ1	130							
HPK2000111	SQ1	131							
HPK2000112	C2	132							
HPK2000113	SQ1	133							
HPK2000114	C2	134	Y						
HPK2000115	C2	135	Y						
HPK2000116	C2	136	Y						
HPK2000117	C1	137							
HPK2000118	C4	138							
HPK2000119	A4	139							
HPK2000120	C3	140							
HPK2000121	C2	141							
HPK2000122	L1	142							
HPK2000123	L1	143							
HPK2000124	C2	144							
HPK2000125	C2	145							
HPK2000126	C3	146							
HPK2000127	L2	147							
HPK2000128	C3	148	Y						
HPK2000129	C4	149							
HPK2000130	C1	150							
HPK2000131	L1	151							
HPK2000132	L2	152							
HPK2000133	C4	153							
HPK2000134	L2	154							
HPK2000135	C4	155							
HPK2000136	C3	156							
HPK2000137	C2	157	Y	Y	ODA007	P3	OLA018	P3	12345678
HPK2000138	L1	158							
HPK2000139	L1	159	Y	Y	ODA011	P2	OLA003	P3	123568
HPK2000140	C4	160							
HPK2000141	C2	161	Y						
HPK2000142	C4	162	Y						
HPK2000143	C3	163	Y	Y	ODA012	P3	OLA015	P4	123568
HPK2000144	C1	164							
HPK2000145	C3	165	Y						
HPK2000146	A4	166							
HPK2000147	A3	167							
HPK2000148	A4	168							
HPK2000149	C1	169							
HPK2000150	A4	170	Y						
HPK2000151	A3	171							
HPK2000152	L1	172							
HPK2000153	C3	173							
HPK2000154	C3	174							
HPK2000155	SQ1	175	Y						
HPK2000156	A4	176							
HPK2000157	C1	177							
HPK2000158	A4	178							
HPK2000159	C4	179							
HPK2000160	C2	180							

PLAN #	PRICE TIER	PAGE	MATERIALS LIST	QUOTE ONE®	DECK	DECK PRICE	LANDSCAPE	LANDSCAPE PRICE	REGIONS
HPK2000161	C2	181							
HPK2000162	C2	182							
HPK2000163	C3	183							
HPK2000164	L2	184							
HPK2000165	L1	185	Y						
HPK2000282	SQ3	186							
HPK2000166	C1	188	Y	Y					
HPK2000167	SQ1	189							
HPK2000168	C1	190	Y						
HPK2000169	C1	191	Y						
HPK2000170	C4	192							
HPK2000171	C2	193							
HPK2000172	C3	194							
HPK2000173	C3	195							
HPK2000174	C1	196	Y						
HPK2000175	C1	197							
HPK2000176	C1	198							
HPK2000177	C1	199							
HPK2000178	A2	200							
HPK2000179	C2	201	Y						
HPK2000180	C2	202							
HPK2000181	C2	203	Y	Y					
HPK2000182	C2	204							
HPK2000183	C3	205	Y						
HPK2000184	C1	206							
HPK2000185	C1	207							
HPK2000186	C2	208							
HPK2000187	C2	209	Y						
HPK2000188	C2	210	Y						
HPK2000189	C2	211	Y						
HPK2000190	C3	212	Y						
HPK2000191	C3	213	Y						
HPK2000192	C4	214	Y						
HPK2000193	C2	215	Y						
HPK2000194	C3	216	Y						
HPK2000195	A4	217	Y	Y					
HPK2000196	C3	218							
HPK2000197	C2	219	Y						
HPK2000005	A4	220	Y						
HPK2000198	C3	222							
HPK2000199	C4	223	Y	Y					
HPK2000200	C3	224							
HPK2000201	C3	225							
HPK2000202	L1	226							
HPK2000203	C3	227							
HPK2000204	C4	228							
HPK2000205	L1	229							
HPK2000206	C1	230							
HPK2000207	A4	231	Y						
HPK2000208	A3	232							
HPK2000209	A4	233							
HPK2000210	A4	234							
HPK2000211	A4	235							
HPK2000212	A4	236	Y						
HPK2000213	A3	237	Y						
HPK2000214	A4	238	Y						

PLAN #	PRICE TIER	PAGE	MATERIALS LIST	QUOTE ONE®	DECK	DECK PRICE	LANDSCAPE	LANDSCAPE PRICE	REGIONS
HPK2000215	A3	239							
HPK2000216	A3	240	Y						
HPK2000217	A3	241							
HPK2000218	A3	242	Y						
HPK2000219	C1	243							
HPK2000220	C2	244							
HPK2000221	A3	245							
HPK2000222	C2	246							
HPK2000223	C1	247							
HPK2000224	C1	248	Y						
HPK2000225	A3	249							
HPK2000226	C1	250	Y			OLA017	P3	123568	
HPK2000227	C1	251	Y						
HPK2000228	A4	252	Y						
HPK2000229	C1	253				OLA005	P3	123568	
HPK2000230	A2	254							
HPK2000231	C3	255	Y	Y		OLA008	P4	1234568	
HPK2000232	L1	256							
HPK2000233	A4	257							
HPK2000234	C3	258							
HPK2000235	C4	259							
HPK2000236	A3	260							
HPK2000237	A3	261							
HPK2000238	C1	262							
HPK2000239	C2	263							
HPK2000240	C1	264							
HPK2000241	C2	265	Y	Y					
HPK2000242	C2	266							
HPK2000243	C2	267							
HPK2000244	C1	268	Y						
HPK2000245	C1	269							
HPK2000246	C2	270	Y						
HPK2000247	C2	271	Y						
HPK2000248	C2	272							
HPK2000249	C1	273							
HPK2000250	C4	274							
HPK2000251	C1	275							
HPK2000252	C1	276							
HPK2000253	A4	277	Y						
HPK2000003	SQ1	278	Y			OLA008	P4	1234568	
HPK2000254	SQ3	280	Y						
HPK2000255	SQ3	281							
HPK2000256	SQ1	282	Y	Y		OLA001	P3	123568	
HPK2000257	A4	283							
HPK2000258	A4	284	Y						
HPK2000259	C1	285							
HPK2000260	A3	286	Y						
HPK2000261	A3	287	Y						
HPK2000262	C3	288							
HPK2000263	C2	289							
HPK2000264	C3	290							
HPK2000265	C1	291							
HPK2000266	C4	292							
HPK2000267	C4	293							
HPK2000268	A4	294							
HPK2000269	SQ1	295	Y						

PLAN #	PRICE TIER	PAGE	MATERIALS LIST	QUOTE ONE®	DECK	DECK PRICE	LANDSCAPE	LANDSCAPE PRICE	REGIONS
HPK2000270	SQ1	296	Y		ODA011	P2	OLA012	P3	12345678
HPK2000271	C3	297					OLA001	P3	123568
HPK2000272	C2	298					OLA012	P3	12345678
HPK2000273	A4	299	Y				OLA012	P3	12345678
HPK2000274	C1	300							
HPK2000275	A4	301	Y						
HPK2000276	C1	302	Y						
HPK2000277	A4	303							
HPK2000278	C1	304							
HPK2000279	A4	305							
HPK2000280	C1	306	Y						
HPK2000281	A4	307							

PLAN #	PRICE TIER	PAGE	MATERIALS LIST	QUOTE ONE®	DECK	DECK PRICE	LANDSCAPE	LANDSCAPE PRICE	REGIONS

Idyllic Escapes

Take the plunge and start building your perfect vacation home. No matter if you are seeking a breathtaking view, a relaxing retreat or a cozy cabin, Hanley Wood has the house plan to fit your every fantasy.

Homes with a View

175 Plans for Golf-Course, Waterfront and Mountain Homes: This stunning collection features homes as magnificent as the vistas they showcase. A 32-page, full-color gallery showcases the most spectacular homes—all designed specifically to accent the natural beauty of their surrounding landscapes.

$14.95 U.S. (*192 pages*)
ISBN 1-931131-25-2

Vacation & Second Homes, 3rd Ed.

430 House Plans for Retreats and Getaways: Visit the cutting edge of home design in this fresh portfolio of getaway plans—ready to build anywhere. From sprawling haciendas to small rustic cabins, this collection takes on your wildest dreams with designs suited for waterfronts, cliffsides, or wide-open spaces.

$11.95 U.S. (*288 pages*)
ISBN 1-931131-37-6

Cool Cottages

245 Delightful Retreats 825 to 3,500 square feet: Cozy, inviting house plans designed to provide the ideal escape from the stress of daily life. This charming compilation offers perfect hideaways for every locale: mountaintops to foothills, woodlands to everglades.

$10.95 U.S. (*256 pages*)
ISBN 1-881955-91-5

Fine Living

130 Home Designs with Luxury Amenities: The homes in this collection offer lovely exteriors, flowing floor plans and ample interior space, plus a stunning array of amenities that goes above and beyond standard designs. This title features gorgeous full-color photos, tips on furnishing and decorating as well as an extensive reference section packed with inspiring ideas.

$17.95 U.S. (*192 pages*)
ISBN 1-931131-24-4

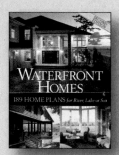

Waterfront Homes, 2nd Ed.

189 Home Plans for River, Lake or Sea: A beautiful waterfront setting calls for a beautiful home. Whether you are looking for a year-round home or a vacation getaway, this is a fantastic collection of home plans to choose from.

$10.95 U.S. (*208 pages*)
ISBN 1-931131-28-7

Getaway Plans

250 Home Plans for Cottages, Bungalows & Capes: This is the perfect volume for anyone looking to create their own relaxing place to escape life's pressures—whether it's a vacation home or primary residence! Also included, tips to create a comfortable, yet beautiful atmosphere in a small space.

$9.95 U.S. (*448 pages*)
ISBN 1-881955-97-4

Hanley Wood
One Thomas Circle, NW | Suite 600 | Washington, DC 20005
877.477.5450 | www.hanleywoodbooks.com

HPK20